D0859120

DUBLINES

Katie Donovan is one of Ireland's most exciting young poets. Born in 1962, she spent her early youth on a farm in Co. Wexford. She studied at Trinity College Dublin and at the University of California at Berkeley, and spent a year teaching English in Hungary. She now lives in Dublin where she works as a journalist. Her first book of poems, *Watermelon Man*, was published by Bloodaxe in 1993.

She is the author of *Irish Women Writers: Marginalised by Whom?* (Raven Arts Press, 1988). With A. Norman Jeffares and Brendan Kennelly she edited *Ireland's Women: Writings Past and Present*, published in 1994 by Kyle Cathie (Britain) and Gill & Macmillan (Ireland).

Brendan Kennelly was born in 1936 in Ballylongford, Co. Kerry. He is Professor of Modern Literature at Trinity College Dublin. In 1983 he achieved international recognition with his shocking epic poem *Cromwell* (Bloodaxe reissue, 1987), following this with the even more notorious *Book of Judas* (1991), which topped the Irish bestsellers list. His latest piece of mischief, *Poetry My Arse* (1995), out-*Judas*es *Cromwell*, sinking its teeth into the pants of poetry itself.

He has published over twenty other books, including *A Time for Voices: Selected Poems 1960-1990* (1990), *Breathing Spaces: Early Poems* (1992) and *Journey into Joy: Selected Prose* (1994) from Bloodaxe, and *The Penguin Book of Irish Verse* (1970). Also available from Bloodaxe are his play-texts: his versions of Euripides' *Medea* (1991) and *The Trojan Women* (1993), with those of Lorca's *Blood Wedding* and Sophocles' *Antigone* due out in 1996.

Richard Pine's Bloodaxe critical anthology *Dark Fathers into Light* (1994) brings together essays on Kennelly by leading critics.

DUBLINES

edited by
KATIE DONOVAN
BRENDAN KENNELLY

BLOODAXE BOOKS

Selection and editors' introductions copyright
© Katie Donovan and Brendan Kennelly 1995, 1996.

Copyright of all other material rests with the authors and other
rights holders as cited in the acknowledgements on pages 313-15,
which constitute an extension of this copyright page.

ISBN: 1 85224 256 6   hardback edition
        1 85224 257 4   paperback edition

First published 1996 by
Bloodaxe Books Ltd,
P.O. Box 1SN,
Newcastle upon Tyne NE99 1SN.

Bloodaxe Books Ltd acknowledges
the financial assistance of Northern Arts.

LEGAL NOTICE
All rights reserved. No part of this book may be
reproduced, stored in a retrieval system, or
transmitted in any form, or by any means, electronic,
mechanical, photocopying, recording or otherwise,
without prior written permission from the copyright
holders listed above and on pages 313-15 of this book.
Katie Donovan and Brendan Kennelly
have asserted their right under Section 77
of the Copyright, Designs and Patents Act 1988
to be identified as the authors of this work.
The views expressed in this book are those
of the contributors, and are not necessarily
shared by the editors or by the publisher.

Cover printing by J. Thomson Colour Printers Ltd, Glasgow.

Printed in Great Britain by
Bell & Bain Limited, Glasgow, Scotland.

CONTENTS

4 Touchstones

CITY OF TALK

Dublin is one of the most fascinating cities in the world. It leaves its mark in a deep and abiding way. Why? After all, Dublin is smallish (though with the second highest growth rate in Europe), congested, polluted, a place where serious matters are quickly reduced to jokes, and jokes are given, with equal speed, a serious status. Dublin has been called the centre of paralysis, the largest village in Europe, the second City of Empire, Scandaltown, Strumpet City, Joycetown and, now and then, the Capital of Ireland. These varying descriptions of Dublin, or aspects of it, may help to account for the city's extraordinary ability to leave its mark on those who live there for even a relatively short time; but there's much more to Dublin than that. It has a character, a personality, all its own. The purpose of *Dublines* is, in my view, to allow that character to emerge in its full, uninhibited glory, squalor and complexity. This book permits Dublin to do what it's best at: talk itself into existence.

City of talk, gossip, rumour, scandal, delight in the destruction of reputation. City of incestuous knowledge and fluent, articulate poison. Crafty, battered, charming, post-colonial prostitute trying to sell her body and soul to the highest or slyest bidder. City of full-time and/or part-time assassins whose weapons are the tongue and the typewriter. Dublin is a cartoon being endlessly re-drawn by a population of cartoonists. All in all, a demonically interesting place with one hell of an appeal. Dante's dream, in part at least. In toto, perhaps.

I've met in Dublin some of the kindest, wittiest people I know. This blend of kindness and wit, of sheer good nature and sharp comment, is one of the city's delights and one of the best reasons for living there. When you pass from that kind of conversation to the resolutely derisive one, teeming with cynical skills, you experience a chilling sense of Dublin's conversational variety and versatility.

And this passion for talk is a tradition. Nowhere in the world have I found an equal delight in derision, an equal charm in good-natured wit and word-play. This runs right through *Dublines*, from 'Talktown' to 'Dublin Destroyed Emerging'. The voices of history support this view of the city.

The walker through Dublin, especially when the city is not obscured by traffic, will discover a place of remarkable elegance as well as scenes of sustained ugliness, drabness and dirt. To explore the endless streets of pre-traffic Dublin early on a summer morning is to experience the variety of this city's character, a character that has survived centuries of misuse and abuse, various forms of tyranny and oppression, crushing poverty, social and political upheaval, violent revolution and terrorist bombings. To stroll through Dublin is to stroll through history. It's easy to see why it was called the second City of Empire: its elegant squares and handsome buildings are a pleasure to the eye. It's easy, too, to understand why so many Dubliners have such pride in, and affection for their city.

Dublin's pub life is the most exhilarating I've experienced anywhere. Arthur Guinness, assisted by various brands of whiskey, is the god of lively conversation. His rule in the pubs of Dublin is timelessly eloquent and benign.

Dublin is more a stage than a city. Life is dramatically intimate there, almost unavoidably congested and familiar. It seems that everybody knows everybody else. What, then, is the point of concealing anything? Something concealed has a special fascination, particularly for those interested in the disclosure of whatever happens to be concealed. The sensational revelation of some hidden event, emotion, misfortune, disease, attractively vicious political shindigging, success, failure, financial skullduggery, neighbourly phone-tapping, love-affair or sexual carry-on has a special lip-smacking relish in Dublin. The glee of disclosure is positively lustful. The Irish love for scandal which is inseparable from our insistence on repectability is at once more concentrated and more prominent in Dublin. Instead of saying 'Good day' to each other, a lot of Dubs prefer the greeting, 'Any scandal, me oul' flower?' Ah, sure where would we be without it?

The deepest impulse in Dublin life is one of cartoonish reductionism, a genius for witty, satirical diminishing of practically everything and everybody burdened with a sense of dignity or self-esteem. James Joyce and Flann O'Brien are the two most ruthless explorers of this impulse. Of the two, O'Brien is the more savage. Yet, in the end, O'Brien himself seemed a cartoon of a cartoon of despair. And is there anything on God's earth that can't be laughed away under the table or out into the Sellafield darkness of the Irish Sea?

There can be, nevertheless, a certain perverse wholesomeness, a healthy mockery in this blackish art of reductionism. Anyone who feels the brunt of it will never 'lose the run of himself' or incline towards the curious belief that 'his shit is ice-cream'!

It would have been easy to give a chronological view of Dublin. Instead, Katie Donovan and I have chosen to let the different centuries jostle, challenge and provoke each other in an arena where time is deprived of its dull despotism to make way for a method and a structure in which contrasts and comparisons, affinities and contradictions, similarities and dissimilarities startle the reader into a fresh apprehension of material he or she may or may not be familiar with. Dublin itself is at times a city of almost crippling familiarity; it is also full of startling surprises. We wish to show this scene in a new, dramatic light. The familiar, seen from a new perspective, can be astonishing. I believe that Dublin, under its mask of implacable familiarity, has a soul full of all kinds of surprises. This book proves it.

Speaking recently to a Dubfriend of mine, I mentioned I was working at *Dublines* with Katie Donovan. 'What's that?' he exploded. 'Katie Donovan is from Wexford and you're from Kerry. Sure, what would you pair o' culchies know about Dublin?' It was in vain I insisted that I'd been living in Dublin for almost forty years. 'Yez are only a pair o' blow-ins' concluded my decent Dubfriend. He meant it too. I liked him for that. And was there, I ask myself, a playful sparkle in his eye as he denounced the culchie blow-ins? Nearly every word uttered in Dublin is touched with humour of one kind or another.

The nature of metropolitan egotism and intolerance is not without comment in this book.

Capital cities have an egotism all their own. It is frequently an unconscious egotism, an unquestioned and unquestionable superiority, a spontaneous gift from the lofty gods of the metropolis. Readers of *Dublines* are invited to scrutinise, savour or reject this divine gift together with its awesome implications, as they will.

Dublin has produced, and continues to produce many colourful characters. But in this fascinating city, there is one character that outshines and outlasts all others, and that is Dublin itself. *Dublines* is an expression of, and a tribute to that (ultimately) lovable character, ever-changing and enduring.

BRENDAN KENNELLY

A REAL DUB

I am not a native of Dublin. The fact that I spent my early years on a farm in Co. Wexford has branded me a yellowbelly for life. I will always be an outsider in the city, although I have lived in its suburbs and its centre on and off since I was nine years old.

There are few denizens of Dublin who don't have one foot outside the Pale. James Joyce, one of Dublin's most famous sons, had an accent with distinctive shades of Cork in it, because his father was from Cork. Yet Dubliners continue to have arguments in pubs and over garden fences about who is a real Dub and who is just a culchie or a blow-in. The never ending dissection of pedigrees which is so much a feature of city gossip inspired our section entitled 'Insiders and Outsiders'.

As we teased the matter out, we realised that few of Dublin's inhabitants have not experienced both sides of this coin. Poverty, for example, can make any native Dubliner feel like an outsider in his or her own city. John McGahern makes this point in his story, 'Doorways', about the two tramps on Abbey Street, Barnaby and Bartleby.

This, then, is our approach. We have taken themes which we feel are close to the heart of Dublin life, and have turned them inside out to find the different nuances they hold. In 'Touchstones', for example, you will find writings about the very stones of the city which bind it physically and historically together. But this section goes further, to include the institutions and customs which are part of the fabric of Dublin life, such as the pub, the café, the love of music, the reading of newspapers and the dazzle of Christmas on Dublin streets.

We also wanted to show the healthy disrespect every Dubliner is capable of feeling towards the 'touchstones' of his or her city. The Abbey Theatre is toppled off its pedestal by the eponymous Murphy in Beckett's novel, who wishes that his cremated remains be flushed down the theatre toilet during a performance.

There is a dark side to Dublin, a sense of insularity and begrudgery so aptly portrayed by Joyce in *Dubliners*, where he sees the city as a centre of paralysis. This quality has chased many talented Dubliners away from their native city. Not only Joyce, but also Beckett, Shaw and O'Casey all felt they could only spread their wings away from the stifling smallness of Dublin life.

The intimacy which Yeats celebrates in 'The Municipal Gallery Revisited' can so often turn into a breeding-ground for smug vindictiveness in Dublin, as evidenced in William Trevor's story 'Two More Gallants', his clever companion piece to Joyce's 'Two Gallants'.

We coined the term 'Grincest' for this tendency of Dublin to don a sneering mask beneath which to devour its own. The 'Grincest' section includes both literal incest, which is a significant problem in the city, as well as all the metaphorical associations the word contains. Dublin's 'political castration' in its long-standing role as second city of the empire is John O'Donovan's explanation for this uglier, 'cynical' face of Ireland's capital city.

The 'Dubs' section has a cornucopia of Dubliners, past and present, with saints, villains, oddities, celebrities and darlin' men all rubbing shoulders together. The legless beggar-turned-robber Billy-in-the-Bowl is in there along with the mother of all the Behans, Kathleen Behan, recalling life in the tenements in Russell Street. Trinity-going Oscar Wilde appears, along with Zozimus, the blind street balladeer. There are familiar faces from present-day Dublin, such as singer Mary Black and boxer Michael Carruth.

The 'Talktown' section speaks for itself. Talking is a favourite pastime among Dubliners in every walk of life, and no matter what he or she might be doing, it is a rare Dub who can't spare the time for gossip, speechifying, jokes, bitchery, debate, the swopping of boasts and insults, and/or endless pontification about the meaning of it all, preferably with the lubrication of 'a pint of plain'.

Our priority in putting together this anthology was to give a spectrum of Dublin life with as much variety as possible. In the end we have only succeeded in skimming the surface due to limitations of space. Inevitably we were drawn to certain writers more than others – Dubliners such as Joyce, Brendan Behan, Sean O'Casey and Nuala O'Faoláin crop up quite frequently. The veteran travel writer, V.S. Pritchett, is also hard to resist. His ability to plumb the city with such endearing insight is due largely to the fact that he stayed in Dublin during the turbulent twenties, and then again forty years later, after the city had changed so much, yet was still just as likely to provide him with examples of the irresistibly absurd. His recollection of Yeats wondering where to empty out a pot of old tea leaves is a priceless example of this.

In the last section, 'Dublin Destroyed Emerging', we have tried to capture the sense of a city constantly fighting to survive in spite of a history of invasions, battles and revolutions, a reputation for poverty and crime, and, more recently, a poor record for planning and conservation. 'Strumpet City', in the words of the playwright Denis Johnston, continually strives to hold her head high 'and unashamed'.

KATIE DONOVAN

1. TALKTOWN

If you don't get up and go down town you'd hear
nothing, nor find what they're saying about you.
And God send they're saying something. Good or
bad, it's better to be criticised than ignored.

BRENDAN BEHAN

The Staple of Wit

Irish wit when exported across the Channel had a certain value. 'Ireland, which one did not suspect,' wrote Horace Walpole in 1756, 'is become the staple of wit, and I find coins *bons-mots* for our greatest men.'

Apart from racial considerations, one may explain the sprightliness of Irish conversation by 'the mixture of ranks' which then distinguished Dublin Society. Politicians, soldiers, divines, and lawyers all rubbed shoulders together in the great houses. The barristers were an especially lively element. They were famous for their eloquence and wit, and had more time for social pleasures than London lawyers.

CONSTANTIA MAXWELL
from *Dublin Under The Georges* (1979)

The Penny-a-Week School

Mr Fogarty brought a gift with him, a half-pint of special whisky. He inquired politely for Mr Kernan, placed his gift on the table and sat down with the company on equal terms. Mr Kernan appreciated the gift all the more since he was aware that there was a small account for groceries unsettled between him and Mr Fogarty. He said:

– I wouldn't doubt you, old man. Open that, Jack, will you?

Mr Power again officiated. Glasses were rinsed and five small measures of whisky were poured out. This new influence enlivened the conversation. Mr Fogarty, sitting on a small area of the chair, was specially interested.

– Pope Leo XIII., said Mr Cunningham, was one of the lights of the age. His great idea, you know, was the union of the Latin and Greek Churches. That was the aim of his life.

– I often heard he was one of the most intellectual men in Europe, said Mr Power. I mean, apart from his being Pope.

– So he was, said Mr Cunningham, if not *the* most so. His motto, you know, as Pope, was *Lux upon Lux* – *Light upon Light.*

– No, no, said Mr Fogarty eagerly. I think you're wrong there. It was *Lux in Tenebris*, I think – *Light in Darkness.*

– O yes, said Mr M'Coy, *Tenebrae*.

– Allow me, said Mr Cunningham positively, it was *Lux upon Lux*. And Pius IX. his predecessor's motto was *Crux upon Crux* – that is, *Cross upon Cross* – to show the difference between their two pontificates.

The inference was allowed. Mr Cunningham continued.

– Pope Leo, you know, was a great scholar and a poet.

– He had a strong face, said Mr Kernan.

– Yes, said Mr Cunningham. He wrote Latin poetry.

– Is that so? said Mr Fogarty.

Mr M'Coy tasted his whisky contentedly and shook his head with a double intention, saying:

– That's no joke, I can tell you.

– We didn't learn that, Tom, said Mr Power, following Mr M'Coy's example, when we went to the penny-a-week school.

– There was many a good man went to the penny-a-week school with a sod of turf under his oxter, said Mr Kernan sententiously. The old system was the best: plain honest education. None of your modern trumpery....

– Quite right, said Mr Power.

– No superfluities, said Mr Fogarty.

He enunciated the word and then drank gravely.

– I remember reading, said Mr Cunningham, that one of Pope Leo's poems was on the invention of the photograph – in Latin, of course.

– On the photograph! exclaimed Mr Kernan.

– Yes, said Mr Cunningham.

He also drank from his glass.

– Well, you know, said Mr M'Coy, isn't the photograph wonderful when you come to think of it?

– O, of course, said Mr Power, great minds can see things.

– As the poet says: *Great minds are very near to madness*, said Mr Fogarty.

Mr Kernan seemed to be troubled in mind. He made an effort to recall the Protestant theology on some thorny points and in the end addressed Mr Cunningham.

– Tell me, Martin, he said. Weren't some of the popes – of course, not our present man, or his predecessor, but some of the old popes – not exactly...you know...up to the knocker?

There was a silence. Mr Cunningham said:

– O, of course, there were some bad lots....But the astonishing thing is this. Not one of them, not the biggest drunkard, not the most... out-and-out ruffian, not one of them ever preached *ex cathedra* a word of false doctrine. Now isn't that an astonishing thing?

– That is, said Mr Kernan.

– Yes, because when the Pope speaks *ex cathedra*, Mr Fogarty explained, he is infallible.

– Yes, said Mr Cunningham.

– O, I know about the infallibility of the Pope. I remember I was younger then....Or was it that – ?

Mr Fogarty interrupted. He took up the bottle and helped the others to a little more. Mr M'Coy, seeing that there was not enough to go round, pleaded that he had not finished his first measure. The others accepted under protest. The light music of whisky falling into glasses made an agreeable interlude.

– What's that you were saying, Tom? asked Mr M'Coy.

– Papal infallibility, said Mr Cunningham, that was the greatest scene in the whole history of the Church.

– How was that, Martin? asked Mr Power.

Mr Cunningham held up two thick fingers.

– In the sacred college, you know, of cardinals and archbishops and bishops there were two men who held out against it while the others were all for it. The whole conclave except these two was unanimous. No! They wouldn't have it!

– Ha! said Mr M'Coy.

– And they were a German cardinal by the name of Dolling... or Dowling...or –

– Dowling was no German, and that's a sure five, said Mr Power, laughing.

– Well, this great German cardinal, whatever his name was, was one; and the other was John MacHale.

– What? cried Mr Kernan. Is it John of Tuam?

– Are you sure of that now? asked Mr Fogarty dubiously. I thought it was some Italian or American.

– John of Tuam, repeated Mr Cunningham, was the man.

He drank and the other gentlemen followed his lead. Then he resumed:

– There they were at it, all the cardinals and bishops and archbishops from all the ends of the earth and these two fighting dog and devil until at last the Pope himself stood up and declared infallibility a dogma of the Church *ex cathedra*. On the very moment John MacHale, who had been arguing and arguing against it, stood up and shouted out with the voice of a lion: *Credo!*

– *I believe!* said Mr Fogarty.

– *Credo!* said Mr Cunningham. That showed the faith he had.
He submitted the moment the Pope spoke.
– And what about Dowling? asked Mr M'Coy.
– The German cardinal wouldn't submit. He left the Church.

JAMES JOYCE
from 'Grace', *Dubliners* (1914)

The Boil's the Boy

Here's a thing I was going to ask for a long time, said Shanahan,
is there any known cure for blackheads?

Plenty of sulphur, said Mrs Furriskey.

Do you mean pimples? inquired Lamont. Pimples take time, you
know. You can't clean pimples up in one night.

Sulphur's very good, of course, Mrs Furriskey, but it's for the
bowels they give you sulphur unless I'm thinking of something
different.

To clear away pimples in the one go-off, continued Lamont, you'll
have to get up early in the morning. Very early in the morning,
I'm thinking.

They tell me if you steam the face, said Shanahan, the pores will
you know – open. That's the man for blackheads, plenty of steam.

I'll tell you what it is, explained Lamont, bad blood is the back
of the whole thing. When the quality of the blood isn't first class, out
march our friends the pimples. It's Nature's warning, Mr Shanahan.
You can steam your face till your snot melts but damn the good it
will do your blackheads if you don't attend to your inside.

I always heard that sulphur was the best thing you could take,
said Mrs Furriskey, sulphur and a good physic.

There would be less consumption in this country, continued
Lamont, if the people paid more attention to their blood. Do you
know what it is, the nation's blood is getting worse, any doctor will
tell you that. The half of it is poison.

Blackheads are not so bad, said Furriskey. A good big boil on
the back of your neck, that's the boy that will make you say your
prayers. A boil is a fright. It's a fright now.

A boil is a fright if you get it in the wrong place.

You walk down the street and here you are like a man with a
broken neck, your snot hopping off your knees. I know a man that

never wore a collar for five years. Five years, think of that!

Well, sulphur is good for that complaint, said Mrs Furriskey, people who are subject to that complaint are never without a pot of sulphur in the house.

Sulphur cools the blood, of course, concurred Lamont.

There was a girl that I knew once, said Mrs Furriskey rummaging anew in the store of her recollections. She worked in a house where they had a lot of silver, pots, you know, and that kind of thing. She used to polish them with sulphur.

Ah, but the boil's the boy, said Furriskey with a slap of his knee, the boil's the boy that will bend your back.

I'll tell you what's hard, too, said Shanahan, a bad knee. They say a bad knee is worse than no knee at all. A bad knee and an early grave.

Water on the knee, do you mean?

Yes, water on the knee is a bad man, I believe. So I'm told. But you can have a bad cap too, a split knee. Believe me that's no joke. A split knee-cap.

Where are you if you are gone in the two, knees? asked Furriskey.

I knew a man and it's not long ago since he died, Bartley Madigan, said Shanahan. A man by the name of Bartley Madigan. A right decent skin too. You never heard a bad word about Bartley.

I knew a Peter Madigan once, said Mrs Furriskey, a tall well-built man from down the country. That was about ten years ago.

Well Bartley got a crack of a door-knob in the knee...

Eh! Well dear knows that's the queer place to get the knob of a door. By God he must have been a bruiser. A door-knob! – Oh, come here now. How high was he?

It's a question I am always asked, ladies and gentlemen, and it's a question I can never answer. But what my poor Bartley got was a blow on the crown of the cap...They tell me there was trickery going on, trickery of one kind or another. Did I tell you the scene is laid in a public-house?

You did not, said Lamont.

Well what happened, asked Furriskey.

I'll tell you what happened. When my hard Bartley got the crack, he didn't let on he was hurt at all. Not a word out of him. On the way home in the tram he complained of a pain. The same night he was given up for dead.

For goodness sake!

Not a word of a lie, gentlemen. But Bartley had a kick in his foot still. A game bucko if you like. Be damned but he wouldn't die!

He wouldn't die?

Be damned but he wouldn't die. I'll live, says he, I'll live if it kills me, says he. I'll spite the lot of ye. And live he did. He lived for twenty years.

Is that a fact?

He lived for twenty years and he spent the twenty years on the flat of his back in bed. He was paralysed from the knee up. That's a quare one.

He was better dead, said Furriskey, stern in the certainty of his statement.

Paralysis is certainly a nice cup of tea, observed Lamont. Twenty... bloody...years in bed, eh? Every Christmas he was carried out by his brother and put in a bath.

He was better dead, said Furriskey. He was better in his grave than in that bed.

Twenty years is a long time, said Mrs Furriskey.

Well now there you are, said Shanahan. Twenty summers and twenty winters. And plenty of bedsores into the bargain. Oh, yes, bags of those playboys. The sight of his legs would turn your stomach.

Lord help us, said Furriskey with a frown of pain. That's a blow on the knee for you. A blow on the head would leave you twice as well off, a crack on the skull and you were right.

I knew a man, said Lamont, that was presented with an accidental skelp of a hammer on the something that he sits on – the important what you may call it to the rear, you will understand. How long did he live?

Is this a man I know, asked Mrs Furriskey.

He lived for the length of a split second, long enough to fall in a heap in his own hall. Something, you understand, gave way. Something – I forget what they call it – but it was badly burst, so the doctors said when they examined him.

A hammer is a dangerous weapon, said Shanahan, if you happen to get it in the wrong place. A dangerous instrument.

The cream of the joke is this, but, continued Lamont, that he got the hammer on the morning of his birthday. That was the present he got.

The poor so-and-so, said Furriskey.

Shanahan gave a whisper from the screen of his flat hand and a privy laugh, orderly and undertoned, was offered and accepted in reward.

FLANN O'BRIEN
from *At Swim-Two-Birds* (1939)

Dublin Street Cries

And first perhaps there was never known a wiser institution than
that of allowing certain persons of both sexes, in large and populous
cities, to cry through the streets many necessaries of life; it would
be endless to recount the conveniences which our city enjoys by
this useful invention; and particularly strangers, forced hither by
business, who reside here but a short time; for, these having usually
but little money, and being wholly ignorant of the town, might, at
an easy price purchase a tolerable dinner, if the several criers would
pronounce the names of the goods they have to sell, in any tolerable
language. And therefore until our law-makers shall think it proper
to interpose so far as to make those traders pronounce their words
in such terms, that a plain Christian hearer may comprehend what
is cried, I would advise all newcomers to look out at their garret
windows, and there see whether the thing that is cried be tripes, or
flummery, buttermilk, or cowheels. For, as things are now managed,
how is it possible for an honest countryman, just arrived, to find
out what is meant for instance, by the following words, with which
his ears are constantly stunned twice a day, 'Mugs, jugs, and por-
ringers, up in the garret, and down in the cellar.' I say, how is it
possible for any stranger to understand that this jargon is meant
as an invitation to buy a farthing's worth of milk for his breakfast
or supper, unless his curiosity draws him to the window, or until
his landlady shall inform him? I produce this only as one instance,
among a hundred much worse; I mean where the words make a
sound wholly inarticulate, which give so much disturbance, and so
little information.

The affirmation solemnly made in the cry of herrings, is directly
against all truth and probability: 'Herrings alive, alive here'. The
very proverb will convince us of this; for what is more frequent in
ordinary speech, than to say of some neighbour for whom the passing
bell rings, that he is 'dead as a herring'. And pray, how is it possible,
that a herring, which, as philosophers observe, cannot live longer
than one minute, three seconds and a half out of water should bear
a voyage in open boats from Howth to Dublin, be tossed into twenty
hands, and preserve its life in sieves for several hours? Nay, we have
witnesses ready to produce, that many thousands of these herrings,
so impudently asserted to be alive, have been a day and a night upon
dry land. But this is not the worst. What can we think of those
impious wretches, who dare in the face of the sun, vouch the very

same affirmative of their salmon; and cry, 'Salmon, alive, alive'; whereas, if you call the woman who cries it, she is not ashamed to turn back her mantle, and show you this individual salmon cut into a dozen pieces. I have given good advice to these infamous disgracers of their sex and calling, without the least appearance of remorse; and fully against the conviction of their own consciences. I have mentioned this grievance to several of our parish ministers, but all in vain; so that it must continue till the Government shall think fit to interpose.

JONATHAN SWIFT
from *An Examination of Certain Abuses, Corruptions, and Enormities, in the City of Dublin* (1732)

Beatles in Dublin

'I'll dream of them tonight,' said the small, fat fifteen-year-old girl whose eyes were shining and forehead damp as she tottered out into O'Connell Street like somebody possessed. There was a tiny man with a red nose and spectacles standing on a wooden box outside the *Evening Press* offices preaching about salvation. But he was talking to himself. Outside the cinema, a row of stout policemen with their arms linked were heaving strenuously against a frantic sea of young people. Girls were screaming inside. They screamed at the pictures in the programmes or if somebody shouted 'Beatles!' The atmosphere was hot and sharp: full of power and perfume and a frightening excitement. But when the curtain finally rose on THEM, the house erupted into one mad, thunderous noise, that continued right until the cries for more were drowned by the National Anthem. This morning it was 'B'-Day plus one as the city began to clean up the debris from the Beatles invasion. Motorists made their way through the shambles of Abbey Street, while workers replaced the plate glass windows which fell victim to teenage hysteria. Trouble began after the first of the two shows when more than two thousand people leaving the cinema 'mingled' with those going in. Members of the St John's Ambulance Brigade attended to injured people on the spot while crowds ran riot around them. Said a Garda sergeant whose cap was knocked off by a flying object, 'I have seen everything now. This is really mad. What can have got into them? You would imagine the country was in the middle of a revolution instead of welcoming four fugitives from a barber's shop.'

DERMOT BOLGER
from *A Woman's Daughter* (1987)

Just One Little Word

I overheard a man discussing cures for the common cold the other day, and he summed up by saying: 'There's nothing to beat *th'owl* ball o' malt.' And as I listened I could not help thinking how hard it would be to explain his full meaning to a foreigner. A 'ball o' malt', of course, is a glass of whiskey; but *owl* is untranslatable.

When a man says 'It'll soon be time to put on *th'owl* overcoat again', he doesn't mean that your overcoat is old, or that his own overcoat is old. He means a whole host of things: that there is comfort in an overcoat; that overcoats have the backing of tradition; that we won't feel it till Christmas; that Time flies and Death approaches.

Owl can mean a lot of things, but it rarely means old: and even when it means *old* it means a dozen other things as well. Indeed it is applied to new things much oftener than to old things. Thus if you praise a friend's brand-new bicycle he will say, as like as not, 'There's nothing like an *owl* bike for getting you about.' This *owl* is Gaelic courtesy, and is half affection, half disparagement – a very useful word indeed in a country where it is bad manners to acquiesce in the praise of your own.

If you want to borrow something, *owl* is almost indispensable: it takes from the shame of asking. A man who has the language from the cradle, for instance, will never ask baldly for the loan of a wheelbarrow. He will look over your fence for a full hour, smoke several pipes, and finish up by saying, as a sort of afterthought, 'I don't suppose you'd have such a thing about the place as an *owl* barrow you wouldn't be wantin' for a little while.' He turns his question into a disinterested, negative statement. He simply refers to what he obviously considers a very remote possibility, and leaves the rest to you. Similarly, if he wants to earth up his potatoes, he will refer obliquely, after a decent interval, to the possible existence of 'an *owl* shovel', and then – with a benign objectivity – reveal the fact that he has 'a few *owl* spuds to earth up'.

JOHN D. SHERIDAN
from *The Best of John D. Sheridan:*
I Have Been Busy with Words (1979)

Voices from the Silence

Gay Byrne's extraordinarily central place in the Irish life of the past three decades is due, not to his own obvious skills – the flow of language, the plausibility, the urbanity – but to their opposite: to the culture of silence which surrounds them. 'I have never,' the letters to him say, 'told this to anyone in my life...' 'I feel very depressed at times and wish I could reveal my secret to somebody...'

'That was ten years ago and since then my mother and I have never mentioned it...Please don't use my name or address as I couldn't stand it if the neighbours knew...'

It is the silences that have made Gay Byrne what he is in Ireland: the silences at the breakfast table, the silences around the fireside, the silences on the pillow. Without them he would be what he so patently is – a superbly professional broadcaster, confident, adaptable, quick thinking and fast talking – and no more. With them, he is something else altogether: the voice in which the unspoken can be articulated, the man who gives permission for certain subjects to be discussed. He is the voice, calm, seductive and passionless, in which things that would otherwise be unbearable can be listened to, things like this letter which he read on the radio in February 1984: 'When I learned that the thing that happened between men and women, as it was locally known, had happened to me, I slowly realised that I might also be going to have a baby...In terror and panic, I tried to find out from newspapers any snippets of information. I learned that babies like the one I might have were usually placed in brown paper bags and left in a toilet and I resolved to do this... For that reason, I started to carry around the one penny I would need to get into the toilet to have the baby...I kept the brown paper bag in my schoolbag and kept the bag under my bed at night... Since I spent most of my time in the chapel praying, the nuns told me I had a vocation.'

Surrounded by that silence, we wanted, in the 1960s, to hear ourselves speak in a charming, sophisticated and worldly-wise voice. And here was a man who had made it in England with Granada TV and the BBC but still wanted to come home, a man who could talk on equal terms with suave foreigners and still be one of our own, who could mention sex and nighties and contraceptives and still be a good Catholic. It is significant that the thing most frequently said about Gay Byrne's broadcasting style, by himself and by others, is that he asks the questions that the audience at home would want to ask but wouldn't dare. His achievement is founded on Irish people's inarticulacy, embarrassment and silence, on speaking for us because we were – and to a degree still are afraid to speak for ourselves.

FINTAN O'TOOLE
from *A Mass for Jesse James* (1990)

The James Joyce I Knew

If I talk about James Joyce I find that I *must* talk about myself: the reason for this will become clear in a minute or two.

The first time that Joyce and I met we disliked each other by what is called instinct, which is always very misleading. We were introduced by a perfect stranger to me.

I was walking up Dawson Street, thinking of nothing, which was and is my favourite form of thinking, when I noticed that two men were coming towards me, and that one of them was deliberating upon me as if I were a life-buoy spotted suddenly in a sea of trouble. Suddenly they stopped, and that one said, 'Stephens, this is Joyce,' and then, turning to his companion, he said, 'I've got to run' – and he ran.

There stood Joyce and I, he stuck with me, and I stuck with him, and the other drowning man was swimming to a reef two streets off. Joyce looked at me without a word in his mouth, and I looked at him with nothing in my mouth except vocabularies. We halted upon each other. We were very different-looking people. Joyce was tall, which I wasn't; he was thin, which I wasn't; he wore specs, which I didn't; he looked down at me, which I couldn't; he rubbed his chin at me, which I wouldn't.

Suddenly I remembered a very cultivated remark which I had

once heard a gentleman in a tall hat make to another in a straw hat
whom he didn't know what to do with, and I repeated it to Joyce:
– 'Come and have a drink,' said I.

He turned, and we walked back toward Grafton Street, and I
regaled him with the gayest remarks that I could think of about what
is known as the weather and this and that: – 'An American,' said
I, 'holds that it never rains in Ireland except between the showers.'

'Ah,' said Joyce.

'But a French lady,' I continued, 'told me that it rains in Ireland
whether there are showers or not.'

'Ah,' said Joyce.

'This is Pat Kinsella's,' I continued, as we halted outside the
first tavern that we came to.

'Ah,' said Joyce, and we went in.

The barman brought the refreshment that I ordered – it was called
a 'Tailor of Malt.' It was larger than a single, and it only escaped
being a double by the breadth of a tram-ticket, and it cost me three
pence. When Joyce had silently dispatched one-third of a tailor
into his system he became more human. He looked at me through
the spectacles that made his blue eyes look nearly as big as the eyes
of a cow – very magnifying they were.

'It takes,' said I brightly, 'seven tailors to make a man, but two
of these tailors make twins. Seven of them,' I went on, 'make a clann.'

Here Joyce woke up: he exploded moderately into conversation.
He turned his chin and his specs at me, and away down at me,
and confided the secret to me that he had read my two books; that,
grammatically, I did not know the difference between a semi-colon
and a colon: that my knowledge of Irish life was non-Catholic and,
so, non-existent, and that I should give up writing and take to a
good job like shoe-shining as a more promising profession.

I confided back to him that I had never read a word of his, and
that, if Heaven preserved to me my protective wits, I never would
read a word of his, unless I was asked to destructively review it.

We stalked out of Pat Kinsella's; that is, he stalked, I trotted.
Joyce lifted his hat to me in a very foreign manner, and I remarked,
'You should engrave on your banner and on your note-paper the
slogan, 'Rejoice and be exceedingly bad.'

'Ah,' said Joyce, and we went our opposite ways, and didn't see
one another again for two years.

JAMES STEPHENS
from *The James Joyce I Knew* (1946)

The Tragedy of Labour in Dublin

To the Editor of *The Times*   DUBLIN
                                                      11 November 1913

Sir, It may seem an audacity on the part of one whose views on the
politics of this city are obviously unpopular to attempt once more,
through you, to influence public opinion. But the most unpopular
council is not necessarily more filled with unwisdom. The masters
of Dublin I have addressed in vain. I now ask the citizens of Dublin
to consider what effect the policy of the masters is going to have.
What has been gained by this resolute refusal of the federated
employers to meet the only body with which negotiations can be
carried on? Are not the forces on the side of labour becoming more
resolute and exasperated week by week?

Nobody in Dublin seems to realise the gigantic power the masters
have challenged. As a disdainful attitude is manifested on the one
side, the leaders of labour have settled into a grim determination
never to submit. The labour leaders, men who have it in their
power to do what they threaten, declare that they will rather hold
up the industrial system of these islands than see the humiliation
of the men completed. Are the citizens content? Do they think it
right they should sit silent and have all this brought on them because
the masters are too proud to meet the representatives of labour in
Dublin? These people seem to read nothing, know nothing, or
think nothing of what is happening in respect of labour elsewhere
in the world. They do not know that organised labour has become
one of the great powers, that its representatives are met by the
representatives of capital in industrial countries with the respect
that the delegates of great nations meet each other. In Great Britain,
the Press, representing all parties, unite in condemning the policy
of the employers. What is the position of the men? They have
declared always that they wanted arbitration boards such as exist in
hundreds in industrial centres where the representatives of organised
labour and the federated employers could meet and to which disputes
over labour could be referred. Agreements entered into after frank
and free discussion as between equals the men will keep. They will
not keep agreements into which they consider they are forced. Labour
has a sense of honour of its own which is as high as the honour of
the masters any day.

I will be met by the famous outburst about contracts and the
nether world. That sentence was never uttered in the sense in which

it was reputed. Mr Larkin was speaking not with reference to the
contracts between masters and men, but about the masters' complaints
that owing to strikes they could not carry out their contracts. It
may have been an unfeeling remark, but it was not the defiance of
all honour between master and employee that an abbreviated report
made it.

Sir, if you will permit me to say something which may irritate
the Irish press, but which, I think, is true and necessary to be said,
if the Dublin journals had not been so manifestly biased on the
side of the employers, reporters would not have come to regard
their work, not as the true gathering of strike news, but the making
up of a case against the men. Nor would it have been so necessary
for me to emphasise one side, as I did in my *Open Letter* and the
much abused speech at the Albert Hall. I am charged with being a
revolutionary, I who for seven or eight years past have week by
week been expounding an orderly evolution of society. I am charged
as being against religion, I the sole poet of my generation who has
never written a single poem which did not try to express a spiritual
mood. But I am not with those who wish to bring about in Ireland
a peace of God without any understanding, and I and all free spirits
will fight with all our power against the fanatics who would bludgeon
us into their heaven, to bow to their savage conception of a deity.
The deity of the infuriated bigot, call him by what holy name they
choose, is never anything but the Old Adversary, who can put on
the whole outward armoury of God. I have known, worked with,
and loved many noble men, true priests of Christ, and they would
not, I am sure assert that the spirit that drives a mob to bludgeon
and kick parents before the eyes of their children is the spirit which
is present at the elevation of the Host. What I say here of the hooli-
gans of religion in Dublin I would say with equal sincerity of the
hooligans of religion in Belfast.

But I do not wish now to explain or defend myself, but to point
out the danger of allowing the present policy to continue. I tell
the citizens of this city that, if the civil authorities, the masters,
and their allies in the Press had been trying deliberately and of set
purpose to make of Dublin another Barcelona, with the bomb of
the Anarchist a frequent blazing terror in the streets, if they wished
to empty the churches, and make of Dublin another Paris, they
could not devise a policy more certain to bring about the result.
The Irish are a gentle people, but history is thronged with evidence
that in long exasperated men, suffering from real or fancied injustice,
gentleness turns to ferocity. To know that is true we can find ample

proof in the story of our own race, whether we begin with mythical Cat Head, in the first far-off uprising of the common people in Ireland, or come nearer our own time to the Dynamitards. Does no one read history nowadays? Is there not a single man in Dublin with knowledge of the human heart? Do not the most kindly and submissive natures change in character through what they believe is injustice or oppression? Natural good is transmuted by some devilish alchemy into hate, and forces are engendered which attract to them all that has been thought by the demoniac outcasts of society, so that the methods of the terrorists seem the only ones which can be adopted.

I ask my fellow-townsmen to think whether it would not have been better for the masters to treat the men as human beings who could be reasoned with than to issue ultimatums like despots to subjects who must be coerced without discussion? I ask whether it is most likely agreements will be kept and good work done if the men are starved into submission or if they are made after the most open interchange of opinions? The state has set up a tribunal which has given its judgement. Ought not public opinion to insist on the recommendation of the Askwith Committee being tried? How can the masters complain of the lawlessness of the workers when they themselves set an example by ignoring the verdict of the only legal tribunal which has tried the case? Dublin seems to be stumbling darkly and blindly to a tragedy, and the silence of those who foresee and do not speak is a crime. It is time for the Chorus to cry out to warn the antagonists in the drama.

Yours, etc., Geo. W. Russell ("AE")

AE (GEORGE RUSSELL)
from *The Times* (1913)

Maud Triumphant

Francis MacManus, who arrived in Dublin as a young man in the year following *The Plough and the Stars* controversy, has left us with a picture of Maud Gonne MacBride and her ability to communicate with an audience.

One afternoon, as he picked his way around the piles of rubble that continued to litter the streets of Dublin, the aftermath of years of warfare, he heard a burst of cheering from a meeting taking place near the Parnell Monument:

> A woman was speaking. Before I could catch a glimpse of her beyond the heads and shoulders of her audience, I heard her voice. It was a voice no man forgets. Never had I heard a voice like it…I had not to be told that she was Maud Gonne MacBride. She appeared to be a tall woman, dressed from head to foot in wispy, lacey black. Black, they say, is absence of colour, she made it as vivid as scarlet or turquoise… What she said I never remembered as words but only the effect of it: an effect of fluent, stern and even slightly theatrical speech; and more than that, an effect of intense feminine vitality and of great hope.

Even when Maud walked along the street afterwards, MacManus continued to be mesmerised by her presence. Although Maud must have been conscious of her effect upon people, the actress within her would never have dreamed of revealing that awareness. That would have shattered all illusions.

> She held herself erect; her pace was stately; her wispy black clothes fluttered. People turned to look after her as I would see them turning to look in the many years to come. She walked as though all her story were around her…Dublin was a battlement on which she, Helen, walked triumphant.

MARGARET WARD
from *Maud Gonne* (1988)

A Dreadful Thing

Francie's accent and mode of expressing herself were alike deplorable; Dublin had done its worst for her in that respect, but unless the reader has some slight previous notion of how dreadful a thing is a pure-bred Dublin accent, it would be impossible for him to realise in any degree the tone in which she said:

'But oh! Tommy Whitty! wait till I tell you what he said about the excursion! He said he'd come to it if I'd promise to stay with him the whole day; so now, see how grand I'll be! And he has a long black mustash!' she concluded, as a side thrust at Tommy's smooth, apple cheeks.

'Oh, indeed, I'm sure he's a bewty without paint,' returned the
slighted Tommy, with such sarcasm as he could muster; 'but unless
you come in the van with me, the way you said you would, I'll take
me ring back from you and give it to Lizzie Jemmison! So now!'

'Much I care!' said Francie, tossing her long golden plait of
hair, and giving a defiant skip as she walked; 'and what's more, I
can't get it off, and nobody will till I die! and so now yourself!'

Her left hand was dangling over Fanny Hemphill's shoulder, and
she thrust it forward, starfish-wise, in front of Tommy Whitty's face.
The silver ring glittered sumptuously on its background of crimson
silk glove, and the sudden snatch that her swain made at it was as
much impelled by an unworthy desire to repossess the treasure as
by the pangs of wounded affection.

'G'long, ye dirty fella'!' screamed Francie, in high good-humour,
at the same moment eluding the snatch and whirling herself free
from the winding embrace of the Misses Hemphill and Brennan;
'I dare ye to take it from me!'

SOMERVILLE & ROSS
from *The Real Charlotte* (1894)

Wilde and Moore

Someone asked Wilde: 'Do you know George Moore?'

Do I know him, is it? Yes I know him so well I have not spoken
to him for ten years...

George Moore on Wilde:

Wilde paraphrased and inverted the witticisms and epigrams of
others. His method of literary piracy was on the lines of the robber
Cacus, who dragged stolen cows backwards by the tails into his
cavern so that their hoofprints might not lead to detection.

The Country Woman

'Tell that to your dirty mother and your friends in America!' Mrs Kinsella screamed.

Mr Bedell, the Relief Man, paused in his rush down the stairs to glare back up at her and, behind her, the greater heaved bulk of Mrs Slattery.

'Ya hoor master!' Mrs Kinsella cried.

'Is that so?' Mr Bedell's fleshless ferrety face twisted with anger. And as he sought for words, Mrs Slattery laughed. 'Go-wan,' he cried, 'you pair of misbegotten bitches with your begging pusses and false pretences!' He shook his fist at the two women on the landing. 'I could have youse up for this.'

Mrs Kinsella roared and darted forward, Mrs Slattery making no effort to restrain her, and in one jump Mr Bedell had cleared the stairs and was shouting his feeble abuse up from the well of the hall.

'Gowan, you filthy Locke Hospital leavin's!' Mrs Kinsella shrieked. 'Go an' stick your lousy seven-an'-six up your la-la!'

'*And* your hungry Monda'!' Mrs Slattery interrupted, and laughed. Cautiously distributing her weight, she went to peer over the bannisters with Mrs Kinsella to make sure Bedell was gone.

He was.

'Mind.' Mrs Kinsella, after listening, eased the other's weight off the bannisters and grinned. 'Well, we made short work of that pox bottle!'

Mrs Slattery laughed back.

'But, Jasus, what'll I use for money now?'

'It was the shaggin' cot,' Mrs Slattery said. 'If only we'd 'membered to take that below.'

Mrs Kinsella exclaimed. 'Ah, but wouldn't you think that dyin' lookin' puke'd have some nature in him? Sure, I had to get that cot if I didn't want the oul' mattress to walk out the door with the weight of them kids' piss. Wasn't it to save the bed I got it?'

Mrs Slattery nodded and sighed. She had expended all the effort she was capable of in a single day, and she would have liked now to go back down to her own room and lie with a wet cold cloth on her head till it was time to get up and go out to the afternoon two-penny rush at the Palace or the Mary-o. But, ahead of her first was the job of lugging back up from her room the contents of Mrs Kinsella's.

'It was the cot,' she said. 'Just the same. Did you not see his oul' galdy eyes rivet themselves onto it the minute he set foot past the door?'

'Ahhh!' Mrs Kinsella screamed now, for no reason. 'Bollix him and the cot!'

'We shoulda hid it,' Mrs Slattery repeated calmly, marvelling at Mrs Kinsella's energy.

'What?' Mrs Kinsella asked incredulously. 'And have that young-wan knocking the nails from the boards with the strength of her t'rottle? No shaggin' fear.'

'Well, it was that what did it,' Mrs Slattery said.

Alice Slattery could be terrible one-track-minded, Mrs Kinsella thought.

'Didn't you hear him say you seemed to have full and plenty, thanks be to God? An' run his hand along the bars of the oul' cot?'

Mrs Kinsella nodded. 'Maybe now I should keep the kids in a shaggin' cage?'

'If only we could!' Mrs Slattery sighed.

PAUL SMITH
from *The Country Woman* (1961)

Goodbye to the Hill

The woman in front of me is killing herself. So is the man beside me. Arms folded, he's sitting back, enjoying himself hugely, glass of beer to hand, under his chair. He chews gum right the way through the show, jaws never faltering. And that's no mean feat because in Lee Dunne's *Goodbye to the Hill*, the one-liners come so fast you're begging for a breather. Most of them are unprintable: funny, bawdy, irreverent, sexist and sad – all at the same time.

The story is Lee Dunne's own: young Paddy Maguire is a lad on the tear, handsome enough to break the heart of every woman, cheeky enough to scald the heart of every mother. He gets advice on how to 'pull the birds' from his mentor – layabout and pub philosopher, Harry Redmond. The trick, says Harry, is to take them up the banks of the Dodder and spout poetry at them. Give them something by that Mexican poet Botticelli, he says. Harry's personal

hope is that God will send his way a female sex maniac, with money.
But it's Paddy who gets that, in the shape of a comely widow woman
from Terenure who is prepared to pay for her pleasure.

It's a familiar tale retold, larded with old jokes, peppered with
archaic sexism, sweetened with compassion – and the audience loves
it. So much so that this, its third production, is now the longest-
running play in Ireland. When it was first put on, in 1978, it ran
for a record 26 weeks but this run, now into its second year, has
long since broken that record. Eat your collective hearts out, Colgan
and Hynes – the play for the people this year, and last, is to be
found at Dublin's Regency Hotel. Six nights a week, they come in
their busloads from Sligo and Skerries, from Drogheda and Dundalk
– not to mention the southside – and then, blow me, if they don't
come back a second time, bringing friends, grandmothers and the
people nextdoor.

Behind the scenes, in the communal dressing room, the cast are
settling down to a game of poker before the show starts. They've
been together for nearly 600 performances. 'We've got beyond acting
now. It's real,' says Claire Mullan, playing Angela, an ageing bar
diva whose singing won't ever be a threat to Barbara Streisand.
Together with Frank Melia and Vincent Smith, she played in the
first production at the Eblana, 14 years ago.

'With a run as long as this,' says Padraig Murray, playing Paddy,
'you get a chance to develop the relationship between Paddy and
the mother.' And indeed, that's where the heartbreak lies as Ma,
played by Anne Kent, watches her handsome son waste his young
life on sex and his money on drink and lurex jackets. While she's
glad of the money he brings in, she does not realise, at first, that
most of it is coming from the Terenure widow.

At the interval, there's an announcement: dinner after the show
will cost a fiver, wine included, and the book is on sale at the back.
In the bar, the orders come up fast – four Guinness, there, please.
And then – same again, another four. Many of the audience have
never been to a play before or, if they have been, it was this one.
During the interval, we all talk to each other. It's not like the Peacock
or the Gate where people at the bar are commenting on the inter-
pretation or the interaction. At the Regency, we're here to enjoy
ourselves. Which is why you hear the occasional bottle being knocked
over as someone makes his or her way out in the middle of the
show for a natural break.

'It's hard for the cast,' says Lee Dunne, 'being on such a small
stage. And with someone edging their way along the row in front

of them, they have to time their speech until the person is settled back in his seat again. Then they can hit the punchline.' And there are plenty of those. When Angela, perched on a barstool, false eye-lashes down to her mini-skirted thighs, drones to the end of her song, Harry shakes his head to get rid of the pain. He'd have preferred something a bit more cultured.

'Culture?' she bawls. 'Culture? The only culture you know is agriculture.' Still, always a gent, Harry raises his glass: 'all the breast,' he says gloomily.

MARY RUSSELL
from *The Irish Times* (1992)

Poetic Licence

In Grafton Street Bernard was surprised to see Fergus Moore, whom he had not met since their visit to Willoughby Towers, coming towards them. He stopped Moore and introduced him to O'Dwyer. The three immediately adjourned to the nearest tea-shop, where Bernard asked Moore what he intended doing in Dublin.

'I've finished with Oxford,' said Moore, and I'm going to take a post graduate course in Philosophy in the National.'

'Good. We're Nationalists too...Medicals...And by the way, what's your present philosophy of life?'

'Much the same as ever. In theory I'm a revolutionary but in practice I'm a hedonist.'

'And what form does your hedonism take?'

'Free Love,' said Moore.

'Good Lord!' said Bernard and O'Dwyer in one breath.

'Don't be startled. I don't mean promiscuity. I said Free Love.'

'Where's the difference?'

'All the difference in the world, my dear boy. Free Love is based on the doctrine that cohabitation without love is immoral. In other words that most marriages automatically become immoral after a few years. Free Lovers cohabit as long as love lasts and not a minute longer.'

'If I wasn't an orthodox Catholic,' said Bernard, 'I might be disposed to favour that doctrine. It's most attractive. But what of the children?'

'I hadn't considered that aspect yet,' said Moore. 'It's certainly a difficulty. That is,' he added, 'under present economic conditions.'

'Present economic conditions,' said Bernard, 'are responsible for the whole of the modern sex problem. Physiologically we ought to marry at twenty. Economically we can't manage it till thirty. Is ten years of voluntary suppression of a physiological function that's as natural as eating and sleeping for a good man? Is it even possible? Half the fellows I've met I know to be unchaste (promiscuously too) and the other half I don't know about. Well, suppression is an evil; prostitution an abomination. Early marriage is impossible owing to the present economic system. Therefore the present economic system must be abolished.

'Very well,' said Moore, 'and what happens then? Hasty marriages of young people who fancy they're in love ending in lives of unhappiness or conjugal infidelity. Those conditions would be as bad as the present, if not worse.'

'The majority of healthy minded people will always be content with monogamy. You can't legislate for exceptions. Besides, even an increase in conjugal infidelity is better than prostitution. I've really only one fixed belief in this matter, and that is that the purpose of sex is to produce children, therefore man's personal comfort must come secondary to the welfare of the children. Children require family life. Therefore, to hell with Free Love.'

'Family life,' said Moore, 'is all very well for creature comforts, but it's ruinous to the mind.'

'Ruin the mind in youth and it'll recover. Ruin the body and it won't. Look at me. I was brought up to be a Tory Imperialist and Capitalist, and you see before you a Cosmopolitan Socialist.'

'Here's to family life!' said O'Dwyer, finishing his tea.

> There was a young fellow called Lascel
> Deserted the fold of the Castle.
>   While Fergus O'Moore
>   Succumbed to the lure
> Of Omar, wine, women, and wassail.

'Why don't you clap?' he asked. 'That was extempore.'

'I hate the way you twist my name to suit your beastly verses,' said Bernard.

'Poetic licence,' said O'Dwyer.

'Licence verging on obsession,' retorted Bernard.

A cadaverous individual in the distance at this moment waved a salutation to Moore who beckoned him over to their table. Moore introduced him to his friends as Austin Mallow.

'Had you a brother, called Brian, at Ashbury?' asked Bernard.

'Yes. Did you know him?'

'Slightly.'

Austin Mallow was a contrast to his burly brother. He was very lean and his shoulder stooped. There was a strange unnatural brightness in his sunken brown eyes.

'Mr Mallow and Mr O'Dwyer,' said Moore, 'you are each meeting a fellow-poet.'

The poets bowed to each other.

'If you can call O'Dwyer a poet at all,' interjected Bernard.

O'Dwyer cast a look of scorn at Bernard.

'Pooh! You've no sense of humour,' he said, 'or criticism either. You always resent the impertinence of my verses, while you ought to be admiring the mind of the person who made them.'

'How old are you, O'Dwyer?' said Bernard.

'Eighteen.'

'If you're not careful you'll develop the artistic temperament.'

'Artistic temperament me neck! I can express all I think.'

'A grave deficiency,' said Austin.

'Not if you think the things I think,'

'Personally,' said Austin, 'I think a lot more than I can express.'

'That doesn't prove that your thoughts are anything wonderful. It merely means that your powers of expression are deficient.'

'Nothing of the sort,' said Austin dogmatically. 'There are thoughts that cannot possibly be put into words. Words are finite and thoughts infinite.'

EIMAR O'DUFFY
from *The Wasted Island*

The DART Accent

It may seem odd, while our larger European future lies in ruins, to be talking about something as trivial as an accent: the accent that children of the Dublin middle classes are using now that is arguably the first new native accent of an independent Ireland. But our idea of ourselves is formed in all kinds of ways.

Just as we are affected by the European currency crisis, so we're affected by the internal realignment of allegiances signalled by this new way of speaking. It is the badge of a new elite. More explicitly than anything else, it expresses that élite's sense of its economically advantaged position in this society. It redraws one of our maps.

I think a lot of people have noticed it. It came up, for example, at an Irish class I went to for a week during the holidays, when there was a general discussion about accent and pronunciation. The teacher mentioned the voice of the young woman who does 'AA Roadwatch' on *Today At Five*. I am struck by her accent myself.

I find myself waiting through the news items until it comes to her, and then hurriedly trying to analyse what it is she is doing to the words she uses; in particular, to the word 'southbound', which is somehow a key to this new accent. I repeat it over to myself – 'southbound,' 'southbound' – but I can't say it the way she says it.

The teacher said that the pupils of Dublin's southside all-Irish schools speak Irish in this 'Roadwatch' accent, too. Or call it a DART accent. Connoisseurs say that it is found along the line of the DART, becoming ever more pronounced the nearer it gets to Glenageary. It is the accent of DART-served schools. I'm told that they don't have it in Belvedere, for instance, and sure enough, Belvedere isn't on the DART.

On the other hand, you hear it all the time in Grafton Street, which isn't on the DART either.

We used to know where we were with accents. Almost precisely. There used to be – just counting the South – about four main ones. There were country accents. They're all different from each other, of course, and they're not even all rural, because they include the cities of Cork, Galway and Waterford, and hundreds of towns. But from the vantage point of Dublin – and accent is all about vantage point – they're all from 'the country' anyway.

Then there were Dublin accents. There were rare Dublin accents, as in the gruesome ads for 'Old Mr Brennan's bread'. There were Trinity accents. And there were anonymous accents.

Mr Haughey, for example, is anonymous Dublin: Gay Byrne is anonymous Dublin; the President, Mrs Robinson, is anonymous Dublin, even though she's from Mayo. Perhaps there's a fifth accent called anonymous rural. MEPs develop anonymous rural. Broadcasters, except for sports broadcasters, are inclined to the anonymous rural. Even James Joyce, astonishingly, on the recording of his voice that survives, has a kind of all-purpose rural accent – Irish, but not from any given place in Ireland.

The anonymity is not about place but about class. Or not exactly, class, in the English sense, but education. Education isn't an indicator of economic privilege, but it is an indicator of privilege, if only the privilege of having parents who care. The less you sound native to wherever it may be, the longer you've spent at school. The exceptions are so obvious that they more or less prove the rule.

Joe Duffy, for example, is highly educated, but he was obviously impervious to any tips about elocution that came his way. Jim Mc-Ardle, of *The Irish Times*, who sometimes reports on cycling for RTE, bends even the most exotic Italian and Belgian names to a robustly Dublin pronunciation. They, and a few others, stand out.

Standard received pronunciation in this country is placeless. It can have a hint of this or that local influence (though Cavan and Monaghan are problematic), but not more than a hint.

No one accent, until this DART one, was expressive of social background. I don't count Anglo-Irish accents because they are not new. As far as I know, they've been the way they are for ever. They are natural, in the sense that they've come down the generations, like all the other accents of the Republic.

But there is one homemade, unmistakable accent which might be proposed as the grandfather or father of the DART accent. This is the one you hear around the Law Library. It is vaguely English, as if its speakers, if they didn't quite go to an English public school themselves, knew a lot of people who did.

As far as the pronunciation of words goes, it is not a progenitor: no other group in Ireland talks like that. (At my most charitable, I believe that it is a necessity forced on advocates by the awful acoustics of the courts, and that the pompous slowness with which they speak is really just an effort to be heard.)

But what the Law Library and the new accent have in common is an absence of timbre – a lightness, a thinness, a kind of sexless-ness, an ostentatious lack of vigour in taking on a sentence. The lawyers may be trying to copy a particular accent but the young people are not. What they appear to aspire to is accentlessness.

They don't sound English or American or Australian, or at least not consistently. They manage not to sound anything – not anything recognisably Irish, and not anything else either. They are, in fact, minimalists – speakers of an English that has about as little personal identity as a spoken language can have. Why this – an accent perfectly suited, say, to the dealing room of an international finance house – should be the preferred accent of our best-placed young people, is wide open to speculation.

But that they would develop a speaking style of their own was predictable enough. Young people used to be just old people who weren't old yet. They wore the same clothes, read the same books, listened to the same music, were involved in the same politics, as their seniors. Drank in the same pubs. Believed older people could be learnt from, for heaven's sake.

All that is over now, and the young now furnish their own ghetto. But there are ghettos within the larger one. You can tell the castes apart even by the gloss of their hair, never mind the cost of their clothes. Now, as soon as they open their mouths, you can also tell which one is going to college, and which one isn't and never dreamt of it. Even which college: the new accent is much more associated with UCD than anywhere else.

I don't know whether DART is spoken only by Dubliners. It would logically be the preferred style also of monied students from rural Ireland – the kind whose parents buy flats and houses in Dublin for their children to use while they're at college. It is, and is meant to be, a 'yuppie' accent. And yuppies, it seems, must eliminate native or traditional elements in their self-presentation. This is ideologically expressive. I see in a report from Zimbabwe in the *Times Literary Supplement* that it happens there, too.

The war of independence, the writer says, is just a memory to young urban Zimbabweans. 'Evidence for this is a curious new fashion among the teenage children of privileged families, whose imitation of English intonation has earned them the sobriquet of 'nose brigades'. In the malls and discos of Harare, they can be seen wearing gaudily decorated pith helmets – solar topis – a fashion roundly condemned by Hove (a Zimbabwean novelist), who told a reporter he would 'soundly beat any child of mine wearing such a thing; it's a sign of disrespect to those who suffered under the colonial regime.'

Well, I don't know that I agree. The only sure way to evade neo-colonialism is to neither know nor care whether you're being neo-colonial or not; to treat the whole thing playfully. Back at that Irish class I mentioned, a man told me that his children – from a comfortable part of Dublin's north side – have taken to speaking in *Commitments* accents, and that, what's more, when they went to a Gaeltacht island this year, the young islanders, too, took to speaking Irish with a *Commitments* accent. That sort of thing comes and goes, I imagine, and adds to the gaiety of nations.

But even if the impulse behind the new accent is liberating, I can't get to like it in itself. I feel a kind of insolence behind all it rejects. I don't like its sectionalism. Especially I don't like how weak it is, how pallid and infantile compared to other full-blooded accents around. It is as featureless as the suburbs from which it comes.

It has none of the originality of underclass speech. In fact, it is determinedly unoriginal, as if the people who speak it have nothing to prove. It expresses nothing except a generalised tedium, which means that words like 'yes', 'Terenure' or 'Heineken' are (a) too boring to pronounce in full, and (b) the property of the caste who pronounce them thus.

It is not that I want everybody to sound like Micheal O Muircheartaigh, but I don't see why the healthiest, best-fed young people in the entire community have to talk as if they're permanently exhausted.

Not that what I might say could make any difference. Isn't the whole point of the new accent that it has nothing to do with the oldies – especially, nothing to do with the pathetic provincials who actually reared the children who speak it? Doesn't it say that they refuse to be the children of any particular home? That if they're at home anywhere, so to speak, it is with each other, in such affluent enclaves as Ireland has to offer?

This isn't the first time or the first way, of course, that one generation has marked itself off from its predecessors. But what is different about this development is that it is, presumably, irreversible. Imagine. This accent is with us for ever. The nose brigades are here to stay.

NUALA O'FAOLÁIN
from *The Irish Times* (1992)

A Tram to Dalkey

By half-past eleven this morning one tram to Dalkey is not far on its way. All the time it approaches the Ballsbridge stop Mrs Kearney looks undecided, but when it does pull up she steps aboard because she has seen no bus. In a slither of rather ungirt parcels, including a dress-box, with a magazine held firmly between her teeth, she clutches her way up the stairs to the top. She settles herself on a velvet seat: she is hot. But the doors at each end and the windows are half-open, and as the tram moves air rushes smoothly through. There are only four people and no man smokes a pipe. Mrs Kearney has finished wedging her parcels between her hip and the side of the tram and is intending to look at her magazine when she stares hard ahead and shows interest in someone's back. She moves herself and everything three seats up, leans forward and gives a poke at the back. 'Isn't that you?'

Miss Kevin jumps round so wholeheartedly that the brims of the two hats almost clash. 'Why, for goodness' sake!...Are you on the tram?' She settled round in her seat with her elbow hooked over the back – it is bare and sharp, with a rubbed joint: she and Mrs Kearney are of an age, and the age is about thirty-five. They both wear printed dresses that in this weather stick close to their backs; they are enthusiastic, not close friends but as close as they are ever likely to be. They both have high, fresh, pink colouring; Mrs Kearney could do with a little less weight and Miss Kevin could do with a little more.

They agree they are out early. Miss Kevin has been in town for the July sales but is now due home to let her mother go out. She has parcels with her but they are compact and shiny, having been made up at the counters of shops. 'They all say, buy now. You never know.' She cannot help looking at Mrs Kearney's parcels, bursting out from their string. 'And aren't you very laden, also.' she says.

'I tell you what I've been doing,' says Mrs Kearney. 'I've been saying goodbye to my sister Maureen in Ballsbridge, and who knows how long it's to be for! My sister's off to County Cavan this morning with the whole of her family and the maid.'

'For goodness' sake,' says Miss Kevin. 'Has she relatives there?'

'She has, but it's not that. She's evacuating. For the holidays they always go to Tramore, but this year she says she should evacuate.' This brings Mrs Kearney's parcels into the picture. 'So she asked me to keep a few of her things for her.' She does not add that Maureen has given her these old things, including the month-old magazine.

'Isn't it well for her,' says Miss Kevin politely. 'But won't she find it terribly slow down there?'

'She will, I tell you,' says Mrs Kearney. 'However, they're all driving down in the car. She's full of it. She says we should all go somewhere where we don't live. It's nothing to her to shift when she has the motor. But the latest thing I hear they say now in the paper is that we'll be shot if we don't stay where we are. They say now we're all to keep off the roads – and there's my sister this morning with her car at the door. Do you think they'll halt her, Miss Kevin?'

'They might,' says Miss Kevin. 'I hear they're very suspicious. I declare, with the instructions changing so quickly it's better to take no notice. You'd be upside down if you tried to follow them all. It's of the first importance to keep calm, they say, and however would we keep calm doing this, then that? Still, we don't get half the instructions they get in England. I should think they'd really pity themselves.... Have you earth in your house, Mrs Kearney? We have, we have three buckets. The warden's delighted with us: he says we're models. We have't a refuge, though. Have you one?'

'We have a kind of pump, but I don't know it is much good. And nothing would satisfy Fergus till he turned out the cellar.'

'Well, you're very fashionable!'

'The contents are on the lawn, and the lawn's ruined. He's crazy,' she says glumly, 'with A.R.P.'

ELIZABETH BOWEN
from 'Unwelcome Idea', *Look at All Those Roses* (1941)

Stations of the Cross

At Blackrock three people got out. His mother had been as good as gold since Tara Street, not opening her mouth to say yes, aye or no. The granny knot in his stomach began to loosen, and as the train slid towards Seapoint he turned from Charlie Chase to Sidney Howard, the Whimsical Wag. It was as if he had let go his grip on a leash, for, on the instant, his mother remarked 'Wasn't it a glorious day?' to two girls sitting opposite.

He put his forehead against the cold glass of the window. He could see the girls' reflection. 'Gorgeous,' one of them said, delighted to be spoken to by a respectable married woman. The other one, thin as a lath and sunburned, said: 'We were in the Phoenix Park.' From the full-of-herself way she said it you would think they had been to England.

'Wasn't that grand for yous,' his mother said. 'Were yous at the a-zoo?'

At this the thin one looked humble and ground her bum into the seat. 'No, only the Furry Glen.' The other one, with thick legs that got even wider as they went up, put on a bold face and said:

'Sure you'd get sick of the old a-zoo.' She had a stuck-on beauty spot on her chin and was a tooth short at the side. The pair of them knew that the Furry Glen was not a patch on the zoo.

His mother was kindness itself. 'And what would yous go near the a-zoo for?' she said, as if only scruff from the slums would set foot in it. Then, having put butter on their bread, she put jam on the butter. 'The Furry Glen? Oh, how well yous went to the right place.' You could see that the compliment put great heart into the girls.

'Were we ever in the Furry Glen, Mag?' his da said, trying to remember.

'We were never out of it,' she said, taking him up short. Jack knew by the dare in her voice that she had never been in the Furry Glen, wherever it was, in her puff. 'Don't mind him,' she said to the girls. She was as grand as the quality of Christmas.

The girls were all smiles and politeness, not knowing that she had a sup taken. He longed for them to get off at Seapoint, but by the look of them and the way they talked he knew they lived in a place like the Tivoli, below Sandycove. The Tivoli was two buildings with iron stairs on the outsides and balconies with clothes hanging over them to dry, like bunting during the Eucharistic Congress. Rough people lived there. The girls would only get out at Seapoint if they were maids for well-off people, and they were not, on account of maids always had country accents.

The one with the thick legs looked at him. 'Is that your young lad, missus?' she asked. He hid behind Film Fun.

His da said with a laugh: 'Oh, that's Jack. Aren't you, son?'

His mother told him to answer people when he was spoken to. The one with the sunburn said: 'The creature. Ah, he's shy.'

'Divil a shy,' his mother said. 'I said, put down that comic.'

She made to tug it down from in front of him and the page tore across. She looked at the comic as if it had torn itself on purpose to make a fool of her. The sunburned one said: 'Ah, his comic.' Then, before he could help it, he let his mother know with his eyes that it was her fault and the fault of the drink. It would surprise you how quick she could be on the uptake: in an instant the good humour was gone and her look bored into him. He was a sleeveen, she was telling him, for having turned against her. She grabbed the comic out of his hands.

'There,' she said to the girls, 'that's the thanks you get. You take them out of Holles Street Hospital when their own didn't want them, and at the end of the road they'd hang you. You slave for

them, and for what? Me good neighbours, me own mother, they
warned me. 'He'll turn on you,' they said. 'He's a nurse-child, you
don't know where he was got or how he was got, you'll rue the day.'
And sign's on it, their words has come true.'

She nodded at her own foolishness. The two girls gawked at her.
He heard his da say with a growl: 'Ah, not at all.'

They were coming to Seapoint. He wiped his eyes with his
sleeve.

'You do your best for them,' she said, 'and they'd stab you. Dr
Enright said to me: 'You'll never rear that child, ma'am,' he said,
'he's delicate.' But I did rear him and he wanted for nothing. He
ought to go down on his bended –' She stopped. Then he heard
her say in a new voice, her looking-for-fight voice: 'Is something up?'

He knew without seeing it that one of the girls had grinned or
given the other one a nudge and she had noticed it.

'I said, is something up?'

The one with the thick legs said 'No.' He looked and saw that
her face was red.

'Make a jeer of someone else, don't make a jeer of me,' his mother
said. 'Pair of faggots.'

'Ah, shush now,' his da said.

'I won't shush,' she said, a scream in her voice. 'Don't tell me
to shush. They won't snigger at me, yella-faced rips the like of them.'

The buffers slammed and there was a gasp of steam. A man
called out 'Seapoint!' Without a word, the two girls were on their
feet and out of the compartment like whippets, the one with thick
legs beginning to wail like a banshee.

HUGH LEONARD
from *Home Before Night* (1979)

Workman's Friend

'The name or title of the pome I am about to recite, gentlemen',
said Shanahan with leisure priest-like in character, is a pome by
the name of the 'Workman's Friend'. By God you can't beat it. I've
heard it praised by the highest. It's a pome about a thing that's
known to all of us. It's about a drink of porter...'

He arose holding out his hand and bending his knee beneath him on the chair.

> 'When things go wrong and will not come right,
> Though you do the best you can,
> When life looks black as the hour of night –
> A PINT OF PLAIN IS YOUR ONLY MAN.'

'By God there's a lilt in that,' said Lamont. 'Very good indeed,' said Furriskey. 'Very nice.'

'I'm telling you it's the business,' said Shanahan. 'Listen now.'

> 'When money's tight and is hard to get
> And your horse has also ran,
> When all you have is a heap of debt –
> A PINT OF PLAIN IS YOUR ONLY MAN.
>
> When health is bad and your heart feels strange,
> And your face is pale and wan,
> When doctors say that you need a change,
> A PINT OF PLAIN IS YOUR ONLY MAN.'

'There are things in that pome that make for what you call *permanence*. Do you know what I mean, Mr Furriskey?'

'There's no doubt about it, it's a grand thing,' said Furriskey. 'Come on, Mr Shanahan, give us another verse. Don't tell me that is the end of it.'

'Can't you listen,' said Shanahan.

> 'When food is scarce and your larder bare
> And no rashers grease your pan,
> When hunger grows as your meals are rare –
> A PINT OF PLAIN IS YOUR ONLY MAN.'

'What do you think of that now?'

'It's a pome that'll live,' called Lamont, 'a pome that'll be heard and clapped when plenty more...'

'But wait till you hear the last verse, man, the last polish-off,' said Shanahan. He frowned and waved his hand...

> 'In time of trouble and lousy strife,
> You have still got a darlint plan,
> You still can turn to a brighter life –
> A PINT OF PLAIN IS YOUR ONLY MAN!

'Did you ever hear anything like it in your life,' said Furriskey. 'A pint of plain, by God, what! Oh I'm telling you, Casey was a man in twenty thousand, there's no doubt about that. He knew what he was at, too true he did. If he knew nothing else, he knew how to write a pome. A pint of plain is your only man.'

'Didn't I tell you he was good? said Shanahan. 'Oh by Gorrah you can't cod me.'

'There's one thing in that pome, *permanence*, if you know what I mean. That pome, I mean to say, is a pome that'll be heard wherever the Irish race is wont to gather...'

FLANN O'BRIEN
from *At-Swim-Two-Birds* (1939)

A Nice Piece of Liver

With two tomes under the arm walking out the back gate of Trinity College. Bright warm evening to catch the train. These business people are bent for their summer gardens and maybe a swim by Booterstown. On these evenings Dublin is such an empty city. But not around the parks and pubs. It would be a good idea to pop onto the Peace Street and buy a bit of meat. I'm looking forward to a nice dinner and bottle of stout and then I'll go out and walk along the strand and see some fine builds. For such a puritan country as this, there is a great deal to be seen in the way of flesh if one is aware and watching when some of them are changing on the beach.

'Good evening, sir.'

'Good evening.'

'And how can I help you, sir?'

'To be quite honest with you, I think I would like a nice piece of calf's liver.'

'Now, sir, I think I can see you with a lovely bit, fresh and steaming. Now I'll only be a minute.'

'Bang on. Wizard.'

'Now here we are, sir. It's a fine bit. On a bit of a holiday, sir? Nice to have a bit of fresh meat.'

'Yes, a holiday.'

'Ah England's a great country, now isn't it sir?'

'Fine little country you have here.'

'Ah it's got its points. Good and bad. And hasn't everything now. And here we are, sir, enjoy your holiday. It's a nice evening now.'

'A great evening.'

'I see you're a man of learning and good-sized books they are too.'

'They're that. Bye bye, now.'

'Grand evening. Good luck, sir.'

Wow, what conversation. Doctor of Platitudes. Holiday, my painful arse. But a nice bit of liver.

J.P. DONLEAVY
from *The Ginger Man* (1955)

Dublin Soul

We're a soul group. We want to make a few bob but we have our principles. It's not just the money. It's politics too, remember. We're supposed to be bringin' soul to Dublin. We can't do tha' an' smoke hash at the same time.

– It's oney hash.

– The tip o' the fuckin' iceberg, Billy. Dublin's fucked up with drugs. Drugs aren't soul.

– Wha' abou' drinkin'?

– That's different, said Jimmy. – That's okay. The workin' class have always had their few scoops.

– Guiness is soul food, said Joey The Lips.

– That's me arse, Jimmy, said Outspan.

– Listen, said Jimmy – For fuck sake, we can't say we're playin' the people's music if we're messin' around with drugs. We should be against drugs. Anti drugs. Heroin an' tha'.

– Yeah, but –

– Look wha' happened to Derek's brother.

– Leave my brother ou' o' this, said Derek.

He nearly shouted it.

– Okay, sorry. But yeh know wha' I mean.

– Wha' happened to Derek's brother? Billy asked.

– Forget it, Billy.

– I was oney askin'.

– Annyway, said Jimmy. – Do yis agree with me?

– Ah yeah – o' course, oney –

– We'll get a Heroin Kills banner for behind the drums, said Jimmy.

– Hang on, said Deco. – Wha' abou' the niggers in America, the real soul fellas, wha' abou' them? They all smoke hash. – Worse.

This was Joey The Lips' field.

– Not true, Brother. Real Soul Brothers say No to the weed. All drugs. – Soul says No.

– Wha' abou' Marvin Gaye?

– Wha' abou' him? said Jimmy.

– He died of an overdose.

– His da shot him, yeh fuckin' sap.

– A bullet overdose, said Billy.

– Sam Cooke then, said Deco.

– I don't know wha' happened to him. – Joey?

– Died under very mysterious circumstances, said Joey The Lips. – A lady.

– Enough said.

– I'm sure he was lookin' for it, said Imelda.

– Phil Lynott, said Deco.

– Fuck off, said Jimmy. – He wasn't soul.

– He was black.

– Ah, fuck off an' don't annoy me. – Get ou' o' my life. – Annyway, do yis agree abou' the hash? An' the heroin, like?

– Yeah

They all nodded or stayed quiet.

– Can we smoke it after the rehearsal, Jimmy? Billy asked.

– Yeah, sure. No problem.

RODDY DOYLE
from *The Commitments* (1988)

Tom Corkery's Dublin

Dublin is not, thank Heaven, a queen among cities. Rather is she a garrulous pleasure-loving provincial lady of good family, settling comfortably into middle-age, putting on too much weight in the wrong places. There is enough malice in her to keep her conversation interesting, and hospitality is for her more a pleasure than a duty.

Like all provincial ladies she loves the fuss of visitors; she will flatter them to their faces, gossip about them behind their backs, and is as much flattered as annoyed if, when they leave, they make snide remarks about her. The only unforgivable thing is to say nothing at all about her.

An old bag of words, but mother and foster-mother of some famous sons and with no intention of letting you forget the fact. She will never tire of showing you where her James used to walk, recalling what her Seán used to say, how her Willie and George and Oscar used to behave; she will breathe her George Bernard down your ear until you scream for mercy. And she will blandly forget that when she had them she used to clip their ears every time they opened their mouths. But you cannot help liking the loquacious old dame, with her long-winded reminiscences and her sentimental keepsakes all over the drawing-room. Whatever her failings parsimony is not one of them; dinner or no dinner, she dines at seven.

Her mornings are still elegant, not too harsh, not too obtrusive. There is not too much rattle, not too much clangour; a gentle susurration, the gently-refined invitation to be up and about. If sirens call they do so in muted half-hearted fashion, as though they are apprehensive of being prosecuted for disturbing the peace, and church bells interpolate occasional reminders that not by bread alone doth man live. People stop and talk to each other, maybe not too worried whether they get to their work on time. Indeed, one suspects, quite a few do not make it at all.

Not to worry. It is the real motto of the town, the explanation of its haphazard growth, and of its survival through a thousand years of very worrying history. For Dublin's was not a natural birth; the Danes who established it did so, not as the capital of Ireland but rather as a defence against Ireland.

TOM CORKERY
from *Tom Corkery's Dublin* (1980)

Ringsend

I will live in Ringsend
With a red-headed whore,
And the fan-light gone in
Where it lights the halldoor;
And listen each night
For her querulous shout,
As at last she streels in
And the pubs empty out.
To soothe that wild breast
With my old-fangled songs,
Till she feels it redressed
From inordinate wrongs,
Imagined, outrageous,
Preposterous wrongs,
Till peace at last comes,
Shall be all I will do,
Where the little lamp blooms
Like a rose in the stew;
And up the back garden
The sound comes to me
Of the lapsing, unsoilable,
Whispering sea.

OLIVER ST JOHN GOGARTY
from *Others to Adorn* (1938)

The Keane Edge

In the magazines circulation war, Nell Stewart-Liberty is intent on running the gamut of limbs from A to B. First she stole a march on her competitors with her legs (the 100 best pins in Ireland). Now she's staging a rear(guard) action with the 100 sexiest bums in Ireland.

On the whole this is a good list – Nell gets it nearly right by giving me a whole category to myself called 'Behind Every Great

Man'. However, those of you who think that my bottom was admired by only one Great Man, I must refer to the files. Michael O'Leary is on the record as proclaiming that mine is the best bottom in Ireland. And on one occasion in Nearys my fans got so carried away that they acclaimed it the best in Western Europe.

These lists are good fun and quite harmless as long as nobody confuses them with the genuine erogenous zones. The real erogenous zone has always been – and for my money, will always be – the head, where sex begins and ends.

*

Many of you may have been taken in by a charmer going under the nom de guerre of Terry Keane on the *Brendan Balfe Show* during last week. This person came across as nice as pie and people rang in to say how much they actually liked her. This column will not have it thought that its incumbent was *nice*, let alone likeable or sympathetic.

Let me enunciate all the reasons that the Brendan Balfe sweetie pie could not have been I. Firstly, in order to appear on a 9 a.m. radio slot one would have to get us at 7 a.m. Now the world and the dawn chorus knows that this is the time I normally get home. Secondly, I'm told by producer Pat Dunne that the person who put the show on the road with Brendan was bright-eyed and freshly scrubbed at that ungodly hour, and looked as if she'd come from a virtuous couch. That, as you all know could not be me: I never look freshfaced – I look fabulous – and my couch knows only the hurly-burly of life after marriage.

Brendan Balfe set himself a mission impossible: to show that Terry Keane was not the '24-carat bitch everyone thinks she is'. Ignoring the fact that this is arrant subversion, let me remind you that I didn't get where I am today by being kind to animals and politicians. It's not easy being a bitch – it's just great fun. You need courage and encore la courage: you need balls, you need nerve, you need wit, élan and style.

So I am not having all I've worked for since the cradle dashed in one fell week of radio, Brendan. You did a very good job with my alter ego all week – but you should remember the strictures of *Mission Impossible*; when the fait was accompli, destroy the evidence. Ms Nice Gal is no more – the bitch that gets the phagocytes going on a dull Sunday morning is back.

TERRY KEANE
from *Sunday Independent* (1993)

The People

'What have I earned for all that work,' I said,
'For all that I have done at my own charge?
The daily spite of this unmannerly town,
Where who has served the most is most defamed,
The reputation of his lifetime lost
Between the night and morning. I might have lived,
And you know well how great the longing has been,
Where every day my footfall should have lit
In the green shadow of Ferrara wall;
Or climbed among the images of the past –
The unperturbed and courtly images –
Evening and morning, the steep street of Urbino
To where the Duchess and her people talked
The stately midnight through until they stood
In their great window looking at the dawn;
I might have had no friend that could not mix
Courtesy and passion into one like those
That saw the wicks grow yellow in the dawn;
I might have used the one substantial right
My trade allows: chosen my company,
And chosen what scenery had pleased me best.
Thereon my phoenix answered in reproof,
'The drunkards, pilferers of public funds,
All the dishonest crowd I had driven away,
When my luck changed and they dared meet my face,
Crawled from obscurity, and set upon me
Those I had served and some that I had fed;
Yet never have I, now nor any time,
Complained of the people.'

              All I could reply
Was: 'You, that have not lived in thought but deed,
Can have the purity of a natural force,
But I, whose virtues are the definitions
Of the analytic mind, can neither close
The eye of the mind nor keep my tongue from speech.'
And yet, because my heart leaped at her words,
I was abashed, and now they come to mind
After nine years, I sink my head abashed.

W.B. YEATS
from *The Wild Swans at Coole* (1919)

Street Talk

– Well, I'll tell ye, Bridie, that wan this morning really had me annoyed, fingering the oranges, sniffing the apples and, finally, doesn't she go over and feel a cucumber for ages.
– What did ye say to her, luv?
– I said, Pardon me, missus, it doesn't get bigger if ye feel it.

*   *   *

– Missus, are them eggs fresh?
– I only laid the counter, luv.

*   *   *

– I think them bananas is turning black.
– Maybe they're pining for Africa, luv.

*   *   *

– Missus, them oranges are very dried up and shrivelled looking.
– Well, listen, if you had to come all the way from South Africa wouldn't ye run outa' juice yerself?

*   *   *

– Have you got any crabs, missus?
– I don't know, luv, I didn't look this morning.

*   *   *

– Them fish is still alive and flappin' about.
– Oh, don't mind them, son, they're auditioning for a part in Moby Dick.

*   *   *

– Oh, he says that he never turned to drink but that it turned to him.
– I wouldn't mind that fella, luv, sure he was born in a glass.

*   *   *

– A hangover! Course I have a hangover, sure what's a hangover?

– As Brendan Behan said, A hangover for me is when the brew of the night meets the dawn of the day.

*　*　*

– That wan says she knows the days that she can do her washing from looking at her husband in the morning. If it's lying to the right she says it'll be a fine day, but if it's lying to the left rain is on the way.

– And what if it's standing up in the middle?

– Sure, Jaysus, luv, who'd want to do anything on a day like that?

*　*　*

– Isn't it terrible all the same, luv, when ye start to put on a few years ye'r left to yerself. I remember well the time when my fella couldn't wait for me to take off me stockings. Jaysus, now I have time to knit a pair.

*　*　*

– Sure how could that wan be expectin' and the husband in prison for the past few years?

– Well, luv, that's now what I'd call a grudge situation. Someone must have had it in for him while he was away.

*　*　*

– Bridie, can you give us the lend of a quid?

– For what?

– Jaysus, I want to open up a supermarket, don't I?

*　*　*

– Jaysus, luv, it's so cold today ye'd need yer terminal underwear on.

*　*　*

Some Dublin Slang

You big long drink of water.
– *Insult, particularly to a tall thin person.*

I will in me hat.
– *I won't do it.*

It was the rale Ally Dally.
– *The genuine article.*

He wouldn't give you the steam off his piss.
– *A mean fellow.*

PAUL RYAN
from *Dublin Wit* (1986)

2. GRINCEST

In a little city like Dublin one meets every person whom one knows within a few days. Around each bend in the road there is a friend, an enemy, or a bore striding towards you, so that, with a piety which is almost religious, one says 'touch wood' before turning any corner.

JAMES STEPHENS

Wing Clipping

In a word, Dublin was politically castrated. It was not just the second city of the Empire but the second city of Ireland, London being the first. The Lord Lieutenant and his court appeared to exercise full regal sway, but the Castle civil servants knew it was largely a sham. Poynings had clipped his successors' wings and had made it impossible for the English "garrison" in Ireland to pursue any policy, no matter how desirable for Ireland, which happened to be against English interests.

One effect of the old situation can be felt to this day: that the only real success recognised by the Dubliner is a London success, although in recent years an American success has also begun to count. Hence the brain drain to London and other places, which has outlasted even the notorious brawn drain that weakened and impoverished the country during two centuries. Swift spoke for all Irish authors and painters, sculptors and scholars, actors, musicians and poets when, after a glorious decade of mingling with the mighty on the banks of the Thames, he described his enforced return to his native city to be dean of its most prestigious cathedral as a going into miserable exile.

All Dublin could hope to be was a place where Ireland's well-to-do enjoyed themselves to the top of their bent, with little need to be concerned with life's whys and wherefores. It wasn't that they were inferior in capability to English people. The English Mrs Delany found most of her Irish acquaintances 'much the same as in England... a mixture of good and bad; all that I have met with behave themselves very decently, according to their rank, now and then an oddity breaks out, but none so extraordinary but that I can match them in England.'

But because Dubliners had little in their social surroundings to give their life much point beyond the incessant pursuit of pleasure, there grew up the sneering cynical attitude towards serious endeavour for which the city is sadly so well-known, an attitude bred by futility and frustration.

JOHN O'DONOVAN
from *Life by the Liffey: A Kaleidoscope of Dubliners* (1986)

Dublin, Fare Thee Well

Like all Dublin writers he was caught up in the perpetual Dublin jealousies and quarrels, for success is not easily forgiven. He was pursued by threats and eventually left Dublin in a rage and never returned. This was a disaster for his talent. He was one of the many for whom the powerful Dublin spell is necessary. The Irish writer works best in his own country, but his countrymen are his worst enemies and he can succeed only outside it, either in England or America. O'Casey preached unity in Ireland at a time when there was, as yet, no feeling for unity.

V.S. PRITCHETT
from *Dublin* (1991)

A Superior Soul

Little Chandler quickened his pace. For the first time in his life he felt himself superior to the people he passed. For the first time his soul revolted against the dull inelegance of Capel Street. There was no doubt about it: if you wanted to succeed you had to go away. You could do nothing in Dublin. As he crossed Grattan Bridge he looked down the river towards the lower quays and pitied the poor stunted houses. They seemed to him a band of tramps, huddled together along the river-banks, their old coats covered with dust and soot, stupefied by the panorama of sunset and waiting for the first chill of night to bid them arise, shake themselves and begone. He wondered whether he could write a poem to express his idea. Perhaps Gallaher might be able to get it into some London paper for him. Could he write something original? He was not sure what idea he wished to express, but the thought that a poetic moment had touched him took life within him like an infant hope. He stepped onward bravely.

Every step brought him nearer to London, farther from his own sober inartistic life.

JAMES JOYCE
from 'A Little Cloud', *Dubliners* (1914)

No Mean City

Though naughty flesh will multiply
Our chief delight is in division;
Whatever of Divinity
We all are Doctors of Derision.
Content to risk a far salvation
For the quick coinage of a laugh
We cut, to make wit's reputation,
Our total of two friends by half.

PATRICK McDONOGH
from *One Landscape Still* (1958)

The Base and Ludicrous

I did not set foot in Ireland again until 1905, and not then on my own initiative. I went back to please my wife; and a curious reluctance to retrace my steps made me land in the south and enter Dublin thrugh the backdoor from Meath rather than return as I came, through the front door on the sea. In 1876 I had had enough of Dublin. James Joyce in his *Ulysses* has described, with a fidelity so ruthless that the book is hardly bearable, the life that Dublin offers to its young men, or, if you prefer to put it the other way, that its young men offer to Dublin. No doubt it is much like the life of young men everywhere in modern urban civilisation. A certain flippant futile derision and belittlement that confuses the noble and serious with the base and ludicrous seems to me peculiar to Dublin; but I suppose that is because my personal experience of that phase of youth was a Dublin experience; for when I left my native city I left that phase behind me, and associated no more with men of my age until, after about eight years of solitude in this respect, I was drawn into the Socialist revival of the early eighties, among Englishmen intensely serious and burning with indignation at very real and very fundamental evils that affected all the world; so that the reaction against them bound the finer spirits of all the nations together instead of making them cherish hatred of one another as a national virtue. Thus, when I left Dublin I left (a few private friendships apart) no society that did not disgust me. To this day my sentimental regard for Ireland does not include the capital. I am not enamored of failure, of poverty, of obscurity, and of the ostracism and contempt which these imply; and these were all that Dublin offered to the enormity of my unconscious ambition. The cities a man likes are the cities he has conquered. Napoleon did not turn from Paris to sentimentalise over Ajaccio, nor Catherine from St Petersburg to Stettin as the centre of her universe.

BERNARD SHAW
from *Composite Autobiography,* edited by Stanley Weintraub (1969)

Rat Trap

After the scum of the offal was skimmed from the top of the huge vats, the tallow was tapped and taken off for soap and candle making. The bones were put into a lime solution which burned off any remaining flesh, and then they were milled into a fine powder. My job was to shovel the bonemeal into sacks for sale to farmers who would feed it to other cattle to fatten them up. But often I had to clean the yard, slopping around through the blood, guts and the crappings of the terrified creatures. It was after this task that I would find the blood beneath my nails. On the bus on the way home I could smell myself and the smell disgusted me. In those days the abattoir became to me like a metaphor for my existence in Dublin.

My chief workmate was a stocky little man called Paul. He carried an axe in his waistband in readiness for the fight he hoped was coming. He was totally without fear, which is a terrifying thing in its ultimate stupidity. It was Paul in Dublin whom I had in mind years later when I wrote 'Rat Trap'. 'Hope bites the dust behind all the closed doors and pus and grime ooze from its scab-crusted sores.'

One Sunday he insisted I went for a drink with him after mass. It wasn't an invitation so much as a summons which it would have been imprudent to ignore. That day he showed me a side of life in Dublin which a boy like me from the soft south side of the city has little conception of, though I had some glimmerings from working with the Simon Community all those years before. There was a stripper in the pub he took me to, but nobody was watching her. Instead he and his mates were concentrating on some heavy drinking to warm up the Guinness consumed the night before. Suddenly Judy, his girlfriend, stood up from her seat, walked across the room, over the table-tops, smashed a glass and, screaming 'you fuckin' whoor', stuck it into another girl's face. That night we went to a club and on the way we passed a parked Mercedes. Its windows were steamed up and the car was rocking from vigorous sexual activity going on inside. As we reached it the door flew open and a girl's head fell out. She looked unconscious. But then a man's head appeared on top of her. As he lunged into her, the girl turned her head sideways and vomited. It went inside the car and it went on to the pavement. The man carried on lunging, and as he lunged, she puked. He came and collapsed on to her, then recovering himself shouted at the drunken woman's face, 'Jaysus, look at the fuckin' mess you've made of my brother's car.' This was the rat trap, this was the future, deadening and dispiriting. I saw clearly then that I would never be able to get started on anything in my life unless I got out of Ireland.

One glum November night with the fog coming in heavy from the sea and the upstairs windows of the No. 7A bus all steamed up with a mixture of dense cigarette smoke and the condensation from damp coats and body heat, I pressed my head against the glass and watched the pale yellow glow of the street lights as we passed. The conductor sang 'Delilah' loudly and continuously as he moved back and forth between the lower and upper decks.

'My, my, my Delilah,' he brayed, and then *sotto voce* added the orchestral counterpoint in words of his own lewd invention: 'Get yer knickers off, get yer knickers off.'

The passengers hunched their shoulders against the assault of his unfailing jocularity. I folded the bus ticket in two and tried to clean my nails.

'Tell you what,' he repeated yet again, as he approached a school-girl for her fare. 'You tell me you haven't got the money, then I'll take your name and address and, you never know, tonight could be your lucky night.'

* * *

The bus continued its unsteady progress along the route which touched the major landmarks of my life so far: Booterstown and the train, Blackrock and the school, Mount Merrion Avenue and our first house, Murray's and the dope, Glenageary Road and the dead hand of the present. I turned from this landscape of unchanging drabness, my forehead damp from the glass. All around me were faces in sullen concentration, faces in empty conversation, faces coughing wetly into *Evening Herald* situation-vacant pages and faces set in the pragmatic resolution which was the only heroism of the times. The bus seemed full that grey evening of the hopeless and the doomed, certainly full of everything I never wanted to be. And here I was with the blood of the abattoir staining my hands. But I was getting out. Again.

BOB GELDOF
from *Is That It?* (1986)

Drunk

Four o'clock on this oblong Tuesday. Sebastian pushing through the door of a secret public house, moved cautiously to an empty space at the bar. Bartender suspiciously approaching him.

'I want a triple Irish, Gold Label. Quickly please.'

'Sir, I'm afraid I can't serve you.'

'You what?'

'Can't serve you, sir, rules of the house, you've had enough to drink.'

'I've had enough to drink? What on earth do you mean?'

'I think, sir, you've had sufficient unto your needs now. I think you've had enough now.'

'This is contemptible.'

'Peacefully sir, now. Keep the peace. When you're sober sir, now, be very glad to serve you. Little sleep. You'll be fine'

'Frightful outrage. Are you sure you're not drunk yourself?'

'Now sir, a place and time for everything.'

'Well for Jesus sake.'

Sebastian turned from the bar pushed out through the door and along the street. In dazed condition. Along the pavement by shop windows with pens and pencils and stone steps to Georgian doors and black spokes of fences and by a tea shop with gray women clustered at the tables. So I'm drunk. Strangled Christ. Drunk. Nothing to do but suffer this insult as I have suffered so many others.

It will die away in a few years, no worry about that. I'm going on
a tram ride. Dalkey. That nice little town out there on the rocks
with pretty castles and everything. A place where I will move when
the quids are upon me. I hate this country. I think I hate this country
more than anything else I know. Drunk. That son of a bitch, take
him up by the ears from behind that bar and beat him against the
ceiling. But must forget the whole thing. I'm at the bottom of the
pile. Admit that I'm in such a state that I can barely think. But I
won't be insulted. Incredible outrage.

He passed in front of the Kildare Street Club, crossed over the
street and waited for the tram, leaning against the railings of Trinity
College.

J.P. DONLEAVY
from *The Ginger Man* (1955)

Tale of Two Cities

The streets of London are not paved with gold,
The streets of London are paved with failures;
They get up and move about when they are filled with drink
Just as in Dublin. Yesterday in Fleet Street
In a pub I met one. He shook my hand
And he was full of poisonous fellowship as he looked into my eyes:
I would have a double whiskey.
I was from Dublin, most wonderful spot on earth.

How was Harry Kelly, Jack Sullivan and Brady
And Galligan the greatest Dubliner of them all?
I'll tell you the name of the greatest living poet, he muttered,
He lives near Manchester and will be heard of yet.
What about Auden, I interrupted. He ignored me –
Yeats was second rate, not a patch on Higgins –
I was back in Dublin as I listened.
You certainly must have another double whiskey, he cried
And once again he gripped my hand in his
And said there was no place like Dublin.

His friendship wounded, but I dare not complain
For that would seem boorish. Yet it was this
Insincere good-nature that hurt me in Dublin.
The sardonic humour of a man about to be hanged.
But London would not hang him; it laid him horizontal
To dream of the books he had written in liquor
Once again he would return to Dublin.
Where among the failures he would pass unnoticed,
Happy in pubs talking about yesterday's wits,
And George Moore's use of the semi-colon.

PATRICK KAVANAGH
from *Collected Poems* (1964)

Inside the Pale

Dublin wasn't Ireland and I kept reminding myself of that. I had
never stopped reading the provincial papers, a habit I developed
in the Irish News Agency because the local notes and news were
often a first class source. As a reporter in Ballina I was not too long
learning that Dublin papers give scant coverage to matters outside
'The Pale' and I made the promise, even then, that if ever I got to
Dublin I'd do what I could to see 'country news' got a fair show.

JOHN HEALY
from *Healy, Reporter* (1991)

A Faint Mortal Odour

Grafton Street, along which he walked, prolonged that moment of
discouraged poverty. In the roadway at the head of the street a slab
was set to the memory of Wolfe Tone and he remembered having
been present with his father at its laying. He remembered with
bitterness that scene of tawdry tribute. There were four French

delegates in a brake and one, a plump smiling young man, held, wedged on a stick, a card on which were printed the words: *Vive l'Irlande!*

But the trees in Stephen's Green were fragrant of rain and the rainsodden earth gave forth its mortal odour, a faint incense rising upward through the mould from many hearts. The soul of the gallant venal city which his elders had told him of had shrunk with time to a faint mortal odour rising from the earth.

JAMES JOYCE
from *A Portrait of the Artist as a Young Man* (1916)

The Primacy of the Factual

It was no accident that Joyce chose to make use of so many characters who had an actual existence of their own and to insert real events into *Ulysses*. He recognised the primacy of the factual, in a society obsessed with self-inquisition, and daringly, almost with disdain, showed how, set in the mosaic of a work of art, it can illumine the final result.

ULICK O'CONNOR
from *Biographers and the Art of Biography* (1991)

Gloomy Respectability

An August Sunday afternoon in the north side of Dublin. Epitome of all that is hot, arid, and empty. Tall brick houses, browbeating each other in gloomy respectability across the white streets; broad pavements, promenaded mainly by the nomadic cat; stifling squares, wherein the infant of unfashionable parentage is taken for the daily baking that is its substitute for the breezes and the press of perambulators on the Bray Esplanade or the Kingston pier. Few towns are duller out of the season than Dublin, but the dullness of its north side neither waxes nor wanes; it is immutable, unchangeable, fixed as the stars. So at least it appears to the observer whose impressions are only eye-deep, and are derived from the emptiness of the streets, the unvarying dirt of the window panes, and the almost forgotten type of ugliness of the window curtains.

SOMERVILLE & ROSS
from *The Real Charlotte* (1894)

Secret Lives

In the house we lived on Baggot Street there was a young woman who was secretly married to the son of a very famous Dublin family. He would sneak over to see her for a few hours every night. Because his family was respectable, and hers was not, the marriage was unknown. There were all kinds of liaisons warrened away in houses. There was a woman who had a baby but she went around with a pillow under her skirt because she had to pretend she hadn't had the baby. The whole dreadful, dreadful 50s thing that there was no sex and that nobody got pregnant before marriage led to so many secret lives. Dublin connived with these secret lives. There were huge houses in Pembroke Street and all along the canal; all the Georgian streets where there were twenty or thirty people, twenty or thirty different secret lives in each of those houses. All of them hiding from official Ireland, all of them ready for the 60s. There were also very respectable business ladies who lived in bedsitters and always had done, and had little coal fires. They were the heads of cosmetic counters or they were something in the civil service and gradually I came across them. They took a little drink privately.

NUALA O'FAOLÁIN
from *Alive, Alive O!*
edited by Mairín Johnston (1988)

Anything To Grasp At

Sean felt that if he stayed in Dublin, life would become embarrassing to meet. Dublin was too close to everyone. All its streets led into the one square where everyone met, where hands were shaken, shoulders clapped, and drinks taken to every other person's health. Sound and happy association, with one reservation – that when one was on the way to a good creation, he might be waylaid, left by the wayside, to die there, unfortified by the rites of the church. He remembered what he had gone through with his last play: Mr Robinson agitated during rehearsals; silent sullenness stiffening the dialogue spoken by the actors; Lady Gregory anxious, and talking to Yeats about what might happen; and gigantic whispers wandering from one room to another in the Abbey Theatre, making the sullen more sullen still. 'I refuse to say the word Snotty,' said F.J. McCormick, while someone, in the background, murmured For righteous men must make our land a nation once again; 'and I,' said Miss Eileen Crowe – having first asked her priest about it – 'refuse to say the words "Ne'er a one o' Jennie Gogan's kids was born outside of th' bordhers of the Ten Commandments",' a chorus in the background chanting,

> Oh, sure you're right, allanna, for decent people know
> That every girl in Ireland, as things at present go,
> Is the soul of truth and of melting ruth,
> With a smile like a summer at dawn;
> Like the colleens that trip up and the colleens that trip down
> The sweet valley of Slieve na Man, amen.

O Yes, O Yes, and there was Mr O'Brien, the Abbey Director, running round moaning, 'The Song, The Song! That'll have to come out; Yeats, you've got to be careful.' And the lights in the pubs went higher and higher, and everything in them was agog and aglow. And Mr Michael Dolan, the theatre's Manager, writing to Lady Gregory beseeching her, with tears in his eyes, beseeching her, of her charity, now that the theatre was booming, to have nothing to do with this play; for the language, oh, the language in it goes beyond the beyonds; and the song at the end of the second act, oh, the song at the end of the second act, sung by the girl of the streets, is, is unpardonable; and we don't want to give any enemy of the theatre Anything To Grasp At...

*   *   *

Sean realised now that the theatre, called the Abbey, as a whole was against him, and that it would be a good thing to put a greater distance between it and him (though it was very ironical to look back to see that some of these very actors, who had so strongly protested against the play, afterwards – when the tumult had died down – carried it all over the United States to their own advantage, bringing back many dollars which happily made their future a little less uncertain for them than it had been).

SEAN O'CASEY
from *Inishfallen, Fare Thee Well* (1949)

Town of Little Stars

Let us arise and mosey
Round clammy, cosy Dublin –
Embellied slowbloat town
Of dole and rain and lichen
Thick, sluggish, thriving
On singers' thin ambitions.

Round the dives we go
Round the Rock Garden, Coffee Inn,
Galleries of clownish grins
Vibrant with the stink
Of drink, the drink, the drink,
Lillies, The Pink
And other tipsy hostelries.

Grinning, grinning,
Like skeletons of strychnine
I hear grinning musicians
Inept with dreaming
And the sound of pints talking
At an inappropriate volume.

Grinning, grinning,
Comfy in the slum
Of singers, strings and drums

Of Temple Lane, crawsick
With the offal breath
Of Dublin prate.

Round the dives we go
Trumpeting our own demise
Puffed with the guff of critics
But no crowds.

Graft? Craft? Rehearsal? Toil?
Please
Don't bore me with details,
I'm a myth in the mind of Grafton Street.
Queen of kitsch, mean, lean sonofabitch
With shades in the rain and leather jeans;
Brother pass the vaseline
I've got another palm to grease,
And brother can you give me a ride?
There's nought so sad a sight
As a tarted star lugging his own gear
Down the ragged arse of Temple Bar.

PETER MURPHY

Dublin Jackeens

His own room behind the shop in South King Street seemed better
to him than it had for a long time. After all, he and Annie had a
range. They had gaslight. And they had the use of the lavatory on
the upper landing. He was pleased to think of the many advantages
he had over those people who had been peeping out at him. He used
to think sometimes that South King Street was a dungeon in which
he was imprisoned for life, while other men went here and went
there, and did this and did that, and some of them even went off
to Paris. But at the moment he felt it was a fine thing after all to
have a place of your own to keep things in, a place where you could
lie down if you were sick or worn out. And it was within a stone's
throw of the Pillar.

He didn't get out enough – that was the trouble. If he got out and about more he'd have the right attitude to the house, and maybe to the shop, too. No wonder he was sick of it, never leaving it except like this, to do a message. He should take an odd day off. Man! What was he talking about? He ought to take a week. He ought to run over to Paris and look up the boys. Then, as if aghast at the magnitude of his revolt, he gave himself an alternative. He should go over to Liverpool, anyway, for one of the weekend race meetings. With a bit of luck he might make his expenses, and that would shut Annie's mouth.

*   *   *

The Dublin people couldn't tell you the difference between a bush and a tree. Manny stood to recover his breath. And he thought of his wife with her yellow elbows coming through the black unravelled sleeve of her cardigan, as she leaned across the counter in the dismal shop, giving off old shaffoge with any shawley who came the way and had an hour, or maybe two hours, to spare. He thought of the bars filled with his cronies talking about the state of the country for all they were fit, men that never saw more of it than you'd see from the top of a tram. He thought of the skitting young fellows and girls outside Whitefriar Street after late Mass on a Sunday, and he thought of the old men standing at the pub ends of the streets, ringing themselves round with spits. He thought of the old women leaning against the jambs of their doorways, with white crockery milk jugs hanging out of their hands, forgotten in the squalor of their gossip. He thought of the children sitting among the trodden and rancid cabbage butts on the edge of the pavements, repeating the gossip they had heard when they crouched, unheeded, under some public-house counter. He thought of the young and the old, the men and the women, and the pale, frightened children, who were shuffling along the kneelers in churches all over the city, waiting their turn to snuffle out their sins in the dark wooden confessionals. And it seemed as if the cool green light of day scarcely ever reached those people, and the only breezes that blew into their lives came from under their draughty doors thickened with the warm odour of boiling potatoes. The loathing he'd felt for the city, years before, when he first came to Dublin, stole over him again as it had done on that night long ago in the little theatre in Mary Street. Dublin jackeens! he thought.

'Dublin jackeens!' he said then out loud, the gibe coming forth from a dim corner in his mind where the memory of a buttercup field, and a cobbled yard pricked with grass, gave him the right to feel different from them. Once more he longed to get away from Dublin. But this time there was a difference. He wanted to get away from Dublin – yes – but not from Ireland. He didn't want to go away from Ireland, he thought with anguish. Not away from her yellow fields. Not away from her emerald ditches. He wanted only to get away from the stuffy Dublin streets and the people that walked them. Even to get away occasionally for an hour like this would satisfy him.

*   *   *

He remembered what he had said to himself up at Sallygap about the people of Dublin: that they were ignorant, with clogged pools in their blood that clotted easily to unjust hate. They hugged their hate. He thought of Paris, with its flashing lights and its flashing hates, its quick flashing knives; but the dangers in Paris seemed vivid and vital compared with the dead anger in the sullen eyes that were watching him. Desperately he thought of the hills, but the thought of them gave him no refuge. The happy hills were fading from his mind already. He would never seek a sanctuary among them again.

For there was no sanctuary from hatred such as he saw in Annie's eyes, unless it came from behind some night, from a raised hatchet brought down with a crack on his skull, or from a queer taste in the mouth followed by a twisting in the guts. She had him imprisoned for ever in her hatred. His little fiddle had crashed on the pier the day he gave up all his dreams for her, and it had floated in splintered sticks on the dirty water. He thought of it for a moment, and then he thought of nothing at all for a while, but just sat watching her as she went about the room.

MARY LAVIN
from 'At Sallygap', *The Stories of Mary Lavin* (1974)

A Helpless Animal

She stood among the swaying crowd in the station at the North Wall. He held her hand and she knew that he was speaking to her, saying something about the passage over and over again. The station was full of soldiers with brown baggages. Through the wide doors of the sheds she caught a glimpse of the black mass of the boat, lying in beside the quay wall, with illumined portholes. She answered nothing. She felt her cheek pale and cold and, out of a maze of distress, she prayed to God to direct her, to show her what was her duty. The boat blew a long mournful whistle into the mist. If she went, to-morrow she would be on the sea with Frank, steaming towards Buenos Ayres. Their passage had been booked. Could she still draw back after all he had done for her? Her distress awoke a nausea in her body and she kept moving her lips in silent fervent prayer.

A bell clanged upon her heart. She felt him seize her hand:

– Come!

All the seas of the world tumbled about her heart. He was drawing her into them: he would drown her. She gripped with both hands at the iron railing.

– Come!

No! No! No! It was impossible. Her hands clutched the iron in frenzy. Amid the seas she sent a cry of anguish.

– Eveline! Evvy!

He rushed beyond the barrier and called to her to follow. He was shouted at to go on but he still called to her. She set her white face to him, passive, like a helpless animal. Her eyes gave him no sign of love or farewell or recognition.

JAMES JOYCE
from 'Eveline', *Dubliners* (1914)

Fighting Like Divils

O, Dublin City, there is no doubting
Bates every city upon the say:
'Tis there you'd hear O'Connell spouting,
And see Lady Morgan making tay.
For 'tis the capital of the finest nation
With charming peasantry on a fruitful sod,
Fighting like divils for conciliation
And hating each other for the love of God.

W.J. FITZPATRICK
from *The Life of Charles Lever* (1884)

Family Man

'Tickle me the way you tickle my Mammy,' I said. I climbed up
on the bed and he smiled down. The colours were runnin' down
his face like a river. Bright splashing colours. 'Go on tickle me,' I
said. An' he tickled my belly with his colours. 'I have a secret,' I
said, 'Mammy says I've to tell no-one 'specially not you.' 'Are you
goin' to tell me it?' he said. 'Tickle me again an' I'll tell.' I said.
'It's a big secret.' 'I swear I won't tell anybody,' he said laughin'.
'Let me in beside you first.' I said. I go in under the covers where
it was soft. 'Well then,' he said. 'What's the big secret?' 'Me an'
Mammy went down the town an' we turned a road an' then another
road. We saw you sittin' in the car with a lady an' Mammy hurt
my arm an' said I wasn't to tell no one. 'Specially not you. I see
your colours Daddy,' I said. 'I see them.' He laughed down an' all
the colours grew bright an' came runnin' down his face. 'Say how
old I am, say?' I said. 'You're three!' he said, an' he tickled me.
'No I'm not. Three is a baby. I'm four now. Say it Daddy. Say how
old I am.' 'Three-and-a-half,' he said. The laughin' came closer.
'I'm not three-and-a-half. I just told you, I'm four now.' He tickled
me again an' I was laughin' into his colours. Then it was dark. I
felt the Dark touchin' me funny an' I was cryin' so Maggie came
an' he touched Maggie funny not me. Not me. Not me.

The Big Dark was grindin' the Little Dark's bones to smithereens.
Then the bones were a white dust an' the dust began to whirl an'
fall on my bed. It came higher an' higher until I was sucked down
under it an' I couldn't breathe.

He was looking down on me and then he pulled the blankets off
me an' touched me funny. Mammy came in an' I thought 'It'll be
all right now. It'll be all right.' It was dark but she didn't turn the
light on. She stood beside my pillow an' looked at him doin' the
funny things. Her eyes were sort of glintin' and she looked real
cold. I went to say 'Mammy stop him hurtin' me,' but she wasn't
mindin' me. She was in the faraway place watchin' him doin' the
funny things so I pretended I wasn't there. Then he went down-
stairs and she went into the toilet. When she came back she switched
the light on an' I started to cry. 'Look,' I said. 'Look is that red
blood on the sheets? Is it Mammy?' She came over an' pulled the
covers up and told me to lie down. 'Go to sleep now,' she said.
'You had a bad dream.' 'It wasn't a dream, Mammy,' I said. 'It was
real.' She bent down over me. 'It was a dream. Now go to sleep.'

'It wasn't Mammy,' I cried. 'Say it wasn't. Look.' I pushed the covers down and showed her the red blood. 'Look at that,' I said, 'It was a dream,' she said. 'Now lie down and go to sleep.' 'It wasn't, Mammy. Say it wasn't. Say it was real.' When she was gone I switched the light on again to look at the blood. 'Look at it, Maggie,' I said. 'She said it was a dream but it wasn't. It was real.' Maggie came to have a look an' she started laughin' mad an' then I laughed too. I kept pointin' at the red blood and laughin' my head off.

DOROTHY NELSON
from *In Night's City* (1982)

Jumping Out At You

O'Connell Street was thick with a grey precarious snow that had packed hard like marble underneath the slush. Roaring groups of Christmas Eve Dublin drinkers spilled out from the pubs and disco bars. Police cars prowled up and down, fishtailing around icy corners, red lights wet in the shop windows, which gaped with sad-eyed mannequins. The water in the Anna Livia memorial – the floosie in the jacuzzi – was frozen solid, crisp bags, Coke cans, condom packets and burger wrappers all fossilised in the translucent ice. The GPO shimmered with pale yellow light and the windows had all been decorated with green sashes that had 'Welcome Home For Christmas' stamped on in gold. Down Henry Street the star-shaped lights glinted suggestively in the purple smog. Talbot Street was the same. Eddie saw a lurching drunk in a Santa Claus uniform hail down a taxi and jump in, pausing only to pull a packet of twenty cigarettes from his breast pocket. Two soldiers waited at a bus stop, fat kitbags by their feet. Queues stretched out from the doors of the fast-food joints. The pool halls and gambling arcades were full of young guys in jeans, cursing, rattling pool balls into pockets. And the whole street seemed to vibrate with the exultant buzz of the jackpot bells and the insistent thud of piped heavy metal. Couples skidded up and down the pavement, Christmas lights in their eyes, laughing, kissing, fighting. Under the statue of Daniel O'Connell, a group of stocky traveller women all wrapped in tartan blankets shared a flask of something steamy, counting out the day's money into a battered mushroom punnet. And all along the Liffey the black water danced with light, all the way down past the silver Halfpenny Bridge and into the Phoenix Park, where the neon rainbow glowed up and down the huge papal cross.

Eddie picked his way down past the black bulk of Trinity College, towards Westland Row, feeling apprehensive and excited in equal measure. Dublin at Christmas was a dangerous town. Too many familiar people, all waiting to jump out of the shadows and wave their latest attitude in your face.

JOSEPH O'CONNOR
from *Cowboys & Indians* (1991)

Two More Gallants

You will not, I believe, find either Lenehan or Corley still parading the streets of Dublin, but often in the early evening a man called Heffernan may be found raising a glass of Paddy in Toner's public house; and FitzPatrick, on his bicycle, every working day makes the journey across the city, from Ranelagh to the offices of McGibbon, Tait & FitzPatrick, solicitors and commissioners for oaths. It is on his doctor's advice that he employs this mode of transport. It is against the advice of *his* that Heffernan continues to indulge himself in Toner's. The two men no longer know one another. They do not meet and, in order to avoid a confrontation, each has been known to cross a street.

Thirty or so years ago, when I first knew Heffernan and Fitz-Patrick, the relationship was different. The pair were closely attached, Heffernan the mentor, FitzPatrick ready with a laugh. All three of us were students, but Heffernan, a Kilkenny man, was different in the sense that he had been a student for as long as anyone could remember. The College porters said they recalled his presence over fifteen years and, though given to exaggeration, they may well have been accurate in that: certainly Heffernan was well over thirty, a small ferrety man, swift to take offence.

FitzPatrick was bigger and more amiable. An easy smile perpetually creased the bland ham of his face, causing people to believe, quite incorrectly, that he was stupid. His mouse-coloured hair was kept short enough not to require a parting, his eyes reflected so profound a degree of laziness that people occasionally professed surprise to find them open. Heffernan favoured pin-striped suits, FitzPatrick a commodious blue blazer. They drank in Kehoe's in Anne Street.

'He is one of those chancers,' Heffernan said, 'we could do without.'

'Oh, a right old bollocks,' agreed FitzPatrick.

' "Well, Mr Heffernan," he says, "I see you are still with us." '

'As though you might be dead.'

'If he had his way.'

In the snug of Kehoe's they spoke of Heffernan's *bête noire*, the aged Professor Flacks, a man from the North of Ireland.

' "I see you are still with us," Heffernan repeated. 'Did you ever hear the beat of that?'

'Sure, Flacks is senile.'

'The mots in the lecture giggle when he says it.'

'Oh, an ignorant bloody crowd.'

Heffernan became meditative. Slowly he lit a Sweet Afton. He was supported in his continuing studentship by the legacy left to him for that purpose by an uncle in Kilkenny, funds which would cease when he was a student no longer. He kept that tragedy at bay by regularly failing the Little-go examination, a test of proficiency in general studies to which all students were obliged to submit themselves.

'A fellow came up to me this morning,' he said now, 'a right eejit from Monasterevin. Was I looking for grinds in Little-go Logic? Five shillings an hour.'

FitzPatrick laughed. He lifted his glass of stout and drank from it, imposing on his upper lip a moustache of foam which was permitted to remain there.

'A minion of Flacks',' Heffernan continued. 'A Flacks boy and no mistake, I said to myself.'

'You can tell them a mile off.'

' "I know your father," I said to him. "Doesn't he deliver milk?" Well, he went the colour of a sunset. "Avoid conversation with Flacks," I told him. "He drove a wife and two sisters insane." '

'Did your man say anything?'

'Nothing, only "Cripes".'

'Oh, Flacks is definitely peculiar,' FitzPatrick agreed.

In point of fact, at that time FitzPatrick had never met Professor Flacks. It was his laziness that caused him to converse in a manner which suggested he had, and it was his laziness also which prevented him from noticing the intensity of Heffernan's grievance. Heffernan

hated Professor Flacks with a fervour, but in his vague and un-
questioning way FitzPatrick assumed that the old professor was
no more than a passing thorn in his friend's flesh, a nuisance that
could be exorcised by means of complaint and abuse. Heffernan's
pride did not at that time appear to play a part; and FitzPatrick, who
knew his friend as well as anyone did, would not have designated
him as a possessor of that quality to an unusual degree. The opposite
was rather implied by the nature of his upkeep and his efforts not
to succeed in the Little-go examination. But pride, since its presence
might indeed be questioned by these facts, came to its own support:
when the story is told in Dublin today it is never forgotten that it
has roots in Professor Flacks's causing girls to giggle because he
repeatedly made a joke at Heffernan's expense.

Employed by the University to instruct in certain aspects of liter-
ature, professor Flacks concentrated his attention on the writings
of James Joyce. Shakespeare, Tennyson, Shelley, Coleridge, Wilde,
Swift, Dickens, Eliot, Trollope, and many another familiar name
were all bundled away in favour of a Joycean scholarship that thirty
or so years ago was second to none in Irish university life. Professor
Flacks could tell you whom Joyce had described as a terrified YMCA
man, and the date of the day on which he had written that his
soul was full of decayed ambitions. He spoke knowledgeably of the
stale smell of incense, like foul flowerwater; and of flushed eaves
and stubble geese.

'Inane bloody show-off,' Heffernan said nastily in Kehoe's.

'You'll see him out, Heff.'

'A bogs like that would last for ever.'

Twelve months later, after he and Heffernan had parted company,
FitzPatrick repeated all that to me. I didn't know either of them
well, but was curious because a notable friendship had so abruptly
come to an end. FitzPatrick, on his own, was inclined to talk to
anyone.

We sat in College Park, watching the cricket while he endeavoured
to remember the order of subsequent events. It was Heffernan who'd
had the idea, as naturally it would be, since FitzPatrick still knew
Professor Flacks only by repute and had not suffered the sarcasm
which Heffernan found so offensive. But FitzPatrick played a vital
part in the events which followed, because the elderly woman who
played the main part of all was a general maid in FitzPatrick's digs.

'Has that one her slates on?' Heffernan inquired one night as
they passed her by in the hall.

'Ah, she's only a bit quiet.'

'She has a docile expression all right.'

'She wouldn't damage a fly.'

Soon after that Heffernan took to calling in at FitzPatrick's digs in Donnybrook more often than he had in the past. Sometimes he was there when FitzPatrick arrived back in the evening, sitting in the kitchen while the elderly maid pricked sausages or cut up bread for the meal that would shortly be served. Mrs Maginn, the landlady, liked to lie down for a while at that time of day, so Heffernan and the maid had the kitchen to themselves. But finding him present on several occasions when she came downstairs, Mrs Maginn in passing mentioned the fact to her lodger. Fitzpatrick, who didn't himself understand what Heffernan's interest in the general maid was, replied that his friend liked to await his return in the kitchen because it was warm. Being an easy-going woman, Mrs Maginn was appeased.

'There's no doubt in my mind at all,' Heffernan stated in Kehoe's after a few weeks of this behaviour. 'If old Flacks could hear it he'd have a tortoise's pup.'

FitzPatrick wagged his head, knowing that an explanation was in the air. Heffernan said: 'She's an interesting old lassie.'

He then told FitzPatrick a story which FitzPatrick had never heard before. It concerned a man called Corley who had persuaded a maid in a house in Baggot Street to do a small service for him. It concerned, as well, Corley's friend, Lenehan, who was something of a wit. At first FitzPatrick was confused by the story, imagining it to be about a couple of fellow-students whom he couldn't place.

'The pen of Jimmy Joyce,' Heffernan explained. 'That yam is Flacks's favourite of the lot.'

'Well, I'd say there wasn't much to it. Sure, a skivvy never would.'

'She was gone on Corley.'

'But would she steal for him?'

'You're no romantic, Fitz.'

FitzPatrick laughed, agreeable to accepting this opinion. Then, to his astonishment, Heffernan said: 'It's the same skivvy Mrs Maginn has above in your digs.'

FitzPatrick shook his head. He told Heffernan to go on with himself, but Heffernan insisted.

'She told me the full story herself one night I was waiting for you maybe the first night I ever addressed a word to her. "Come into the kitchen outa the cold, Mr Heffernan," she says. D'you remember the occasion it was? Late after tea, and you didn't turn up at all. She fried me an egg.'

'But, holy Christ, man – '

'It was the same night you did well with the nurse from Dundrum.'

FitzPatrick guffawed. A great girl, he said. He repeated a few details, but Heffernan didn't seem interested.

'I was told the whole works in the kitchen, like Jimmy Joyce had it out of her when she was still in her teens. A little gold sovereign was what she fecked for your man.'

'But the poor old creature is as honest as the day's long.'

'Oh, she took it all right and she still thinks Corley was top of the bill.'

'But Corley never existed –'

'Of course he did. Wasn't he for ever entertaining that fine little tart with the witticisms of Master Lenehan?'

The next thing that happened, according to FitzPatrick, was that a bizarre meeting took place. Heffernan approached Professor Flacks with the information that the model for the ill-used girl in Joyce's story 'Two Gallants' had come to light in a house in Donnybrook. The Professor displayed considerable excitement, and on a night when Mrs Maginn was safely at the pictures he was met by Heffernan at the bus stop and led to the kitchen.

He was a frail man in a tweed suit, not at all as FitzPatrick had imagined him. Mrs Maginn's servant, a woman of about the same age, was slightly deaf and moved slowly owing to rheumatism. Heffernan had bought half a pound of fig-roll biscuits which he arranged on a plate. The old woman poured tea.

Professor Flacks plied her with questions. He asked them gently, with courtesy and diplomacy, without any hint of the tetchiness described so often by Heffernan. It was a polite occasion in the kitchen, Heffernan handing round the fig-rolls, the maid appearing to delight in recalling a romance in her past.

'And later you told Mr Joyce about this?' prompted Professor Flacks.

'He used come to the house when I worked in North Frederick Street, sir. A dentist by the name of O'Riordan.'

'Mr Joyce came to get his teeth done?'

'He did, sir.'

'And you'd talk to him in the waiting-room, is that it?'

'I'd be lonesome, sir. I'd open the hall door when the bell rang and then there'd be a wait for maybe an hour before it'd ring again, sir. I recollect Mr Joyce well, sir.'

'He was interested in your – ah – association with the fellow you mentioned, was he?'

'It was only just after happening, sir. I was turned out of the place in Baggot Street on account of the bit of trouble. I was upset at the time I knew Mr Joyce, sir.'

'That's most understandable.'

'I'd often tell a patient what had happened to me.'

'But you've no hard feelings today? You were badly used by the fellow, yet – '

'Ah, it's long ago now, sir.'

Heffernan and FitzPatrick saw the Professor on to a bus and, according to FitzPatrick, he was quivering with pleasure. He clambered into a seat, delightedly talking to himself, not noticing when they waved from the pavement. They entered a convenient public house and ordered pints of stout.

'Did you put her up to it?' FitzPatrick inquired.

'The thing about that one, she'd do anything for a scrap of the ready. Didn't you ever notice that about her? She's a right old miser.'

It was that that Heffernan had recognised when first he'd paid a visit to Mrs Maginn's kitchen: the old maid was possessed of a meanness that had become obsessional with her. She spent no money whatsoever, and was clearly keen to add to what she had greedily accumulated. He had paid her a pound to repeat the story he had instructed her in.

'Didn't she say it well? Oh, top of the bill, I'd say she was.'

'You'd be sorry for old Flacks.'

'Oh, the devil take bloody Mr Flacks.'

Some months went by. Heffernan no longer visited the kitchen in Donnybrook, and he spoke hardly at all of Professor Flacks. In his lazy way FitzPatrick assumed that the falsehoods which had been perpetrated were the be-all and end-all of the affair, that Heffernan's pride – now clearly revealed to him – had somehow been satisfied. But then, one summer's afternoon while the two idled in Stephen's Green in the hope of picking up girls, Heffernan said: 'There's a thing on we might go to next Friday.'

'What's that?'

'Mr Flacks performing. The Society of the Friends of James Joyce.'

It was a public lecture, one of several that were to be delivered during a week devoted by the Society to the life and work of the author who was its *raison d'être*. The Society's members came from far afield: from the United States, Germany, Finland, Italy, Australia, France, England and Turkey. Learned academics mingled with less learned enthusiasts. Mr James Duffy's Chapelizod was visited, and Mr Power's Dublin Castle. Capel Street and Ely Place were investigated, visits were made to the renowned Martello Tower, to Howth and to Pim's. Betty Bellezza was mentioned, and Val from Skibbereen. The talk was all Joyce talk. For a lively week Joyce reigned in Dublin.

On the appointed evening FitzPatrick accompanied his friend to Professor Flacks's lecture, his premonitions suggesting that the occasion was certain to be tedious. He had no idea what Heffernan was up to, and wasn't prepared to devote energy to speculating. With a bit of luck, he hoped, he'd be able to have a sleep.

Before the main event a woman from the University of Washington spoke briefly about Joyce's use of misprints; a bearded German read a version of 'The Holy Office' that had only recently been discovered. Then the tweeded figure of Professor Flacks rose. He sipped at a tumbler of water, and spoke for almost an hour about the model for the servant girl in the story, 'Two Gallants'. His discovery of that same elderly servant, now employed in a house in Donnybrook, engendered in his audience a whisper of excitement that remained alive while he spoke, and exploded into applause when he finished. A light flush enlivened the paleness of his face as he sat down. It was, as Heffernan remarked to his dozy companion, the old man's finest hour.

It was then that FitzPatrick first became uneasy. The packed lecture-hall had accepted as fact all that had been stated, yet none of it was true. Notes had been taken, questions were now being asked. A voice just behind the two students exclaimed that this remarkable discovery was worth coming two thousand miles to hear about. Mental pictures of James Joyce in a dentist's waiting-room flashed about the hall. North Frederick Street would be visited tomorrow, if not tonight.

'I'd only like to ask,' Heffernan shouted above the hubbub, 'if I may, a simple little question.' He was on his feet. He had caught the attention of Professor Flacks, who was smiling benignly at him. 'I'd only like to inquire,' Heffernan continued, 'if that whole thing couldn't be a lot of baloney.'

'Baloney?' a foreign voice repeated.

'Baloney?' said Professor Flacks.

The buzz of interest hadn't died down. Nobody was much interested in the questions that were being asked except the people who were asking them. A woman near to FitzPatrick said it was extraordinarily moving that the ill-used servant girl, who had been so tellingly presented as an off-stage character by Joyce, should bear no grudge all these years later.

'What I mean, Professor Flacks,' said Heffernan, 'is I don't think James Joyce ever attended a dentist in North Frederick Street. What I'm suggesting to you, sir, is that the source of your information was only looking for a bit of limelight.'

FitzPatrick later described to me the expression that entered Professor Flacks's eyes. 'A lost kind of look,' he said, 'as though someone had poked the living daylights out of him.' The old man stared at Heffernan, frowning, not comprehending at first. His relationship with this student had been quite different since the night of the visit to Mrs Maginn's kitchen: it had been distinguished by a new friendliness, and what had seemed like mutual respect.

'Professor Flacks and myself,' continued Heffernan, 'heard the old lady together. Only I formed the impression that she was making the entire matter up. I thought, sir, you'd formed that opinion also.'

'Oh, but surely now, Mr Heffernan, the woman wouldn't do that.'

'There was never a dentist by the name of O'Riordan that practised in North Frederick Street, sir. That's a fact that can easily be checked.'

Heffernan sat down. An uneasy silence gripped the lecture-hall. Eyes turned upon Professor Flacks. Weakly, with a hoarseness in his voice, he said: 'But why, Mr Heffernan, would she have made all that up? A woman of that class would hardly have read the story, she'd hardly have known – '

'It's an unfortunate thing, sir,' interrupted Heffernan, standing up again, 'but that old one would do anything for a single pound note. She's of a miserly nature. I think what has happened,' he went on, his tone changing as he addressed the assembly, 'is that a student the Professor failed in an examination took a chance to get his own back. Our friend Jas Joyce,' he added, 'would definitely have relished that.'

In misery Professor Flacks lifted the tumbler of water to his lips, his eyes cast down. You could sense him thinking, FitzPatrick reported, that he was a fool and he had been shown to be a fool. You could sense him thinking that he suddenly appeared to be unreliable, asinine and ridiculous. In front of the people who mattered to him most of all he had been exposed as a fraud he did not feel himself to be. Never again could he hold his head up among the Friends of James Joyce. Within twenty-four hours his students would know what had occurred.

An embarrassed shuffling broke out in the lecture-hall. People murmured and began to make their way into the aisles. FitzPatrick recalled the occasion in Mrs Maginn's kitchen, the two elderly puppets on the end of Heffernan's string, the fig-rolls and the tea.

He recalled the maid's voice retailing the story that he, because he knew Heffernan so well, had doubted with each word that was uttered. He felt guilty that he hadn't sought the old man out and told him it wasn't true. He glanced through the throng in the lecture-hall at the lone figure in porridgy tweeds, and unhappily reflected that suicide had been known to follow such wretched disgrace. Outside the lecture-hall he told Heffernan to go to hell when a drink in Anne Street was suggested – a remark for which Heffernan never forgave him.

'I mean,' FitzPatrick said as we sat in College Park a long time later, 'how could anyone be as petty? When all the poor old fellow ever said to him was "I see you are still with us?" '

I made some kind of reply. Professor Flacks had died a natural death a year after the delivery of his lecture on 'Two Gallants'. Earlier in his life he had not, as Heffernan had claimed, driven a wife and two sisters mad: he'd been an only child, the obituary said in the *Irish Times*, and a bachelor. It was an awkward kind of obituary, for the gaffe he'd made had become quite famous and was still fresh in Dubliners' minds.

We went on talking about him, FitzPatrick and I, as we watched the cricket in College Park. We spoke of his playful sarcasm and how so vehemently it had affected Heffernan's pride. We marvelled over the love that had caused a girl in a story to steal, and over the miserliness that had persuaded an old woman to be party to a trick. FitzPatrick touched upon his own inordinate laziness, finding a place for that also in our cobweb of human frailty.

WILLIAM TREVOR
from *The News from Ireland* (1986)

Dosh and Josh

'That deal is worth 38k. Was worth 38k,' yelled Denis as he swerved the car around the bend on Christchurch Place. 'Effin buses. Think they own the road,' he yelled and thumped on the horn. 'We could have closed him. We could have closed him for 38k.' He thumped the horn again. He screeched the car off Dame Street onto Crow Street, turned right and handbraked the car in the middle of Cecilia Street.

'Keep your mouth shut. Tell them it went fine. I'll cover. Out.'
'Aren't you coming in?' Kevin asked quietly.

'No, Kevin, I'm not. I've another appointment. Do telesales up to lunch. Update me at two.' Denis accelerated up Fownes Street, across onto Trinity Street and then onto Andrew Street. He snaked around onto Exchequer Street. Never meant for cars. You'd get fed up in Dublin. Ireland. Everything too small. No room for mistakes. Past Aungier Street church. Hopes she's in. Maybe I should ring. Could say no. Better just to arrive. Harder for her then. Wexford Street always crazy with traffic. So many people. Henry Street and Moore Street rolled into one on the southside. Into Montague Street. Jesus you could hardly stuff a sausage up it. Tiny. Into Montague Lane. Beautiful, a space. Something went well today.

MARTIN ROPER
from *The Close* (1992)

The Municipal Gallery Revisited

I

Around me the images of thirty years:
An ambush; pilgrims at the water-side;
Casement upon trial, half hidden by the bars,
Guarded; Griffith staring in hysterical pride;
Kevin O'Higgins' countenance that wears
A gentle questioning look that cannot hide
A soul incapable of remorse or rest;
A revolutionary soldier kneeling to be blessed;

II

An Abbot or Archbishop with an upraised hand
Blessing the Tricolour. 'This is not,' I say,
'The dead Ireland of my youth, but an Ireland
The poets have imagined, terrible and gay.'
Before a woman's portrait suddenly I stand,
Beautiful and gentle in her Venetian way.
I met her all but fifty years ago
For twenty minutes in some studio.

III

Heart-smitten with emotion I sink down,
My heart recovering with covered eyes;
Wherever I had looked I had looked upon
My permanent or impermanent images:
Augusta Gregory's son; her sister's son,
Hugh Lane, 'onlie begetter' of all these;
Hazel Lavery living and dying, that tale
As though some ballad-singer had sung it all;

IV

Mancini's portrait of Augusta Gregory,
'Greatest since Rembrandt,' according to John Synge;
A great ebullient portrait certainly;
But where is the brush that could show anything
Of all that pride and that humility?
And I am in despair that time may bring
Approved patterns of women or of men
But not that selfsame excellence again.

V

My mediaeval knees lack health until they bend,
But in that woman, in that household where
Honour had lived so long, all lacking found.
Childless I thought 'My children may find here
Deep-rooted things,' but never foresaw its end,
And now that end has come I have not wept;
No fox can foul the lair the badger swept –

VI

(An image out of Spenser and the common tongue).
John Synge, I and Augusta Gregory, thought
All that we did, all that we said or sang
Must come from contact with the soil, from that
Contact everything Antaeus-like grew strong.
We three alone in modern times had brought
Everything down to that sole test again,
Dream of the noble and the beggar-man.

VII

And here's John Synge himself, that rooted man,
'Forgetting human words,' a grave deep face.
You that would judge me, do not judge alone
This book or that, come to this hallowed place
Where my friends' portraits hang and look thereon;
Ireland's history in their lineaments trace;
Think where man's glory most begins and ends,
And say my glory was I had such friends.

W.B. YEATS
from *New Poems* (1938)

Too Small a City

'I suppose it won't be long now till your friend is here,' the barman said as he held the glass to the light after polishing.

'If it's not too wet,' I said.

'It's a bad evening,' he yawned, the rain drifting across the bandstand and small trees of Fairview Park to stream down the long window.

She showed hardly any signs of rain when she came, lifting the scarf from her black hair. 'You seem to have escaped the wet,' the barman was all smiles as he greeted her.

'I'm afraid I was a bit extravagant and took a taxi,' she said in the rapid speech she used when she was nervous or simulating confusion to create an effect.

'What would you like? '

'Would a hot whiskey be too much trouble?'

'No trouble at all,' the barman smiled and lifted the electric kettle. I moved the table to make room for her in the corner of the varnished partition, beside the small coal fire in the grate. There was the sound of water boiling, and the scent of cloves and lemon. When I rose to go to the counter for the hot drink, the barman motioned that he would bring it over to the fire.

'The spoon is really to keep the glass from cracking,' I nodded toward the steaming glass in front of her on the table. It was a poor attempt to acknowledge the intimacy of the favour. For several months I had been frustrating all his attempts to get to know us, for we had picked Gaffneys because it was out of the way and we had to meet like thieves. Dublin was too small a city to give even our names away.

JOHN McGAHERN
from 'Sierra Leone', *Getting Through* (1979)

Deadlock

Rashers set out with the determination to try everything he knew. He was hungry. He had been hungry for weeks. It was a miserable kip of a city at the best of times. It had gone to hell altogether now. Day in and day out he stood in the gutter and played his whistle. Nobody minded him. Occasionally, when he had made certain there were no police to see him, he begged. They turned aside from him. He knocked at door after door for odd jobs. There were none, or some locked-out unfortuante had got there before him. Once he met Hennessy. He was aggrieved at the perversity of fate, the obduracy of the employers, the supiness of the Government, the stubbornness of the strikers, the deadlock that looked like paralysing the city for ever.

JAMES PLUNKETT
from *Strumpet City* (1969)

Escape

Welcome, O life! I go to encounter for the millionth time the reality of experience and to forge in the smithy of my soul the uncreated conscience of my race.

JAMES JOYCE
from *A Portrait of the Artist as a Young Man* (1916)

3. DUBS

A Dubliner is an inhabitant of that city who may
or may not have been born there, whereas the
trueborn native with the city in his blood will
always proclaim himself to be a Dublinman.

GERRY O'FLAHERTY

Apples and Quares

There was what we called The Lawn, a big sort of wasteland at the back of Earlsfort Terrace and around the back of Adelaide Road and Harcourt Street. It ran right around the back of all the gardens of the big old houses. There were orchards there. We used to rob orchards, as all kids do. We used to look over this wall that was the back of a house on Harcourt Terrace and whose was it, but Micheál mac Liammóir's and Hilton Edwards'. I often remember on a summer evening you would see them sitting out with their straw hats in the garden, sipping tea or drinking cocktails. We used to all sit peering over the wall. They didn't mean anything to us, they were just rich people. I didn't know who the hell they were. We used to see them walking up and down Charlemont Street, especially Micheál, and you would always know he was coming because you would get the smell first. He always had this very strong, perfumed aftershave, a spicy smell. It was lovely, and he always held his head really high. We had a kind of respect for him. He definitely had a presence, that even the children were aware of.

I remember him catching me robbing his orchard. One day we thought there was nobody in the house and the other kids slipped me over the wall. I was the lightest, and I had to run over and pick up the apples, the ones that had fallen on the ground: Next thing didn't he come running out and just as I was getting to the wall he caught me. He gave out and said he was going to bring us round to the police, but he didn't. He said I was not to be coming in over the wall. I'll never forget the fright I got. I don't think I ever got into a garden to rob an orchard again. He was just one of the characters.

I suppose having a shop you came across them more than the average person. A fella used to come in called Christy, I don't know what his surname was, we just knew him as Christy. He came in every morning for his half pint of milk, the little triangular ones. When, at certain times, his behaviour changed, my mother always knew there was going to be a full moon. There was this picture on the wall, it was a cat advertising coal or something and he'd walk straight in and have a conversation with the cat. He had a name on the cat and all. On these particular mornings my mammy said, 'It's going to be a full moon tonight, Christy's gone a bit...' He was always very gentle, a lovely man, but he would go completely loopy at that time and as soon as the full moon would pass he'd be back, quite normal again. So there is certainly something to be said about the full moon, it was so obvious, it really was.

My mammy would have loads of stories to tell about the different characters. There was one woman in the street, Emily was her name, and she was a little bit simple. She used to go around and do all the messages for the old people. She was middle-aged when we were young. She had a great way with the younger kids and always sang to them. When Sé, my oldest brother, was born my mother used to have him sitting out in the pram and as soon as he'd see Emily coming he'd start to sing Daisy or whatever she was singing. He was only about nine or ten months old and my mother used to say the talent was coming out even then. Before he was one year old he could sing four songs. Everybody knew and everybody loved her. All the kids used to chase her and slag her and she'd come running after us and we used to think it was great fun. There were lots and lots of characters, that's what I liked about Dublin. No matter where you went there was some character or another. Even now it's still quite obvious, people are very much themselves.

MARY BLACK
from *Alive, Alive O!*
edited by Mairín Johnston (1988)

Tiers in Their Eyes

Larboy said he knew a place off the quays where we could get free cakes. We all barrelled down and Larboy had to get in this window to open the door for the rest of us. When we got inside it was a whole factory full of cakes...gur cake, fruit cake, jam log, chocolate log, cream slice, cream doughnut, coffee cakes, birthday cakes...it was like being in a film to me...and there in the centre, pride of place, towering over everything else, an eight tier wedding cake with a plastic man and woman at the top. Larboy had told us to be quiet and we were for the first minute but now everybody was shouting...

– What'll we take, what'll we take...

I just stood there, pointing to the iced monument...

– This is the one...this one...

Five minutes later I was back with Nellser's pram. I navigated and the others held various parts of it as we made our way up Constitution Hill to the Temple at the back of the Kings Inns. We removed the top four tiers in order to get the heaviest part over the railings. Then we replaced them and in the space provided under the plastic bride and groom, directly below the words 'the marriage of' I wrote Jean Costello and Larboy McDermott. Annie Clarke was the bridesmaid and I forget who was the best man and the priest, but when Larboy was asked, 'do you take this woman...' I turned to Annie Clarke and said I am a woman. Annie Clarke said, but is Larboy a man, and the two of us went into hysterics that lasted for about fifteen minutes. When the fellas accused us of spoiling the wedding, we went into even worse hysterics.

After three tiers of wedding cake we all felt as sick as dogs. Not even a small bottle of lemonade between us to wash it down. Then the others accused me of being stupid I threw a lump of cake at someone and started a full scale war. Five tiers of wedding cake turned into two stone of snowballs. And wedding cake hurts, I can tell you that. It's all those small lumpy bits of fruit. And icing is murder to get out of your hair. Well, the police broke up our wedding party. Lucky Larboy spotted them and we made it out of the temple before we were caught.

PETER SHERIDAN in collaboration with **JEAN COSTELLO** from *Shades of the Jelly Woman* (1986)

Other Lives

I went – everything was so simple – I went into a bar and bought a drink. Each sip was like a sliver of metal, chill and smooth. It was a cavernous place, very dark. The light from the street glared whitely in the open doorway. I might have been somewhere in the south, in one of those dank, tired ports I used to know so well. At the back, in a lighted place like a stage, some youths with shaven heads and outsize lace-up boots were playing a game of billiards. The balls whirred and clacked, the young men softly swore. It was like something out of Hogarth, a group of wigless surgeons, say, intent over the dissecting table. The barman, arms folded and mouth open, was watching a horse-race on the television set perched high up on a shelf in a corner above him. A tubercular young man in a black shortie overcoat came in and stood beside me, breathing and fidgeting. I could tell from the tension coming off him that he was working himself up to something, and for a moment I was pleasurably alarmed. He might do anything, anything. But he only spoke. *I've lived here thirty-three years,* he said, in a tone of bitter indignation, *and everyone is afraid.* The barman glanced at him with weary contempt and turned back to the television. Blue horses galloped in silence over bright-green turf. I am afraid, the young man said, resentful now. He gave a tremendous twitch, hunching his shoulders and ducking his head and throwing up one arm, as if something had bitten him on the neck. Then he turned and went out hurriedly, clutching his coat around him. I followed, leaving my drink half-finished. It was blindingly bright outside. I spotted him, a good way off already, dodging along through the crowds with his elbows pressed to his sides, taking tight, swift little steps, nimble as a dancer. Nothing could stop him. In the thickest surge of bodies he would find a chink at once, and swivel deftly from the waist up and dive through without altering his pace. What a pair we would have made, if anyone had thought to link us, he in his tight shabby coat and I with my fancy hat and expensive clutch of carrier bags. I could hardly keep up with him, and after a minute or two I was puffing and in a sweat. I had an unaccountable sense of elation. Once he paused, and stood glaring into the window of a chemist's shop. I waited, loitering at a bus-stop, keeping him in the corner of my eye. He was so intent, and seemed to quiver so, that I thought he was going to do something violent, turn and attack someone, maybe, or kick in the window and stamp about among the cameras and the cosmetic displays. But he was only waiting for another shudder to pass through him. This time when he flung up his arm his leg shot up as well, as if elbow and knee were connected by an invisible string, and a second later his heel came down on the pavement with a ringing crack. He cast a quick look around him, to see if anyone had noticed, and gave himself a casual little shake, as if by that he would make the previous spasm appear to have been intentional too, and then he was off again like a whippet. I wanted to catch up with him. I wanted to speak to him. I did not know what I would say. I would not offer him sympathy, certainly not. I did not pity him. I saw nothing in him to merit my pity.

No, that's not true, for he was pathetic, a maimed and mad poor creature. Yet I was not sorry for him, my heart did not go out to him in that way. What I felt was, how shall I say, a kind of brotherly regard, a strong, sustaining, almost cheerful sense of oneness with him. It seemed the simplest thing in the world for me to walk up now and put my hand on the thin shoulder and say: *my fellow sufferer, dear friend, compagnon de misères!* And so it was with deep disappointment and chagrin that at the next corner I stopped and looked about me in the jostling crowd and realised that I had lost him. Almost at once, however I found a substitute, a tall fat girl with big shoulders and a big behind, and big, tubular legs ending in a pair of tiny feet, like a pig's front trotters, wedged into high-heeled white shoes. She had been to the hairdresser's, her hair was cropped in a fashionable, boyish style that was, on her, grotesque. The stubbled back of her neck, with its fold of fat, was still an angry shade of red from the dryer, it seemed to be blushing for her. She was so brave and sad, clumping along in her ugly shoes, and I would have followed her all day, I think, but after a while I lost her, too. Next I took up with a man with a huge strawberry mark on his face, then a tiny woman wheeling a tiny dog in a doll's pram, then a young fellow who marched resolutely along, as if he could see no one, with a visionary's fixed glare, swinging his arms and growling to himself. In a busy pedestrian thoroughfare I was surrounded suddenly by a gang of tinker girls, what my mother would have called *big rawsies,* with red hair and freckles and extra-ordinary, glass-green eyes, who pushed against me in truculent supplication, plucking at my sleeve and whining. It was like being set upon by a flock of importunate large wild birds. When I tried to shoo them away one of them knocked my hat off, while another deftly snatched out of my hand the carrier bag containing my new jacket. They fled, shoving each other and laughing shrilly, their raw, red heels flying. I laughed too, and picked up my hat from the pavement, ignoring the looks of the passers-by, who appeared to find my merriment unseemly. I did not care about the jacket – in fact, the loss of it chimed in a mysteriously apt way with that of its discarded predecessor – but I would have liked to see where those girls would go. I imagined a lean-to made of rags and bits of galvanised iron on a dusty patch of waste ground, with a starving dog and snot-nosed infants, and a drunken hag crouched over a steaming pot. Or perhaps there was a Fagin somewhere waiting for them, skulking in the shadows in some derelict tenement, where the light of summer fingered the shutters, and dust-motes drifted under lofty ceilings, and the rat's claw in the wainscoting scratched at the silence, scratched, stopped, and scratched again. So I went along happily for a little while, dreaming up other lives, until I spotted a wheyfaced giant with rubber legs clomping ahead of me on two sticks, and I set off after him in avid pursuit.

What was I doing, why was I following these people – what enlightenment was I looking for? I did not know, nor care. I was puzzled and happy, like a child who has been allowed to join in an adults' game. I kept at it for hours, criss-crossing the streets and the squares with a drunkard's dazed single-mindedness, as if I were tracing out a huge, intricate sign on the face of the city for someone in the sky to read. I found myself in places I had not known were there, crooked alleyways and sudden, broad, deserted spaces, and dead-end streets under railway bridges where parked cars basked fatly in the evening sun, their toy-coloured roofs agleam. I ate a hamburger in a glass-walled café with moulded plastic chairs and tinfoil ashtrays, where people sat alone and gnawed at their food like frightened children abandoned by their parents. The daylight died slowly, leaving a barred, red and gold sunset smeared on the sky, and as I walked along it was like walking under the surface of a broad, burning river. The evening crowds were out, girls in tight trousers and high heels, and brawny young men with menacing haircuts. In the hot, hazy dusk the streets seemed wider, flattened, somehow, and the cars scudded along, sleek as seals in the sodium glare. I got back late to the house, footsore, hot and dishevelled, my hat awry, but filled with a mysterious sense of achievement.

JOHN BANVILLE
from *The Book of Evidence* (1989)

Grannie and Grandma

A visit to Grannie Collins always promised adventure. Married to the General Manager of the Hibernian Bank, she lived in the large and rather grandiose house with immensely high rooms over the bank, which is right in the middle of the city in College Green. For a small child living in the wilds of Howth, this grandstand view of life in the big city was an excitement in itself. The frequent presence of my cousins Betty and Dorothy added spice to my visits. On one occasion, we couldn't resist the temptation of squirting soda-water from a syphon onto the bowler-hatted businessmen passing along the footpath below. Not getting sufficient reaction, since the jet was dissipated in the wind, we resorted to buckets of water. This resulted in the immense satisfaction of an outraged crowd of gesticulating victims, and we rolled about in a fit of laughter which was quite uncontrollable until a loud knocking at the hall door announced the ominous arrival of the police. We fully believed we would be sent to prison, and that Grandpa would be dismissed from his exalted position, and were greatly relieved when nothing more serious happened than banishment to our bedroom, where we discovered the delightfully pungent perfume produced by toasting orange-peel on the spiral coils of the electric heater.

Grandpa Collins would emerge from the boardroom for meals. His enormous tabby cat would sit on the table just to his right on a special mat, and with the utmost delicacy would transfix a pat of butter with one claw and lick it with the decorum necessary to pass the test for the Indian Civil Service – a standard of table manners much quoted for the benefit of us children in those days, since two of the Collins daughters had married successful candidates. The great tabby cat was called Guinness, after the immense cart-horses that used to draw the wagons of stout barrels around Dublin. He was never known to utter a sound until he fell out of the window on the first floor onto the street below. After a lengthy and anxious convalescence, he gained a healthy baritone voice and a purr like an engine.

The big drawing-room window from which Guinness fell was the scene of a more dramatic episode during the 'troubles'. Grandpa used to sit with his back to the window after breakfast, reading the paper; and his bald head was too tempting a target for the soldiers stationed on top of the Bank of Ireland across the street. Taking a pot-shot at his head, the bullet just missed it, went through the top of the *Irish Times* and the parrot's cage, and lodged in the walnut case of the piano, where it created a fascinating wiry clank on a couple of notes in the bass. Surviving this near miss, my grandfather flourished until well on in his nineties, refusing to retire until a few years before his death. He had the appealing habit of calling me over to him on quite unexpected occasions, asking whether I liked portraits. Where-upon he would produce as a tip a golden half-sovereign, pointing out the portrait of Queen Victoria or King Edward or George.

Trips to the Zoo and the Metropole cinema added to the excitement of these city visits; though a nightmarish fear of things not understood intruded upon the adventure of the journey on top of the open tram to Phoenix Park. As we passed the ruins of the Four Courts, only recently blown up, the grotesquely twisted lamp-bracket over the porch seemed somehow to distil the essence of this fear in its ominously symbolic image.

Grannie-in-the-bank was great fun. Curiously enough I was never conscious of her going to church. By contrast, Grandma was grave, and her house was like an extension of the Moravian church. Just like Queen Victoria she dressed in widow's black, with black beads all down her front, for the decade or so that she survived Grandfather Boydell. She wore a black bonnet when she ventured out to sit in the rustic summerhouse under the weeping willow in the garden in Raglan Road, and when she went for drives in her carriage driven by the coachman Tye, who had a big lump on his neck and wore a top hat with a black cockade. I adored travelling in the carriage with the smell of leather, and the soothing sound of the horse's hooves and the rumble of the rubber-tyred wheels on the wooden street-sets. Pulling down the blinds and letting them flip up again was great fun – though gravely discouraged.

A special entertainment at Raglan Road was the speaking tube which enabled one to communicate from one floor to another. If you blew strongly down the tube a little yellow stained ivory whistle would pop out and whistle a summons in the domestic quarters. The great game was to make the whistle pop out into someone's mouth when they were talking into the tube. I can remember its curious taste.

Other activities when visiting Grandma were of a more serious nature. In the drawing room, which was furnished and decorated in real Victorian style with curio cabinets and masses of photographs, was a superb Bechstein grand piano at which I would spend hours 'making up' music inspired by an old travel book of America, with engravings of Niagara Falls and other famous sights. The quite characteristic smell of a Bechstein and the sound of the bells of nearby St Bartholomew's church are vividly associated with Grandma's gravy – a culinary ideal which has never since been attained.

Beside Grandma and the loveable cook who taught me to make currant scones, the other inhabitants of the house were my maiden aunt Edie and auntie (pronounced 'anti') Hurst, the widow of my grandmother's brother, who must have done something awful, for his name was never mentioned. As far as I was concerned auntie

Hurst had no first name: in fact she was more like an item of vast black furniture than a person, though she had the horribly fascinating attribute of a large mole on her chin with very long hairs sprouting from it. I often seemed to be there on Sundays, when the only allowable entertainment was to 'play church' with Grandma and the two aunts as my personal congregation. I actually enjoyed this in a curious way, though this had nothing to do with my childhood propensity for devotional fervour. Rather, my enjoyment probably centred on acting the part of a leader, imagining I had the same authority and power as Mr Hutton, the Moravian minister, whom I remember commanding his flock in Kevin Street from the immense height of the pulpit, thumping the red velvet upholstery as he declared the word of God. I also enjoyed providing what I considered the appropriate music on the Bechstein, and taking up a collection from my congregation of three. I can't remember whether I was allowed to pocket the proceeds.

One Sunday in the summer it was unusually warm, and it was deemed appropriate to sit quietly in the garden. A veil must be drawn over that occasion, and the shame of it shadowed me for many years. I actually turned 'head-over-heels' on the lawn, revealing – on Sunday, remember – that even very small children possessed a part of their anatomy which, when very much older, they might refer to in naughty whispers as a 'bottom'. I fear the horror took many years off Grandma's life.

BRIAN BOYDELL
from *Irish Childhoods,*
edited by A. Norman Jeffares & Antony Kamm (1987)

His Own Man

Tony Gregory, TD, is quite bemused by his new status. He is now the darling of the media. He is the 'young socialist' from the deprived inner city area of Dublin. He is of the 'Left', according to the terminology of the commentators. He has just secured a Dáil seat and everybody is surprised. Everybody suddenly wants to know who he is.

Yet, Tony Gregory has been around for a long time. The only difference is that nobody was watching him, nobody was listening, he was the lonely young man, the man without a party. Nobody bothered to read his excellent contributions to city council debates. When he spoke about the city's housing crisis, the poverty in the inner city, the need for jobs, land speculation and the breaking up of communities, nobody cared. When he said there was need to double the housing output in the city from 1500 to 3000 dwellings a year, his words fell on stony ground. When he said it this week it was news.

Yes, Tony Gregory has been there, ploughing a long furrow, quite unfettered by party allegiance for quite some time now. He is his own man. He has implicit belief in his own judgement; he conducts his own crusade. And helpers flock to support him.

He ran his campaign on a shoestring but what the campaign lacked in finance it made up for in endeavour. On top of that Gregory is always around. He is a very "visible" politician, a high-profile politician who is always accessible. A politician of another era, the late Frank Sherwin, used to say, 'vote for the man you know, the man you can see every day.'

I have seen Gregory come through the political nursery of the City Council. For one so young, he shows an incredible political maturity. He possesses an amazingly quick political mind. He is highly articulate. He can express his case with clinical brevity and lethal effect. It is done in a quietly effective manner. He never rambles, and does not like to see others waffling. Time is too important to be wasted.

In the City Council he keeps to the point and makes his case well. He does not always win or get what he wants (who does?), but in his case he is back again the week after fighting his corner again. And he does it in the nicest possible way, without offending anyone.

His tremendous political energy has borne fruit in a spectacular fashion. To get his seat in the Dáil he stepped over the bodies of some prominent candidates, including two Fine Gael heavyweights.

And he will not give up his seat easily. Mr Haughey and Dr FitzGerald should not underestimate him when they meet him. They will quickly find they are dealing with a unique new-style Irish politician.

FRANK KILFEATHER
from *The Irish Times* (1982)

He Liked His Gargle

Tone was himself a Dublinman and was born behind the Four
Courts in what is now called Wolfe Tone Street. He was captured
during the rebellion and was brought to Dublin and sentenced to
death. As he was a soldier – a Chef de Brigade in the French Army
– he asked that he should be shot but this was refused and he was
condemned to be publicly hanged. On his last night in prison, he
was mysteriously found dying – some say his gaolers had tried to
kill him, some say he committed suicide rather than face the indignity,
for a soldier, of hanging. He died that night anyway and he was
waked near where he was born – in the Cornmarket. Although he
is held in the utmost affection by every Irishman, the clergy have
always been against him, and I remember some bishop referring
to him as recently as 1934 or so as the 'cut-throat Tone'.

His autobiography makes great reading for he was a very human
person with a great deal of affection and humour in his make-up.
He liked his gargle, too, and makes no secret of the fact, and Frank
MacDermot in his biography says that he was temperate by the
general standard of the time and was never as footless as Pitt. He
had a great smack for the people of his own city. He tells of how
one day he was recruiting for France among captured British sailors,
many of whom were press-ganged men from Ireland who were
only too glad to throw over the King of England and to fight for
the French. But one man didn't want to; and Tone tells: 'I heard
a voice from the back in the accents of Ormond Quay call out
impatiently, "If he won't enlist voluntarily and of his own free will,
throw him in the wather, admiral".'

The area where Tone was born, and the area across the river
immediately south, are two of the oldest parts of Dublin. They
used to be the fashionable areas, but the opening of O'Connell Street,
further down the river, drew the wealthier parts of the population
down to the Georgian squares that were built about the same time
– Merrion Square, Fitzwilliam Square, Parnell Square and the
rest.

BRENDAN BEHAN
from *Brendan Behan's Island: An Irish Sketch-book* (1962)

Saluting the Poet

I am used to being mistaken for a priest and so I am no longer embarrassed by the respect paid to my cloth. As a provincial youth, ignorant of new literary ways, I believed that a poet must wear a wide-brimmed black hat and grave suit. Sometimes as I cycled along country roads, I was saluted by carter or stonebreaker, so I consulted a clerical student, who was an intimate friend of mine. He told me what to do in order to spare the feelings of passers-by who might salute me. For a year or so after his ordination, a young priest always raises his hat; gradually he learns only to touch it; then he moves his hand only as far as his shoulder – and at last a mere showing of his right palm suffices. With the increasing ruralising of Dublin and the spread of religious action since the Civil War, my hand is kept busy. In particular, the Cork men who live here now are a daily problem. When they are in a bus, they spend much time raising their hats, or if they are bare-headed, crossing themselves as ostentatiously as possible, not only at every church we pass, but at unseen oratories and private chapels in convents, orphanages, colleges, Magdalen Homes, hospitals and industrial schools, some of them not less than a quarter of a mile away. When they get off the bus, they seem to be looking around for the nearest clergyman to reverence. Frequently therefore, as I walk along the city streets, I am saluted, and in the suburbs, motorists, lorry-drivers, cyclists and small boys pay me undue respect. Clergymen on their autocycles give me a professional nod, or glance at me quickly, as the come out of the city cinemas in the afternoon. Sometimes I am tempted to take vicarious advantage of my old-fashioned poetic garb. When I draw my black muffler closer to hide my lack of celluloid collar, I am offered a seat immediately in an over-crowded bus, receive attention in tea-shops, quicker sherries in the larger hotels – and I need never wait more than a few seconds outside a telephone booth.

AUSTIN CLARKE
from *Twice Round the Black Church* (1962)

A Rub of the Relic

My first job when I left school was in Eason's. I went to so much trouble for the customers, tearing up parcels in the wholesale to see what book had come in and looking up the catalogue numbers. No one has ever done that for me in there. Eason's was a real Dublin place. The girls in there were real Dublin and the discussion in the canteen at the break was who had had a rub of the relic. I was absolutely shocked by this talk. They were great. I didn't last that long because the work was so blooming hard. But while I was there I made use of the fact that there were magazine stands. I read all the magazines I could lay my hands on to see what they published. I sent stories off to them and that was really how I started.

I think that when we were growing up, although we weren't great readers, there was more of a naturally cultural environment. There was no Concert Hall then but people went to the opera or the theatre or the circus. They went out a fair bit and they discussed a lot.

My grandfather was knocked down and killed on his way to the circus, when he was ninety. He was a man who constantly went to every kind of entertainment and enjoyed it. He was an opera singer. In his early youth he sang with Count John McCormack. When he was in his eighties somebody told him that Gigli was on in town. He was incredibly excited because he loved Gigli. He was asked if he wanted to go and he said, 'Oh lovely that would be wonderful.' Of course his hearing wasn't the best and it turned out that it wasn't Gigli at all, it was the film *Gigi*. 'Ah sure it was lovely anyway,' he said. He enjoyed it just as much.

Dublin was never really Venice for opera, where the audience would shout their heads off, as if they were at a soccer match. In Dublin you knew that if they hadn't liked the opera they would throw eggs or tomatoes at the performers. It wasn't that they knew opera, simply that they listened to it and rejoiced in it.

Dubliners had a great vulgar sense of humour. They still have. I think it's marvellous. But they were a very discreet people, never asked questions about money, didn't ask direct questions. The other side of that I suppose is that they minded their own business a bit too much. Apart from the centre of Dublin there probably wasn't much of a community spirit. But I think there's a feeling of invasion now. That feeling of privacy and natural gentility and delicacy has been invaded. It could be the level of bureaucracy. People just seem to talk about politics and money all the time.

Certainly this would not have been done in my time. It would have been considered really bad form. You told a few stories and you sang a few songs and you pretended things weren't serious. It's got a bit dull now, heavy handed and self-conscious. A lot's been lost.

From what I remember when I was growing up there wasn't any money, and there were never any clothes bought. My parents never seemed to say, 'Her shoes are worn down,' or, 'Her dress is worn out. What are we going to do?' If there was a communion, a confirmation, or a school uniform needed, then the money was found. But other than that there were never any clothes bought.

We used to go to the Iveagh Market with our pocket money. When we got there, instead of buying a nice cotton dress, we'd buy floor length silk nightdresses and evening dresses smelling of moth balls. They were so irresistible. The smell was terrible but the clothes were wonderful. We loved the Iveagh Market.

CLARE BOYLAN
from *Alive, Alive O!*
edited by Mairín Johnston (1988)

The Liberties King

Jonathan Swift, the Dean of St Patrick's Cathedral from 1713 to 1745 and virtual dictator of the Liberties in his time, must have been a difficult person at close-range. 'What a bundle of inconsistencies is man,' he once wrote. He himself was the kind of person you loved devotedly or else hated bitterly. When he first arrived as Dean in Dublin he was loathed. It was partly politics, and I should think, partly personality, so that they stuck rude poems on the cathedral door the day he was being installed.

As a new broom Dean he bulldozed his chapter of dignitaries and canons during his first two months. It was like Jove letting off thunderbolts, until they were subdued, said Lord Orrery, his first (and rather acid) biographer. No doubt the canons remained rebellious underneath. But nobody up against Swift dared to show rebellion. Everything indicates that Jonathan Swift was a man who loved power and could make himself thoroughly unpleasant in order to get it. On the other hand, once he had got his power, he did try to use it to good purpose.

This kind of paternalism is something we moderns cannot tolerate – neither in ex-colonial countries nor in business management nor in everyday social relationships. But where it can be accepted – and not everyone will agree with me – there are times when it is not without good results, depending on the quality of the ruler. If the ruler is loved and trusted his bossiness can be accepted. This was what happened to Swift.

The loathing turned to near-worship. It was to make a new man of him. Once his people were docile and showed that they liked him, he seems to have been kindly, hardworking and generous. He said that although he hated people in bulk and found humanity corrupt and greedy, nevertheless he heartily loved Tom, Dick and Harry. His work in the Liberties was very personal ministry, and it clearly was not sectarian. As soon as he was seen to be a patriot, and especially when he had stood out against the scandalous racket of the Wood's Halfpence, so that he became a champion of the Irish interest, he was idolised by everyone in the heart of Dublin. This gave him scope to try to do good, and in his paternalistic way he was very successful because people would now accept it from him.

Perhaps this new relationship affected his inconsistent nature and brought a gleam of sunniness to him (I am reminded that his rural Parish Clerk, Roger, one of the heroes of the many 'Swift-and-his-man' stories, wrote a charming poem about his good nature, saying

> I love to see the Doctor smile
> For its the sunshine of our isle

The result was that his friend Dean Delany (in spite of being a member of the chapter!) went so far as to say that in his pastoral care and generous benefactions Swift 'literally followed the example of his blessed Saviour and went about doing good'. If this is laying it on a bit heavily, Swift's own humorous grumble is attractive that Liberties ought to buy him a couple of beaver hats annually to make up for all those worn out by acknowledging salutations as he went around!

With his ingrained inconsistency, it was typical that Swift should combine meanness and generosity in his charities. He was known to give away one third of what he had every year. When he saved a coach fare by walking instead, he gave away what he had saved to a beggar. On the same system he drank beer for dinner instead of wine, and then gave away the price of a pint of wine to some one of his old women.

He had come to Dublin away back in 1713 feeling like a poisoned rat in a trap. He was to find that Dublin in general, and the Liberties in particular, suited his temperament well, and he grew into them. Providing enough subjects for a somewhat tyrannical kindness, the Liberties became a sort of Swiftian Happy Family. He grew to be both loved and trusted, and in the end he could do anything here. The people here believed everything he told them – like the solemn and splendid fictions of the Drapier Letters. Again, such is the incident of the eclipse – a typical piece of Swiftian humour. The people of the Liberties had assembled to see an eclipse of the moon. Swift sent out a bellman to say that the eclipse had been postponed at the order of the Dean. Accordingly, everyone went home.

His "seraglio" of crippled old women was famous, and he helped those who helped themselves. Thus, having saved the price of a coach by getting home before a shower, he said to Mrs Pilkington, 'Thank God, I have saved my money...carry this sixpence to the lame old man that sells gingerbread at the corner because he tries to do something and does not beg'. On the other hand having himself a Freudian passion for cleanliness his rebukes to unwashed beggars were savage and his reactions unrewarding.

This is all casual charity. His organised care for the Liberties was equally important. He was anxious that the deserving should get on, and so in 1716 he started a school for boys, and later paid apprenticeship fees for them. Again, poor tradesmen in that era of economic pressure, found it very difficult to buy equipment. With the first five hundred pounds he owned, the Dean started a loan bank. He gave out grants of £5 to be repaid weekly at the rate of 2 shillings, free of interest. Mrs Brent the deanery housekeeper (contradicting Dr Johnson on the subject) said 'You cannot imagine what numbers of poor tradesmen who have even wanted proper tools to carry on their work, have, by this small loan, been put in a prosperous way and brought up their families in credit.'

There was more to Swift in the Liberties than just a benevolent old gentleman handing out sixpence to old ladies. There was the Irish agitator, as we have said, who earned the street ballads. This sort of thing:

> Since the Drapier's set up and Wood is cried down,
> Let ballads be made by the bards of the town,
> To thank the brave Drapier for what he has done,
> Which nobody can deny, brave boys,
> Which nobody can deny.

Or the personal ballads which indicated his complete invulnerability in a district which cherished him so completely:

Fair liberty was all his cry;
For her he stood prepared to die,
But not a traitor could be found
To sell him for six hundred pound.

And it seems to me, there was a third aspect; the Swift of the economics of the Liberties. The big windows of its tall Dutch style houses held the weavers. In Swift's time the weaving was a basic trade here. But is was harassed by competitive English legislation, and, like all industries in any case, it went through its periods of extreme depression. Here Swift was to the fore, and he was looked on as the man of power who could influence the rulers to do something.

Mark you, the weavers did not always play ball with Swift in his efforts for them. Thus, during one periodic slump, he asked them to give him patterns, so that the Archbishop might instruct his clergy that they were to wear Dublin-made gowns. Swift specified a black woollen material at about eighteen pence per yard. The specified time came and a fortnight passed. Where were the patterns? At last someone came to Swift. No, we do not actually have any patterns, Mr Dean, but we think it would be a good idea if you would very kindly write a pamphlet in favour of Irish manufacture.

For Swift all this must have been extremely frustrating. But he did persist in his efforts for the Liberties, and that should never be forgotten to him. Dictatorial, yes – but also deeply concerned for people, and very especially, for the people of the Liberties, to whom to the end of his mental capacity, he felt a special responsibility. And they all knew it. When he was seventy and failing, they gave a birthday celebration for him around the Deanery, lighting bonfires and tar barrels to do him honour.

It is clear that Swift's business abilities were competent. Thus his scheme for the betterment of the Liberty weaving trade was more and better than just forcing clergy to wear Irish made cassocks. One proposal made by the Dean was this – that a group of manufacturers should join together to advertise their cloths and stuff at fixed retail prices, and of a guaranteed width and quality, 'so that if a child of ten years old were sent with money and directions what stuff and cloth to buy, he would not be wronged in any one article.' The range of price and quality should have a money-back guarantee given by all the members of his projected association, and any firm which let the standard down or refused to honour the conditions would immediately be expelled from the group. It does not appear that the scheme was adopted; on the other hand the time-honoured policy of agitation continued as before.

Of course, the distresses of the Liberty Weavers were by no means always their own fault. Foreign competition, often subsidised, made things very difficult.

In the Liberties, under creaking shop signs, there were dozens of shops selling all kinds of textiles. The advertisement of one such encouraged the public to buy 'arras, baize, bewpers, bombazines, busyarns, blankets, callamancoes, carrells, chamblettes, domicks, durance, and damasks' – materials which will baffle the most scholarly minded housewife today. When there were too many of foreign origin, and too few of Irish make being sold, the men of the Liberties let off steam in colourful protests. Thus, in *Pue's Occurrences* of 31 May 1735 – (that most informative and curious Dublin newspaper of the day) – it is recounted that the weavers dragged the figure of a man and woman dressed in 'Calico and other Indian Goods' to the Market Square in the Coombe and happily hanged them on a gibbet especially put up for the purpose. After this, (no doubt with pipers and balladeers) they marched to St Stephen's Green where the public gibbet stood and draped it with imported cloths 'to prevent these goods from being worn here'. (All that one fears is that the ladies of the wealthy classes, who were the buyers of such stuff, were, alas, not likely to be converted by the angry Liberty dwellers and their protest marchers).

Swift had written for the seventeen hundred or so weavers of the Liberties a diatribe against the iniquitous policy of forbidding the export of Irish manufactures. This law had been laid on in 1699, and was on all fours with the Penal Laws. Of it, Swift said 'Ireland is the only kingdom I have ever heard or read of, either in ancient or modern history, which was denied the liberty of exporting their native commodities and manufacturers wherever they pleased, except to countries at war with their Prince and State'.

As some small attempt to help the Liberty families starving as a result of the economics war of the day, a play was produced for their benefit. Swift wrote an epilogue about home industries – a more positive one than his famous 'burn everything English except the coal!' This composition advised that –

> We'll dress in manufactures made at home,
> Equip our kings and gen'rals at the Comb.
> We'll rig in Meath Street Egypt's haughty Queen
> And Anthony shall court her in ratteen
> In blue shallon shall Hannibal be clad
> And Scipio trail an Irish purple plad.'

Jonathan Swift has been described as 'absolute Monarch of the Liberties and King of the Mob'. So far so good. But I believe that he made himself also Father of the Liberties. I hope so, at any rate.

BISHOP WYSE JACKSON
from *The Liberties of Dublin*,
edited by Elgy Gillespie (1973)

Billy-in-the-Bowl

The 'poor mouth' has long been a noted Irish characteristic, and in Dublin begging became an art form. Some beggars were celebrities, like Bill-in-the-Bowl who flourished in the 1780s and pursued his vocations in the Stoneybatter-Grangegorman area.

Billy was literally in a bowl made of iron and fitted with wheels, for he had been born without legs. But nature, with a touch of remorse, gave him soulfully luminous dark eyes, a fine nose and mouth, and a mop of rich brown curly hair. His combination of misfortune and charm made him a special pet with the women of Stoneybatter and Grangegorman. When he appeared the servant girls would raise the cry 'It's Billy-in-the-Bowl, ma'am,' and housewives were said to authorise the packing of his bowl with beef, bread and dainties.

But Billy supplemented these alms with a sinister sideline. He used to spend some evenings hidden behind a hedge on a lonely path beyond the city, emerging to beg from the solitary traveller. If the traveller ventured within reach, Billy seized him – he had phenomenally strong arms – killed him and robbed him. The killing would have been necessary because Billy was so easily identifiable, and since Billy would have struck only when there were no witnesses he remained unsuspected.

But one evening he pushed his luck too far. Two well-to-do ladies with gold watches, bracelets and diamond rings were strolling along what was then known as Richardson's Lane (now part of Collins' Barracks). Billy appeared with his customary plea and managed to seize both women. But one managed to wind her hand in his hair and press her thumb into his eye. Billy had to let go and the women fled back to their friends in Manor Street. A posse was sent after him and he was caught hiding behind a hedge. His was a capital offence, but he was let off with life imprisonment and spent the remainder of his days in Newgate in Green Street, performing such hard labour as his disability allowed.

JOHN O'DONOVAN
from *Life by the Liffey: A Kaleidoscope of Dubliners* (1986)

The Twangman

Come listen to my story,
'Tis about a nice young man.
When the militia wasn't wanting
He dealt in hawking twang.
He loved a lovely maiden
As fair as any midge
And she kept a treacle billy depot
One side of the Carlisle Bridge.

Now another one came courting her
And his name was Mickey Bags.
He was a commercial traveller
And he dealt in bones and rags.
Well he took her out to Sandymount
For to see the waters roll
And he stole the heart of the twangman's mot,
Playing Billy-in-the-Bowl.

Now when the twangman heard of this
He flew into a terrible rage,
And he swore by the contents of his twang cart
On him he'd have revenge.
So he lay in wait near to James's Gate
And when poor oul Bags came up
With his Twangknife sure he took the life
Of the poor oul gather-em-up.

And it's now yis have heard my story
And I hope yis'll be good men

And not go chasing the Twangman's mot
Or any other oul hen.
For she'll leave you without a brass farthing,
Not even your oul sack of rags
And you'll end up in the gutter there
Like poor oul Mickey Bags.

ANONYMOUS

Shawlie to God

Jimmy O'Dea's Biddy Mulligan was a closely observed character study without any exaggerations. She was meticulously clean and neat with shining black hair parted in the centre, tightly combed into little curls over the ears, and crowned with a fussy little hat. She had a long skirt and apron and a checked shawl over her shoulders. Her blouse and shawl changed over the years according to the dictates of fashion but that was her basic costume which was completed by black elastic-sided bootees which were, like the wigs and the clothes, specially made. Although she never displayed them under any circumstances she wore long old fashioned bloomers underneath (a sure laugh for lesser comics). Asked by Vernon Hayden why he went to the trouble to complete the costume with bloomers that nobody knew about, Jimmy, the perfectionist, replied 'I know!'.

The character he portrayed was the typical Dublin shawlie, witty and sharp-tongued though she could assume an air of gentility with a quasi-refined accent until, goaded by her errant husband, Mick, her mood and accent suddenly changed and she poured on him a torrent of restrained invective. She had a genuine dignity in the face of adversity and was ever optimistic. Much of the material in the Mulligan sketches was true to life, and both Jimmy and Harry frequented the pubs used by their models and listened in on the conversations of the shawlies. In fact, Jimmy always drank in the public bar for preference in whatever pub he might find himself. To Jimmy, Biddy Mulligan was a real character, in the theatrical sense, and rather than give the usual superficial performance of a dame comedian he played her as a real woman, drawing on the reserves of the femininity in his own nature. And he drew a fine line between a recognisable comic creation and the overblown reality of the real thing. Jimmy was aware of the trap of being too perfect and never lost touch with his own personality.

When he visited Canada in 1961 the critic of the *Toronto Dáily Star* was to write:

> His appearance as Mrs Mulligan – a woman from the fish market of Dublin entertaining an American visitor – was hilarious and excellently worked out. His movements and intonation were so genuinely feminine that for a while, not having been able to consult the programme in the dark, I assumed that his supporting cast included a low voiced and boisterous actress.

Jimmy had the knack of turning laughter into tears and many compared him in that respect to Chaplin and, while it is true that many of his sketches have a Chaplinesque twist in them, mingling pathos with comedy, the comparison is not a completely satisfactory one. Granted that both men often achieved similar effects, the means by which they arrived at them were completely dissimilar. A possible exception to this is the sketch 'Buying A Turkey,' in which the important detail depends upon action rather than dialogue as in Chaplin's silent films. In the sketch Mrs Mulligan is forced by penury to buy a thin, famished turkey for her Christmas dinner. Due to a mix-up with identifying labels, a messenger boy, on his way to deliver of a fine plump bird to a well-heeled customer, puts the wrong label on Mrs Mulligan's bird and takes it for delivery by mistake, leaving the big bird on the counter. The stage directions read:

> Mulligan is about to call him back. He is off. Music plays softly. She moves towards the turkey. Puts out a hand gingerly and takes it. Turns slowly and walks a couple of slow steps...suddenly makes a dash and runs off. (*Blackout.*)

Audiences silently watching this sketch were consciously sympathetic to the poverty-stricken Mrs Mulligan, and anxiously willed her to take the fine fat turkey. Gabriel Fallon described it as comparable to the Fall.

PHILIP B. RYAN
from *Jimmy O'Dea: The Pride of the Coombe* (1990)

The Reluctant Nun

The order of the Sisters of Mercy, the largest religious community in the English-speaking world, owes its existence to three Dublin houses, Stormanstown House (now demolished) at Ballymun, Coolock House and the house in Baggot Street that became the first Mercy convent. The young lady who became the first Mercy sister did not really want to found an order or become a nun herself but because of the religious politics of the Dublin of her time there was no other way for her to do the work she wished, of educating young girls, of protecting the morals of older ones and of nursing the sick poor.

Catherine McAuley was born in Stormanstown House on 29 September 1778 of moderately rich parents. Her father died when she was five and her mother who was easily influenced by rich friends lost all her money and her religion. When she died Catherine was twenty and was adopted by William and Catherine Callahan of Coolock House, a Quaker couple, who loved and respected her but tried to make her give up 'Romish practices'. William Callahan had, however, become a Catholic by the time of his death in 1822 and he left Catherine his house and fortune.

It was while she lived in Coolock that she began to understand how much work needed to be done to alleviate the misery of the village poor, to say nothing of the conditions in the nearby city. Advised by local priests she built a 'house of mercy' in Baggot Street. The women who helped her were to be free to give up the work when they felt inclined to do so but she decided, for reasons of continuity and to counter the clerical opposition she met at every turn, to formalise her community.

Her Order of Mercy was established in 1835 but it was difficult for the rich, fifty-year-old woman to undergo the discipline of novitiate training. The order was finally approved by Pope Gregory XVI five months before its founder's death on 10 November 1841. By then there were ten convents in Ireland and two in England (in London and Birmingham). Since then the order has spread worldwide and with 23,000 sisters it is the largest congregation of women in the church. The process for the canonisation of its remarkable founder is well advanced.

ART BYRNE & SEAN McMAHON
from *113 Great Irishwomen & Irishmen* (1990)

Hard Men

Hot Potato was a smallish inoffensive ruddy-faced man who walked the streets minding his own business, respectably dressed in a black overcoat and wearing a bowler hat. He kept himself to himself. Until somebody shouted 'Hot potato', whereupon he raged into attempted assault on whoever had shouted. Maybe he had been hypnotised and those were the keywords? Otherwise his behaviour was inexplicable, because we often lit fires in the back lanes, throwing potatoes into them until they were burned black and covered with soot. Then we ate them. They tasted lovely too.

Dingers lived up the Lane. He was the companion and minder of a well-known lady of the night and day, and he was a hard man. 'Twas said that when he had no money and needed a drink, he'd walk into the pub and spit into the nearest pint on the counter. If the owner objected he'd get a punch that would fell him, and Dingers would drink the pint. If the owner didn't object, Dingers drank the pint and left him alone. I once saw the peelers arresting him and bringing him up the North Circular Road to Mountjoy station. It took six big DMP men and they had to cut his belt and let his trousers drop around his ankles before they could manage it.

Maybe ten or twelve years later, five of us from the club were having a co-operative pint in the former McAuley's pub when Dingers came in looking for free drink. He bumped against Dick spoiling for a row, but the years had caught up with him. With as sweet a right uppercut as I've seen outside the ring, Dick floored him.

By a peculiar coincidence, Terry and I were coming from work about 11 p.m. and as we passed through Summerhill, Dinger's lady was sitting on a step, she wrapped in a shawl, her hand wrapped about a wine bottle. She asked us did we want to do business. I felt a strange sort of sadness for the two of them. Escape from the environment was, I should imagine, on everyone's mind all the time.

BILL KELLY
from *Me Darlin' Dublin's Dead and Gone* (1983)

The Buck Stops Here

Let us begin with No. 86 Stephen's Green, South, next door to Clanwilliam House and, since 1908 part of University College. This granite house has one of the most handsome fronts in Dublin, five bays wide, virile and well-proportioned, with an admirable lion couchant over the door. Its only fault is that it clashes in scale with Clanwilliam House which was there first. Internally it is equally admirable, spacious planning and flowing plasterwork bespeaking the hand of Robert West, its probable designer and builder in about 1765. Though extremely palatial, it was built for a commoner, Richard Chapell Whaley, MP for Co. Wicklow, who died in 1769, leaving, among other children, a son Thomas, the famous Buck Whaley who made the celebrated journey to Jerusalem. Richard Chapell Whaley was commonly called Burn-Chapel Whaley, and was a magistrate and a notorious priest-hunter. But the Dublin tradition that he swore no Papist should ever darken his threshold, has doubtless been preserved, if not created, by the circumstance of Cardinal Cullen's having bought the house in 1853, after which it was for many years the Catholic University of Ireland. He is also renowned for having written a cheque in rhyme in favour of his wife:

> Mr La Touche
> Open your pouch
> And give unto my darling
> Five hundred pounds sterling:
> For which this will be your bailey,
> Signed, Richard Chapell Whaley.

His son the Buck is much more famous. He entered Parliament at the age of eighteen in 1785, but he seems to have spent much more time gambling in Daly's Club in College Green, than in the House next door. The story of his leaping for a wager out of a first-floor window and over a standing coach is sometimes placed here and sometimes in Stephen's Green, but he himself places the incident at Dover on his way to or from the Continent. It is a very typical Dublin Buck exploit. His renowned journey to Jerusalem to win a wager incurred at dinner in Leinster House is perfectly authentic: indeed he left an amusing account of it in MS, which was printed in 1906. It was also the subject of contemporary Dublin balladry:

> Buck Whaley lacking much in cash,
> And being used to cut a dash,
> He wagered full ten thousand pound
> He'd visit soon the Holy Ground.

In Loftus's fine ship
He said he'd take a trip,
And Costello so famed,
The captain then was named.

The journey took him from 1788 till the summer of the following year, and cost him £8000, leaving a net profit of £7000 from the wager, 'the only instance in all my life before, in which any of my projects turned out to my advantage'. In spite of his wild reputation, the account shows him to have been an observant traveller and even something of a scholar.

In Dublin he was known as the boon companion of the Sham Squire Francis Higgins and John Scott (Copper-Faced Jack), Earl of Clonmell: as rascally a pair as could be found anywhere. These three were frequently to be seen promenading in the Green, whether on Leeson's Walk (their own side) or the more fashionable Beaux Walk (Stephen's Green, North): Whaley the Buck, Higgins the gutter journalist and government informer, and Scott, the obese and unscrupulous Chief Justice of the King's Bench. Whaley's sister married Fitzgibbon, and he himself married, a year before his death, the sister of Valentine Browne Lawless, second Lord Cloncurry.

Buck Whaley's gambling debts finally became so embarrassing that he withdrew from Dublin and ended his days in the Isle of Man, where he wrote his Memoirs in a spirit of commendable contrition. He built a large house there known as Whaley's Folly, subsequently the Fort Anne Hotel, which is said to have been built on Irish earth imported in shiploads sufficient to underlie the whole mansion to a depth of six feet to satisfy a wager – a typical part of the Buck Whaley legend. His last patriotic action was to accept a bribe of £4000 from the Grattan party to vote against the Union. He died at a coaching inn in Cheshire on 2 November 1800, at the age of thirty-four.

MAURICE CRAIG
from *Dublin 1660-1860* (1980)

The Duck Stops Here

I don't intend to be a prisoner of my past.
CHARLES HAUGHEY, October 1982

Several days after he had become leader of Fianna Fáil in December 1979, Charles Haughey was having lunch in the restaurant in Leinster

House. Among the company at his table was Martin O'Donoghue. The menu was passed around and O'Donoghue ordered duck for his main course. The waitress told him the duck was off: O'Donoghue selected something else. Haughey remarked that he had some of the finest duck in Ireland on his lands at Kinsealy. There were polite expressions of interest and the conversation moved on to other topics. Several weeks later, Haughey's garda driver called to O'Donoghue's house in Dartry in south Dublin. O'Donoghue was not at home but the driver left a package with his wife Evelyn. Inside, she found a dead duck and a card from Haughey. The card read: 'Shot on Saturday'.

The incident encapsulated one of the central features of the new Taoiseach. His actions gave rise to wildly diverging interpretations while his own motives remained enigmatic. Haughey's friends said that the gift of the duck was a gesture of reconciliation to O'Donoghue, who had been dropped peremptorily from Haughey's first cabinet. Haughey's enemies within Fianna Fáil saw it as a Mafia-style message, rubbing home the fact that O'Donoghue's ministerial career was as dead as the duck. Both interpretations may be unjust to Haughey. But his studied mannerisms and his instinct for the telling gesture suggested that most of his actions were calculated. In any event, after the most controversial career in modern Irish politics, few people were prepared to grant Haughey the benefit of innocence.

JOE JOYCE & PETER MURTAGH
from *The Boss* (1983)

In the Hot Seat

Noel Purcell claimed that on a cold winter's day it was cheaper to go to the Theatre Royal in the afternoon than light a fire. Patrons booked permanent seats for Sunday nights, and it was known for some to bequeath their seats to favoured relatives after their death.

PHILIP B. RYAN
from *Jimmy O'Dea: The Pride of the Coombe* (1990)

Whip Round

On Saturday afternoons, the Ha'penny Bridge was reserved for side shows and mini carnivals. Blondini the Sword Swallower, Houdini who got himself tied up with a straight jacket and nearly burst his eyes getting out of it. The Cart Wheel man who balanced a heavy cart wheel on his chin and then lay on broken bottles for an encore. The Whip man who whipped cigarettes out of his wife's mouth. The wife used to look at him as if she was saying, 'If you miss I'll brain ye'. When the act was over, him and the wife used to smoke all the half cigarettes. But the wife held on to the money that was thrown into the ring.

EAMONN MacTHOMÁIS
from *Janey Mack Me Shirt is Black* (1982)

Humane Act

The passage of the Sexual Offences Bill by Dáil Eireann yesterday evening was an historic event, not just for gay people, but for all citizens of Ireland who take seriously the noble words of the Easter Proclamation of 1916 that the State should seek to cherish all the children of the nation equally.

The great advocate of Catholic emancipation, Daniel O'Connell, uttered a profound truth when he said that by extending freedom and dignity to others one enhances rather than diminishes one's own dignity and freedom.

When, next week, this Bill is passed by Seanad Eireann and sent to the President for signature I will, for the first time in my life, feel that I am at last a full and equal citizen of my own country. I will be just 49 years old and for exactly half that period I have campaigned for just this kind of a civilised change in the law.

The attempt to seek a liberalisation of the draconian British imperial statutes has not always been popular, even within the gay community. When we embarked on this campaign in the early 1970s there were many in the gay community itself who understandably wanted a quiet life and felt that we were foolhardy to draw attention to our existence at all.

Nevertheless right from the beginning there was a substantial group, by no means all gay themselves, who felt that it was important that the stigma of criminality should be removed.

Because of my personal circumstances, I had an unusual freedom of manoeuvre. I was employed by the University of Dublin, a liberal environment; and both my parents were dead, so that neither family nor employer could bring undue pressure to bear.

For this reason I was able, as many others were not, to speak out publicly early on. As a result I have received a disproportionate amount of praise for the tenacity with which we have fought for our rights, but I should like to place on the record my gratitude to the very many courageous people in the various organisations such as the Irish Gay Rights Movement, the National Lesbian and Gay Federation, the Campaign for Homosexual Law Reform and the Gay and Lesbian Equality Network who selflessly, and for the most part anonymously, dedicated themselves to the task of social reform.

Apart from the outspoken gay activists there are some figures who deserve my public thanks. First of these must be Dr Noel Browne who, as long ago as 1977, asked the then Minister for Justice to consider reform of the law and was quite literally laughed out of the Dáil.

Further those who have recently maintained that there have been no prosecutions for consenting sexual relations between males in this country for the last 40 years must be unaware of the selfless and dedicated work of people like Garrett Sheehan, solicitor, who in a series of unreported cases defended gay people. My own solicitor, the late John Jay, undertook the preparation of the initial constitutional case and I remember also with gratitude the early brief prepared for me by that wise and humane judge, Donal Barrington, then a senior counsel, who indicated that while we had a very strong moral and intellectual case, the political battle would be a long and difficult one.

Most of all, of course, this matter could never have been brought to a successful conclusion without the unique legal ability and passionate humanity of Her Excellency, Mary Robinson, President of Ireland, who so brilliantly represented me as a barrister in the various legal cases both in Ireland and Europe. There is a particular appropriateness, and I hope pleasure, for the President in signing into law a Bill whose passage she was herself obliquely instrumental in securing.

As I sat in the gallery of the Dáil listening to the debate over the last two days, I felt immensely proud to be a citizen of this Republic.

SENATOR DAVID NORRIS
from *The Irish Times* (1993)

Parnell Takes Office

In fact the Dublin visit was to be capped with violence. Earlier in the day Parnell had visited the *United Ireland* offices and dismissed the editor, Matthew Bodkin, who had gone over to the anti-Parnellite side. During the Rotunda meeting some anti-Parnellites had retaken the office. When he learned of this Parnell drove there and drew up his horse so quickly in front of the building that the animal fell flat in the street. Parnell leapt through the waiting crowd and seemed to hurl himself over the area railings to effect an entrance. Dissuaded by his supporters, he seized a crowbar, battered the door in, and then, as one onlooker reported:

> One of the windows on the second storey was removed and Parnell suddenly appeared in the aperture. He had conquered. The enthusiasm which greeted him cannot be described. His face was ghastly pale, save only that on either cheek a hectic crimson spot was glowing. His hat was off now, his hair dishevelled, the dust of conflict begrimed his well-brushed coat. The people were spellbound, almost terrified, as they gazed on him. For myself, I felt a thrill of dread, as if I looked at a tiger in the frenzy of its rage. Then he spoke and the tone of his voice was ever more terrible than his look. He was brief, rapid, decisive, and the closing words of his speech still ring in my ear: 'I rely on Dublin. Dublin is true. What Dublin says today Ireland will say tomorrow.'

The Parnell of the Rotunda meeting and of the battle for the *United Ireland* offices seemed a far cry from the aloof, remote, sometimes passive figure of the past ten years. It is true that when relating the incident to Katie, he sounded like the easy and low-keyed Parnell of old: 'all, or nearly all, I could get out of Parnell himself on the subject was a soft laugh and, 'It was splendid fun. I wish I could burgle my own premises every day!'

But had the struggle of Committee Room 15 changed him? In Dublin, there seemed to appear a different Parnell. There had been charges in recent months that he was actually mad, and it was remembered that there was eccentricity, even insanity, in his family. Even Davitt wrote, 'Well may it be asked: 'Is Mr Parnell mad?' That there are evidences of insanity in his actions no one can doubt.' And it is not merely the Irish Party leaders or the Liberals who looked on with the nonplussed awe of the bystander outside the *United Ireland* offices. Summing up Parnell's state of mind during the following months of stress and tension, even the judicious historian F.S.L. Lyons wrote:

> The deliberate breach of faith with Gladstone, the breaking off of the Liberal alliance, the aspersions hurled at his former colleagues, the violence of his behaviour in Dublin, the invective poured upon his opponents at Kilkenny – all these suggested hidden depths which made men shudder and fear for his reason.

In the heroic stories, it is not unusual to find that at some late point the hero – a Roland, a Launcelot, a Cuchullain – descends to madness, to a kind of uncharacteristic frenzy. And in the tragedies the hero – a Macbeth, a Richard III – is sometimes no more vehement than in the moments just before his death. Yet while it is true that Parnell in his last months sometimes spoke and acted with an alarming and strange violence, it would be well to note what one of his most astute opponents, John Dillon, wrote in his diary: 'Men say here that Parnell is mad, but it seems to me that his astuteness is absolutely infinite...'

MARY ROSE CALLAGHAN
from *Kitty O'Shea* (1989)

She's So Modern

Later in 1977 we released a second single from the album. It was called 'Mary of the Fourth Form'. It was the imaginary life I'd made up for a schoolgirl I'd fancied in Murray's called Mary Preece. The record went to Number 14. We decided, after a triumphant year, we'd return to Ireland as the conquering heroes. The day after we arrived in Dublin I was sitting in the promoter's office working on tour plans when this weird girl walked in. She was about seventeen and dressed in an outfit of ragged lace, which made her look like a cross between a hippy and a punk. She was small and waif-like, her hair was platinum blonde, and she was gorgeous. When she spoke, she sounded like an upper-class English person.

'Hi,' she said, looking straight at me.

'Hi, I'm Bob Geldof.'

'I know, we've met before.'

'Have we? Where?'

'In that restaurant in the Fulham Road, at the party for "Lookin' After Number One", remember?'

'Oh yeah, I remember.' I didn't.

'How are you?' she said.

'OK. Don't stand at the door, come in.'

'There's nowhere to sit.'

'Come over and sit on my knee.'

She did. Great, I'm going to get fucked tonight, I thought. Her name was Paula Yates. She'd just finished doing her 'A' Levels at St Clare's in Oxford and was now a charlady in London.

'I have my own squeegee,' she said.

I invited her to the concert that night. The promoter hired a row of Daimler limousines to transport us. We were in Dublin, we were going to flaunt it. Half-way down Grafton Street she leaned over and unzipped my trousers. I looked up towards the driver. 'Don't do that,' I said. He wasn't looking. Outside the limousine, familiar places were passing the window. 'Stop it, will you?' I said half-heartedly. Christ, this one has been around, I thought. Afterwards she told me she thought she'd better do it, because she imagined that's what all rock stars expected.

After the concert that night, we all went to a night club. She was sitting talking to Fachtna when a shifty and embarrassed young man approached. 'Hi,' he began awkwardly. 'I'm Bono. I'm the singer in a band called U2.' 'So what?' said Paula. Bono walked away crushed. At the end of the evening I said, 'Well, are you coming back with me, or not?' It wasn't really very romantic.

I was staying with the tour promoter. We were sleeping on the floor. It was Christmas and it had been an incredible year, but there was no money coming in yet from the record and we were living pretty frugally. Other people may have been surprised: after all we'd been on telly, had two records in the charts, had limos, so we must have been bona fide "pop stars". My bed was three cushions and an afghan coat. 'Listen to the rain on the skylight,' I said, as we lay there. It was my attempt at a romantic pause. The next morning we found it hadn't been raining – the toilet cistern had burst.

BOB GELDOF
from *Is That It?* (1986)

The Dubs

Oh we're the Dubs, the rub-a-dub Dubs
Sometimes called 'Jackeen'
We're Prod and Papist all in one
We're Orange, White and Green!
Not King nor Pope, despair nor hope
Can make us bend the knee
From Liffeyside we draw our pride
Of Norseman pedigree.

Yes we're the Dubs, the rub-a-dub Dubs
Each mot we'll gladly coort her,
But first things first, we'll slake our thirst
With pints of thick, black porter.
We'll barrel along with many a song
And raise a glass to mine host
For life is short – let's have a snort!
And the dhivil take the hind most.

Oh we're the Dubs, the rub-a-dub Dubs
And we're a breed apart,
Don't give two shits for Gaels or Brits
No malice in our heart.
So come what may on the Judgement Day
The saints will sing our praises
No other place can boast a race
On first name terms with Jaysus.

VINCENT CAPRANI
from *Vulgar Verse & Variations, Rowdy Rhymes & Rec-im-itations* (1987)

Cops and Jobbers

On the day of his retirement, Jim was paid glowing tributes in all the Courts. In Court No.6, Chancery Street, District Justice 'Dinny' Ua Donnchadha said he wished to be associated with his colleagues on the Bench in paying a tribute to Sergeant Branigan, who was one of the best witnesses to have appeared before him. He was clear in his diction from the witness box, competent, and fair to everyone. 'Dublin citizens will miss your work in the detection and prevention of crime,' the Justice said. Mr Ted McCarthy, Court Registrar; Mr G. Ward, solicitor; Mr Don Rooney, *Evening Herald* and Mr Maurice Liston, *Evening Press*, joined in the tributes. Earlier Justice Robert 'Bob' O'hUadhaigh (there always was great repartee in Court between Jim and the legendary Justice O'hUadhaigh) had paid him a great tribute, saying to a Court packed with Senior Counsel, Junior Barristers, Solicitors, Court Clerks and Press Men that Jim had been of great assistance to him personally and to the Courts all down the years of his Garda service. 'I want it to be known that I consider you to be one of the pillars of the law who saw that justice was done. You will be missed by the Courts and myself and my colleagues wish you good health and every happiness in your well earned retirement'. In the Circuit Court a few days later I had the honour of joining with Judge Charlie Conroy, to whom I acted as Court Clerk in No.7, in paying a tribute to Jim, on behalf of the Circuit Court staff. Charlie Conroy paid Jim a tremendous tribute and had earlier arranged for the press to be in attendance. To a packed Court he said that 'not only he but all of Dublin will sadly miss what was part and parcel of this city of ours – Jim Branigan'.

The tributes flowed from every quarter – a special ceremony in honour of Jim was held in the Dalkey Sports Centre when he was made a life member of the centre. The Commissioner, Mr Edmund Garvey, paid tribute at a special Garda function held in his honour, but of all the tributes and presentations that were made to Jim, the one which touched his heart and which he treasured most was that paid by the 'Pavement Hostesses' – Dublin's prostitutes. They clubbed together and on Jim's last night, presented him with a beautiful canteen of cutlery (which he today proudly displays in his home) and a good luck card signed by them all. Jim takes up the story:

'I was patrolling the city with Sonny and the Riot Squad boys in Branno 5 on the eve of my retirement from the force. Everything was fairly quiet. Just after midnight we got a call from patrol to go to the Pepper Canister Church, Upper Mount Street, where "there is something wrong". A 999 call had been received but I did not understand why it had not been dealt with by Donnybrook station.

'When we got to the church there was not a soul around, but being thorough in my methods, I prowled around the area. I thought a girl might be in trouble or lying in an alleyway after an assault. We drove around and circled back to the church. Then I saw seven girls, whom I knew to be "Street girls", standing in a bunch. This is highly illegal and if they are caught congregating in twos or threes the girls know they are liable to be taken in.

'The girls were in good spirits and one said: "Mr Branigan, you would not arrest us on your last day, would you?" It being the duty of every Garda to "keep the streets clean", I said: "Come on now girls, move along, there are complaints about this place." Then I was amazed when the girls said they had made the bogus 999 call so they could wish me "God Speed" in my retirement. I was moved. It was a nice thought, but I was amazed and surprised when one of the girls then said: 'And we have a little something for you to remember us by.'

'Then they gave me this very nice and expensive present. Most of the regular girls on the beat must have contributed towards it. I thanked them, took the present and drove off telling them to disperse, for I still had to keep up a brittle, tough exterior. On my way home that night I tossed in my mind why I should have been the recipient of such an unorthodox present. I must be the only Irish policeman to have received such a gift.'

At the end of that month James Cantwell and Jim Farrelly of the *Evening Herald* wrote Jim Branigan's story which ran for a week in the paper. In the 25 January 1973 edition of the *Herald* a spokeswoman for the 'street girls' who made the presentation told why he deserved his special thank you.

'Let us get one thing clear from the start – policemen and girls of the street are enemies. I for one would certainly never, under any circumstances, give a present to a policeman and if one came around to chat me up I would wonder what he had on his mind or what information he was fishing for. But Mr Branigan was something special. Though he is only a few weeks retired we all (over fifty of us) miss him very much. On an average five nights out of seven he and his crew would pull up the police van beside the pavement and inquire after our welfare. If we were depressed or browned off he would cheer us up or give us a pep talk. He was always in good humour. To be frank when I came from England four years

ago and started soliciting in Dublin I thought Mr Branigan was a
fruit and nut case. I mean it is highly unusual for a policeman to
stop a prostitute and ask her how she is. I know he was not part
of the street girls detective unit but even in England I had never
seen anything like him. Other Dublin cops would land us in Donny-
brook or Harcourt Terrace if they caught us soliciting. My suspicions
of him vanished after four weeks. I realised he was genuine and
not fishing for information. My respect for him began to grow as
I heard more and more stories of his acts of kindness. We spent
long hours discussing whether or not we should give him a present.
Would it be embarrassing for him because of his position? It was
never heard of before for streetgirls to band together to say "thank
you" to a policeman. Eventually we decided at the risk of being
arrested, to meet at Upper Mount Street Church and make the
presentation. We phoned for him. When we handed over the present
[a canteen of cutlery] and card signed by us all, Dolores said: "Here
is something to remember us by. There is nobody to take your place
and you will be missed very much." I could see that he was moved.
And we were all very glad that we had decided to say "thank you"
in this way.'

Jim never arrested a Pavement Hostess (as he called them, con-
sidering the term prostitute vulgar) during his long Garda career.

BERNARD NEARY
from *Lugs: The Life & Times of Jim Branigan* (1985)

The Big Fellows

The 'big fellows' were the men who couldn't or wouldn't find regular
work. They lived by their wits, picking up five shillings here or
there to increase – or more often to lose – it on the horse races.
When they hadn't any money, they would stand on the corner beside
Jemmy Gill's pub, waiting to see what the day's luck would bring.
They could be coarse, and would fight and use bad language on a
Saturday night. But they had the good rebel spirit all right.

Another din could be heard as the children of the Street followed
the lamplighter. 'Billy with the lamp, Billy with the light, Billy with
his sweetheart out all night,' they chanted as they followed him

like the Pied Piper from lamp post to lamp post. At the pub corner
was the newspaper man – short, stout, red-faced, with a ginger
moustache twirled up at the corners army-style, a flat greasy cloth
cap and a scarf knotted round his neck. *'N'Girrell!...Hella Mail!'*
he shouted. That meant *Evening Herald* and *Evening Mail.* You know,
he had been a sergeant-major in the British Army. He was the one
Englishman in *The Quare Fellow* – apart from the hangman.

And as for the Rustlers, as they called themselves – I'd never
known people like those slum-dwellers of Russell Street. They
called me Lady Behan, because I wouldn't sit on the steps gossiping
all day as they did. They were as common as ditchwater, but in
the things that really mattered they were the cream of the earth.
They looked after each other in sickness, and for all their poverty
they had a grand time. We used to sing and dance every opportunity
we got. Yes, the slums were bad, but are the new housing estates
any better? There the mothers sit in the pubs all day, and have no
idea half the time where their children are. That's how you get this
vandalism. The Russell Street children were bold lumps enough, but
there was always someone on the Street keeping a watch on them.

Not that people didn't take a drink, you understand, and it was
a rough place on a Saturday night – a drunken night. Then the
people would get very drunk and use foul language swearing at
anything and everybody they came across. I didn't like it much, but
I had to put up with it – I lived there. When they were drunk they'd
forget 'Lady Behan' and call us 'Bloody old Fenians'.

KATHLEEN BEHAN
from *Mother of All the Behans* (1984)

Cycle of Crime

We would meet in St Patrick's Park in Bride Street and off we
would go for the day, up along the canal and down to the cats' and
dogs' home in Grand Canal. We would have a good look at the dogs,
petting them, feeding them and all the time trying to find a way
to open the cages and let them out. But in the back of my mind, I
could not help thinking about the vicious dogs, the ones that had
gone mad, so if you let one out, you had to let them all out. And

I was fucked if I was letting any mad dog out to bite the bleeding arse off me. But it always was good fun. Off we would go down to Boland's Mills and Bakery for our cakes. We used to sneak into where they loaded up the vans and stuff our jumpers with goodies and out the gate we would go, hanging off the back of the van.

We used to go everywhere, Blackrock, Bray, shops, parks, everywhere but school, and when we would get tired from walking, we would go up to Jacob's Factory and get ourselves two nice bicycles and off we would be, gone again. I was mad on bikes. I think I would have been quite happy as a messenger boy, so long as they gave me a bike, but my mother would not even let me look at a bike for fear I would be killed on it. I remember one time, my father brought home two three-wheel bikes that he had found in the dump. One of the bikes had only two wheels, and the other had no chain. My father got this great idea one day. He put the bike that had only two wheels into the back of the one that had three. I think the O'Neills of St Patrick's House were the first kids in the world to have a five-wheeler bike and it carried everybody from one to twenty-one.

I never liked going to school. It was boring, and there was never anything interesting to do. The school masters had lost interest in me at an early age, because I happened to be trouble and also because there was more kids than me in the school who wanted to learn. Anyhow, they would be lucky to see me at school for half an hour.

My sister, Evelyn, who was in charge of the family, used to bring me any morning she could by the scruff of the neck to school, but more times than not, I would break free of her grip and have it off on my toes. And if I could not break free and had to go to school, then I would wait my chance and get over the school wall, bringing half a dozen others with me. All our family went to the same school. They went from sitting on seats to climbing over the wall. Sometimes the master would send for my younger brother, Bernard, and ask him 'Where is your brother Gerard?' 'Comen,' Bernard would say, and the master's reply would be, 'And so is Christmas.' The master wasn't a bad bloke. He knew the hopelessness of the situation. There were about 40 boys in the class, half with more nits than brains. On the rare occasions that I was in class, he would call me up to the front and in a high voice, he would say: '1-2-3-4-5-6-7, all good children go to heaven; 1-2-3-4-5-6-7, all bad boys go to Letterfrack.' As far as I was concerned at the time, I thought he was a madman, but I soon found out that what he was saying was my future, that the wallop of the duster would

soon be replaced by the wallop of the drumstick on the knuckles
and that the roaming would soon be replaced by moaning.

I remember the day that I got sent to Letterfrack. My mother
came with me to the court, all nice and clean new shoes and a
nice neat suit, leaving the house. That morning was like any other
morning. The Corpo were cleaning out the chutes, and all the
kids were in school. I think my mother had an idea where I was
going. Passing down Aungier Street, people from the flats would
stop my mother and say 'God help you, Chrisso. Your heart must
be broke going in and out of courts. I don't blame you getting
drunk, but God is good. Maybe he will learn his lesson and be a
good boy.' I nor my mother never paid any attention to what they
were saying for they never stopped reporting my mother to the
Corpo, and could not wait to see the back of me. Anyhow, on we
went. Me ma used to always let me smoke when I was going to
courts. So here we were, my mother's heart broke and me with a
king-size Rothmans in my mouth at the manly age of ten. I don't
know who spent the most time in the Children's Courts, me or
the Judge, Christine Kenny. I had been there so often for mitching
and other carry-on that there was not an inch of the kip that I did
not know. There was not a name on the walls that I did not know
and those that I did not know, knew me.

The Courts were situated in the Lower Yard of Dublin Castle.
The building consisted of an ugly waiting room on the left as you
went in the door; straight in front of you were the stairs leading
to the courtroom, and underneath the steps was the cell. It was a
large room with two big windows with bars, mesh wire and plastic
glass. It also had a big bench which was affixed to the floor for fear
it might be used as a battering ram to smash down the cell door.
Outside the cell to the left were the jax for the prisoners. Anytime
you wanted to have a piss, you were escorted by the jailer who
watched you closely just in case you might nick the jax roll and
use it as a rope to hang yourself, and believe me, there were enough
spacers mad enough to try it. The other rooms on the ground floor
were the gardai waiting room and the court registrar.

The first person I saw as I entered the building was the School
Inspector who nodded to myself and said 'Hello' to my mother.
Me ma brought me into the waiting room. Everybody knew every-
body else. All the mothers sat and talked together about their hearts
being broken and smoked like chimney pots, while the accused,
like children in a play-pen, scribbled their case histories on walls,
doors and floors. Some were more artistic than others and drew

nude ladies with tits as big as weather balloons. Between the smoking and pen work, everybody was on edge, nervous and frightened. Case after case was called, every mother wishing each other all the best as they climbed the stairs holding the hands of their children tightly, hoping that they would walk home the same way. Every now and again the courts would go into uproar as someone got sent down. Everyone would go into a cold sweat, the jailer taking the boy from his mother, tears and cries, mother screaming at policemen, cursing them, prisoners making feeble attempts to escape as a forest of policemen stand between him and the birds. Into the cell, order restored, justice being done and law maintained.

The charges I had to answer were one of non-attendance at school and one for the larceny of a bicycle. I was called: Garda Kennedy and Gerard O'Neill. I put out my cig as did my mother, took a deep breath and climbed the steps, getting more and more frightened. I had been warned by the Judge before, that if she saw me again in her court, she would send me away. I thought to myself, 'Run, have it in your toes, don't be a fool. Your last chance, don't throw it away,' I was caught between fear of escaping and the thought of Letterfrack. I could see my mother's face was pained and drawn, nothing but strength keeping her together. A woman was standing at the top of the steps with a prayer book in her hand. It was the woman who owned the push-bike that I had taken. She was an oldish woman with a religious face, but if the Pope himself was to pray for me that day, it would not have mattered a bollox.

MANNIX FLYNN
from *Nothing to Say* (1983)

Dub in the Blood

Now, how to go about presenting your vampire? This was not a difficult task; a little research soon revealed that legends of vampires existed throughout Europe. So did ample evidence of their characteristics; they were most commonly people whose eyebrows met, who had stubby fingers, or hairs in the palms of their hands; or who were seventh sons of seventh sons, or had committed suicide. And generally they were very, very old.

But Bram's idea was for no ordinary vampire; his creation was to be a master ghoul. And after a long search he found him.

He discovered that the Voivode Drakula or Dracula, who ruled Walachia in 1455-62, had earned for himself the title of 'the Impaler', and that the story of his ferocity and hair-raising cruelty in defiance of the Turks was related at length in two fifteenth-century manuscripts, one of which spoke of him as a 'wampyr'. Immediately, Bram sought the help of Arminius Vambery in Budapest.

Vambery was able to report that 'the Impaler', who had won this name for obvious reasons, was spoken of for centuries after as the cleverest and the most cunning, as well as the bravest of the sons of the 'land beyond the forest'. He was a soldier, statesman and alchemist, who took his mighty brain and iron resolution with him to the grave. The Draculas were also held by their contemporaries to have had dealings with 'the Evil One'; the old records, besides labelling Dracula a 'wampyr' using such words as 'stregoica' – witch; 'ordog' and 'pokol' – Satan and Hell.

This, then, was the remarkable man Bram decided to resurrect, four hundred years after his death. How to portray him? Well, he would retain an impression of age and be given a generous number of agreed vampire characteristics.

So Count Dracula took shape in the book as a tall old man, clean shaven save for a long white moustache, and clothed from head to foot in black. His face was a strong aquiline, with high bridged thin nose and arched nostrils. His hair grew scantily round his temples but profusely elsewhere; his bushy eyebrows were massive, almost meeting over the nose. The mouth under the heavy moustache was hard and cruel, and peculiarly sharp white teeth protruded from lips which showed a remarkable ruddiness in an other pallid face. His ears were extremely pointed at the top, and other vampire signs were his hands – rather coarse and broad, with squat fingers, hairs in the centre of the palm, nails long and fine and cut to a sharp point.

He did not eat ordinary food, of course. He cast no reflection in a mirror and threw no shadow. He could appear as a wolf, or as a bat flapping at the window; he could come in a mist, which he would create, or on moonlight rays as elemental dust; and he could see in the dark. He had the strength of twenty men and could direct the elements, the storm, the fog and the thunder, and command all the meaner things – rats, owls, bats, moths, foxes and wolves; but his power ceased, as did that of all evil things, at sunrise.

Restoring Dracula to a natural home in Transylvania, in a vast ruined castle perched on the edge of a great precipice, took Bram many hours of research among books and maps in the British Museum. Most of his information about the country was gleaned from an old guide book; but when, after publication of 'Dracula', he was congratulated by all sorts of people on his first-hand knowledge of Transylvania, and the settings so eerily true, he found it prudent not to spoil the illusion. He carefully placed Count Dracula's district on the borders of three states – Transylvania, Moldavia and Bukovina, in the midst of the Carpathian mountains, a demon-tossed area that seemed to breed every known superstition in the world.

HARRY LUDLUM
from *A Biography of Dracula: The Life Story of Bram Stoker* (1962)

Somewhat Like Himself

As aesthete Wilde found it essential to cultivate more than one art. At Trinity, Sullivan indicates, when Wilde was not living at home, he had rooms in a building known as Botany Bay. These were evidently dingy after Merrion Square, and Wilde made no effort to keep them clean or to receive friends there. Sometimes, however, a visitor called, and would find in the sitting room an easel prominently placed, which held an unfinished landscape in oils by the host. 'I have just put in the butterfly,' Wilde would say, indicating that he was familiar with Whistler's already famous signature. At Oxford he used the same easel for the same purpose. Sullivan also establishes that Wilde continued at Trinity the elaborate style of dressing which he had invented at Portora. He came into Sullivan's rooms one day wearing an outlandish pair of trousers. When Sullivan started to tease him about them, Wilde begged him with mock solemnity not to make them an object of jest. He was planning a trip to Umbria, he explained: 'These are my Trasimeno trousers, and I mean to wear them there.' Happily, his taste in clothing was not so fastidious as to prevent him from smiling (as he told Sullivan) at the recollection of a down-at-heels classical scholar, John Townsend Mills, who had tutored him for the Berkeley Prize. Mills wore a tall hat, which one day was covered with crêpe; on Wilde's commiserating with his supposed loss, Mills explained that he was simply covering a hole in the hat.

Wilde can be seen slowly accumulating at Trinity the elements of his Oxford behaviour – his Pre-Raphaelite sympathies, his dandiacal dress, his Hellenic bias, his ambiguous sexuality, his contempt for conventional morality. These positions were taken, at least on occasion, with a slight air of self-mockery, just as his delight in Swinburnian passion would continue to be mitigated by that 'chaffable innocence' which his Oxford friend J.E.C. Bodley (who first met him in Dublin during the summer of 1874) ascribed to him. One further change in his behaviour – also to persist – was his dallying with the idea of turning Catholic. Much to his father's displeasure, Wilde made friends with some priests in Dublin. The doctrine of papal infallibility had just been declared, and this, and the rise of the Catholic University in Dublin which Cardinal Newman had founded, had given new alarm to members of the (Protestant) Church of Ireland. No doubt Newman's prose style, its beauty just demonstrated again in his *Grammar of Assent* (1870), had as much to do with Wilde's interest as papal infallibility; and a delight in the forms of Catholicism, rather than its content, accounted for his newfound admiration, just as it probably explained his mother's arrangement for his Catholic baptism years before. Yet he preferred to ascribe his remaining a Protestant to his father's threat of disinheriting him. His father need not have worried. Wilde was fostering self-contradictory inclinations.

In any event, he had other interests, other ambitions. His reading made the Irish scene parochial, and his excitement over Pre-Raphaelitism – an English movement – was regarded in Dublin as an amiable folly, not to be entertained, without derision in that city. The claustral quality of Irish life, which Yeats would describe as 'great hatred, little room', rendered the possibility of promulgating some new aesthetic evangel at home exceedingly remote. If Wilde was beginning to leave Ireland spiritually, he had still to leave it physically. The particular suggestion may have come from Mahaffy: another excellent pupil of his, Leech, after taking a Trinity degree had gone on to Gonville and Caius College, Cambridge, for a second undergraduate degree. Mahaffy did not think that the study of the classics could be carried out better in England than at Trinity College, but he had a worldly respect for the older English universities, and would send one of his own sons to Oxford, the other two to Cambridge. He knew that Wilde, brilliant classicist though he was, could not be sure of being offered a fellowship in classics at Trinity in preference to his fellow student Purser. On the other hand, if he should be conspicuously successful at Oxford, he might return to Ireland, as Leech eventually did, to take up a chair.

It was necessary to persuade not only Oscar Wilde but his father. Mahaffy is said to have concerted with Sir Henry Acland, Regius Professor of Medicine at Oxford and a friend of Sir William, for this purpose. But Sir William had his own reason for agreeing, the mistaken hope that the move to Oxford would cause his son to break off his dalliance with Catholicism. England would keep him Protestant. Willie was already in the Middle Temple in London, 'ready,' as his mother said, 'to spring forth like another Perseus to combat evil'. She added, 'His hope is to enter Parliament and I wish it also. He has a good prospect and can be anything if he cares to work,' a qualification which is the first warning of Willie's inadequacies. (He left the Middle Temple in a few months, and was called to the Irish bar on 22 April 1875.) Sir William made no objection to his second son's going off too.

So Wilde was free to respond to the announcement in the *Oxford University Gazette* of 17 March 1874, that Magdalen College would award two Demyships (scholarships) in classics by examination on 23 June. Each paid £95 a year and could be held for five years. Wilde felt confident enough of success not to bother to take the Trinity examinations for his third year. He presented himself at Magdalen on the day, bearing the required testimonial of good conduct and certification that he was under twenty years of age. One of the four other candidates, G.T. Atkinson, who came second to Wilde and was also awarded a Demyship, recalled fifty-four years later how Wilde, older than the others and much more assured in manner, kept coming up to the invigilator for more paper, because he wrote only four or five words to a line. Atkinson remembered Wilde's writing as 'huge and sprawling, somewhat like himself'.

RICHARD ELLMANN
from *Oscar Wilde* (1988)

The Finding of Moses

On Egypt's banks, contagious to the Nile
The Ould Pharoah's daughter, she went to bathe in style.
She took her dip and she came unto the land,
And to dry her royal pelt she ran along the strand.

A bullrush tripped her whereupon she saw
A smiling baby in a wad of straw;
She took him up and says she in accents mild
'Oh taranagers, girls, now, which of yis owns the child?'

She took him up and she gave a little grin
For she and Moses were standing in their skin,
'Bedad now,' says she 'It was someone very rude
Left a little baby by the river in his nude.'
She took him to her oul lad sitting on the throne
'Da,' says she, 'Will you give the boy a home?'
'Bedad now,' says he, 'Sure I've often brought in worse.
Go my darlin daughter and get the child a nurse.'

An oul blackamore woman among the crew
Cried out 'You royal savage, what's that to do with you?
Your royal ladies is too meek and mild
To beget dishonestly this darling little child.'
'Ah then,' says Pharoah, 'I'll search every nook
From the Phoenix Park down to Donnybrook
And when I catch hoult of the bastard's father
I will kick him from the Nile down to the Dodder.'

Well they sent a bellman to the Market Square
To see if he could find a slavey there
But the only one now that he could find
Was the little young one that left the child behind.
She came up to Pharoah, a stranger, mareyah,
Never lettin on that she was the baby's ma.
And so little Moses got his mammy back
Shows that co-in-ci-dence is a nut to crack.

ZOZIMUS

Zozimus was a legendary Dub, a blind
gleeman who sold sheets of his songs and
ballads on Carlisle (now O'Connell) Bridge.

Rovers Return

Rovers is a city institution. In the language of the street nobody says Shamrock Rovers, that's unnecessary. When you mention Rovers all kinds of images spring to mind: power, grandeur, style, success, excitement, crowds, in fact everything that League of Ireland football – Famous Chicken Football – does not possess.

The images evoked belong to the past. Which past depends on who you were talking to. Old men remember Rovers in the 20s and 30s. They recall the packed trams, John Joe Flood, Fulham and Fagan. Somewhat younger men remember Paddy Moore, Peter Farrell, the war years, rations and Rovers.

A younger generation still, my generation, which grew up in the 50s and early 60s remember the Rovers of Paddy Coad. Coad was a genius. He was a great inside forward – delicate, powerful, imaginative.

To a city of young men obsessed with soccer he was the best player we had ever seen. We knew that great football was played in England and further afield in mysterious places like Brazil. We had photos and cigarette cards with heroic yet distant names written on them. But we had no television. We had never actually seen the greats.

Occasionally you would meet The Boy Who'd Been to England, who'd seen Tom Finney play. This boy was envied in much the same way as later you would envy The Man Who Always Got The Pretty Girl.

*   *   *

Those legendary men won everything, if you wanted to see them you would have to have an early Sunday lunch, then to College Green where a vast anxious crowd would throng to await CIE's Football Specials. Many would walk from town on fine days and as your bus crawled along Appian Way and agonisingly slowly through Ranelagh the pavements were awash with hurrying people.

And so on up to Milltown Road to Glenmalure Park past dozens of hawkers selling apples, orr–emm–ges and chocolate. Rovers' place in Irish football meant that they were the team to beat. For every other city team, especially my beloved Drums, and for every country team as well, the big day of the year was the day you played Rovers. They in their majesty were the yardstick by which we could measure our own heroes and thus our own small selves.

*   *   *

The Great Rovers Revival happened. But it made no difference. Time had moved on, we were in another age, the age of television. And it was over. Rovers' success in the 80s proved that the world *does* change, some things die and can never be reincarnated.

Jim McLaughlin won four League of Ireland championships and three FAI cups. As far as cups and medals went you couldn't have asked for more. Sadly, cups and medals are not really what football is truly about. The game is about magic. These days magic comes from the box in the comer of your living-room. It comes from Jack Charlton and his Irish soccer team with which we are now familiar, as indeed we are with the game in Britain.

The more Shamrock Rovers won in the 80s the fewer people went. The League of Ireland was dead. Part of the reason was that we had grown up. The most important change was, however, rooted in reality; football reality and the changing culture of our time. The sporting reality is that soccer is a street game. All the great players, the Coads, Touhys, McCanns and Mickey Bourkes learnt to weave magic on the streets. Kids don't play soccer on the streets anymore. They watch videos, go to McDonalds for their birthdays and have their own computers. They don't have to invent or improvise the way we used to in the bad old 50s. The consequence is that the magicians aren't bred anymore. The game has died or at least is dying. Old assumptions no longer hold, beauty now means something different.

EAMON DUNPHY
from 'The Great Shamrock Rovers Revival',
Invisible Dublin, edited by Dermot Bolger (1991)

Cockles and Mussels

In Dublin's fair city,
Where the girls are so pretty,
    I first set my eyes on sweet Molly Malone.
She wheeled her wheelbarrow
Through streets broad and narrow,
    Crying, 'Cockles and mussels, alive, alive, oh!
        Alive, alive, oh!
        Alive, alive, oh!'
Crying, 'Cockles and mussels, alive, alive, oh!'

She was a fishmonger,
But sure 'twas no wonder,
  For so were her father and mother before.
And they both wheeled their barrow
Through streets broad and narrow,
    Crying, 'Cockles and mussels, alive, alive, oh!
      Alive, alive, oh!' *etc.*

She died of a fever,
And none could relieve her,
  And that was the end of sweet Molly Malone.
But her ghost wheels the barrow,
Through streets broad and narrow,
    Crying, 'Cockles and mussels, alive, alive, oh!
      Alive, alive, oh!' *etc.*

ANONYMOUS

First Dance

In 1935 I went to work for Jimmy O'Dea. Prior to this I went to the Connie Ryan school of dancing after being to Dewy Byrne's school of dancing, in the CYMS in Phyllisburg Avenue, Fairview. Miss Byrne, a lovely woman, thought I had outgrown her school and recommended me to Connie Ryan, who took me over. It was great. She used to teach the O'Dea girls, you know, Jimmy O'Dea's dancers, and she was also a soubrette, as they called them then, out in the front doing the high kicks and singing, 'I'm goin' back to Inverary,' and all sorts of Scottish songs that had nothing to do with anything.

We'd work in extraordinary places like the Esplanade. We'd get the tram up from Ballybough to the old Esplanade where they held the Carnivals up by Collins Barracks, at Kingsbridge. The Esplanade was a great place, famous for its merry-go-rounds. In the tent they had competitions for dancing and singing and I always came away with something. All the mothers would say, 'That's not fair! She's a professional. She's goin' to Connie Ryan. She's been on the Royal. That's not fair. Don't give it to that one...' You know the usual.

But we went to do this little show in the Star Cinema, Bray which is no longer there. Jimmy O'Dea came along to see the show and he put me in a pantomime in the Olympia in 1935. That is when I used to see the sunburst of the Bovril advertisement, there at the corner of D'Olier Street and Westmoreland Street. I played Alfie Byrne, who was the great Lord Mayor at the time. Jimmy O'Dea got a lovely little suit made for me, but he used to keep losing the moustache and we'd find it on the sole of my shoe and there'd be bloody murder. That was my first professional job.

MAUREEN POTTER
from *Alive, Alive O!* edited by Mairín Johnston (1988)

Good and Bad

WOMAN. All I remember we was always movin'. Here in Rutland Street. Over to Aldeborough near to the barracks. Summerhill, Newcommon Court, offa the North Strand, Monto Street, Byrne's Lane offa Potter's Alley, back to Summerhill again, out to Love Lane beyond Ballybough. Sticks o' furniture on top of a hand-cart, the small wans perishin' with the cauld. Runnin' from the Landlords. But what in the name o' God were we runnin' after? Was it anything better?

TALBOT. *(Brusquely.)* I don't remind meself of it. 'Tis all dead now.

WOMAN. Mammy 'n us twelve childer. 'N auld Charlie me father roarin' 'n cursin' 'n drinkin'.

TALBOT. *(Almost to himself.)* I pray for his Eternal Peace.

WOMAN. Who?

TALBOT. Me father.

WOMAN. He was no worse than another.

TALBOT. *(Cry.)* He was a great sinner.

WOMAN. Matt, it's our own father you're taking about.

TALBOT. I seen him in torments! I seen Charlie Talbot among the dammed!

WOMAN. You're very hard, Matt. And hardest on yourself.

TALBOT. He marked others.

WOMAN. What others?

TALBOT. All me brothers. All dead, now. It takes another to bring out the worst in everyone.

WOMAN. What class of livin' is that? Don't we all need others? Isn't the good an' and the bad mixed in everywan?

TALBOT. If there's any meanin' to the life beyond it's that we'll all be alone in Gawd.

WOMAN. Oh, and you're the runner to end us all, Matt. Movin' when the rest of us came to a kinda stop. Wan bit of a room to the next. Drivin' yerself into the ground. God Almighty it's beyond me. Shouldn't we rest in peace?

TALBOT. Not in the flesh, Susan.

WOMAN. *(Sniff.)* Indeed an' it's easy talk when ya haven't others to care.

TALBOT. *(Looks closely at her. Fumbles in a pocket. Holds out his hand.)* Forgive me, sister. I'd forgotten. Take this. G'wan. Buy somethin' for the childer.

WOMAN. What is it?

TALBOT. Only a coupla coppers.

WOMAN. I will not. Ya haven't a bit o' bread yerself. I couldn't. *(Shakes her hand, looking at his hand.)*

TALBOT. Go on, Susan. I don't have the need of it. Take it for the childer.

WOMAN. I couldn't so I couldn't.

TALBOT. Go on now with ya.

She hesitates. She takes the money. She weeps.

THOMAS KILROY
from *Talbot's Box* (1979)

Golden Boy

This time last year Michael Carruth could have walked down O'Connell Street in Dublin or any any other street in any other town in Ireland and he would not have raised an eyebrow. Nowadays he might be in danger of blocking the traffic. He has become a celebrity overnight and will remain so as long as the romance of sport prevails.

In *Ring of Gold*, Carruth with Peter Byrne of this parish, recalls his passion for boxing which has brought him to the pinnacle of the sport. Together they have brought off a considerable feat. It cannot have been easy for a professional writer and an amateur boxer to gel as they have done in this book published by Blackwater Press.

Carruth emerges as a very thoughtful young man, single-minded and determined and always aware of what is going on around him. Those who were privileged to be in Barcelona on that Saturday morning when he and Wayne McCullough won gold and silver medals will probably be aware already of these characteristics, but many will be impressed by Carruth's grasp of his own role in what was a major sporting occasion which had the entire country in ecstasy, and the Badalona area of Barcelona in something akin to carnival mood as the Irish supporters took over the streets.

The dedication required to achieve what Carruth has achieved is captured in a well-produced and printed book with liberal use of photographs. The detail is often fascinating, giving an insight into the mind of an athlete in what must be one of the most searching disciplines in sport. Those who decry the sport would do well to read and study this account of one young man's dedication in pursuit of his aim.

At no stage, has he anything derogatory to say about an opponent, although he does have some fairly pithy thoughts about petty official-dom – so often the bane of the sportsman's life. It is no secret in the amateur boxing scene in Ireland that there was some conster-nation when the IABA ordered a "box off" test to decide who would represent Ireland in the welterweight division in the Irish squad which was to contest the qualifying tournament. Carruth had beaten his very close friend Billy Walsh in the National finals yet, in spite of that and because of boxing politics, a "box off" was ordered much to the astonishment of the boxing fraternity.

As things turned out, Carruth won the bout without a lot of trouble but the annoyance lingered on and even surfaced, albeit amusingly, at the annual general meeting of the IABA in Wexford when Carruth's father and coach, Austin, clashed verbally with Tommy Murphy of Drogheda who had been instrumental in the decision to have the "box off".

Carruth does not shirk his responsibilities in this regard nor yet in reference to the training camp in Germany which prompted Wayne McCullough to fly home in protest. He also deals frankly with three different incidents in Barcelona involving the boxing squad.

There was the Paul Griffin debacle which was, in my view, disastrously handled by the boxing authorities, then the problem which arose when Phil Sutcliffe managed to get Kevin McBride's accreditation badge in a bid to get in touch with his clubmate Paul Griffin before his ill-fated bout, thus causing a security crisis and also the problem which arose because of horseplay by some of the boxers which upset other athletes, and which earned the boxing squad a rap on the knuckles from Pat Hickey, the president of the Olympic Council of Ireland.

Naturally enough, Barcelona overwhelms everything in the book, but Carruth does have time to be philosophical, a trait he obviously inherits from his unflappable father Austin. It was Austin who took the precaution of taking a Tricolour to Barcelona, 'just in case' and Austin who draped the national colours over Michael's shoulders when he went back to the corner at the end of the third round of his final with the Cuban, Hernandez.

He deals also with the controversy over the refusal of the Belfast Lord Mayor to invite him to Belfast to share in Wayne McCullough's homecoming. 'Over the years I've sat down with Irish team-mates and discussed, constructively, the things which separate the two communities in Northern Ireland and debate like that can only be good. That is why I was so disappointed when they declined to invite me to join Wayne in Belfast. One day I plan to go to Belfast to meet at least some of the people (who supported McCullough and myself in Barcelona).'

By and large, this book is well above the average for such publications. Carruth has carved a niche for himself in Irish sport and his book will always remain a record of how it was at the time, how he felt about it, how he reacted and how he thought. It is a valuable document insofar as it gives a keen insight into the life of a sportsman and what it takes to reach the top. Carruth's plans for the future are in abeyance for the moment. Injuries to his right hand and left arm which required surgery are the price he has paid for that success. If he never steps into a competitive ring again he will have achieved what no other Irish boxer has achieved – an Olympic gold medal and the admiration of all Irish sports people.

SEAN KILFEATHER
from *The Irish Times*

Duel in the Crown

The Right Honourable Henry Grattan, leader of the House of Commons, was ever ready to sustain with his pistols the force of his arguments. His cool ferocity, on such occasions, was a fearful display. He began by fighting Lord Earlsfort, and ended by shooting the Honourable Isaac Corry, Chancellor of the Exchequer. He called him, in the debate on the Union, 'a dancing-master', and while the debate was going on, went from the house to fight him, and shot him through the arm.

So general was the practice, and so all-pervading was the duel mania, that the peaceful shades of our university could not escape it. Not only students adopted the practice, but the principal and fellows set the example. The Honourable J. Hely Hutchinson, the Provost, introduced, among other innovations on the quiet retreats of study, dancing and the fashionable arts. Among them was the noble science of defence, for which he wished to endow a professorship. He is represented in *Pranceriana* as a fencing-master, trampling on Newton's *Principia*, while he makes a lunge. He set the example of duelling to his pupils, by challenging and fighting Doyle, a Master in Chancery; while his son, the Honourable Francis Hutchinson, Collector of the Customs in Dublin, not to degenerate from his father, fought a duel with Lord Mountnorris.

As if this was not a sufficient incentive to the students, the Honourable Patrick Duigenan, a Fellow and Tutor in Trinity College, challenged a barrister, and fought him; and not satisfied with setting one fighting example to his young class of pupils, he called out a second opponent to the field.

JOHN EDWARD WALSH
from *Rakes & Ruffians* (1979)

Dublin Jack of all Trades

On George's Quay I first began and there became a porter,
Me and my master soon fell out which cut my acquaintance shorter
In Sackville Street a pastry cook – in James's Street a baker,
In Cook Street I did coffins make, in Eustace Street a preacher.

In Baggot Street I drove a cab and there was well required,
In Francis Street had lodging beds to entertain all strangers.
For Dublin is of high renown or I am much mistaken,
In Kevin Street I do declare sold butter, eggs and bacon.

In Golden Lane I sold old shoes – in Meath Street was a grinder
In Barrack Street I lost my wife – I'm glad I ne'er could find her,
In Mary's Lane I've dyed old clothes of which I've often boasted
In that noted place Exchequer Street sold mutton ready roasted.

In Temple Bar I dressed old hats, in Thomas Street a sawyer,
In Pill Lane I sold the plate – in Green Street an honest lawyer.
In Plunkett Street I sold cast clothes – in Bride's Alley a broker,
In Charles Street I had a shop, sold shovel, tongs and poker.

In College Green a banker was – and in Smithfield a drover,
In Britain Street a waiter and in George's Street a glover,
On Ormond Quay I sold old books – in King Street a nailer,
In Townsend Street a carpenter and in Ringsend a sailor.

In Cole's Lane a jobbing butcher – in Dame Street a tailor,
In Moore Street a chandler and on the Coombe a weaver.
In Church Street I sold old ropes – on Redmond's Hill a draper,
In Mary Street sold 'bacco pipes – in Bishop Street a Quaker.

In Peter Street I was a quack – in Greek Street a grainer,
On the harbour I did carry sacks, in Werburgh Street a glazier,
In Mud Island was a dairyboy where I became a scooper,
In Capel Street a barber's clerk – in Abbey Street a cooper.

In Liffey Street had furniture with fleas and bugs I sold it,
And at the Bank a big placard I often stood to hold it.
In New Street I sold hay and straw and in Spitalfields made bacon,
In Fishamble Street was at the grand old trade of basketmaking.

In Summerhill a coachmaker, in Denzille Street a gilder,
In Cork Street was a tanner – in Brunswick Street a builder,
In High Street I sold hosiery, in Patric Street sold all blades,
So if you wish to know my name they call me Jack of all Trades

ANONYMOUS

A Fine Mayor

Seventy-one per cent of Dubliners want to see Alderman Carmencita Hederman re-elected to serve a second term as the city's Lord Mayor, according to the findings of an *Irish Times*/MRBI opinion poll which surveyed people's perceptions of Dublin and its problems in this Millennium year.

The poll found that most people in Dublin and throughout the country now regard the city as untidy, neglected, unsafe and – to some extent – divided. And while a majority of Dubliners believe it is a pleasant place to live, they also hold the view that the city has changed for the worse in recent years.

Though battered by "progress", Dublin is still a source of pride and affection for an overwhelming majority of its citizens. However, the vast bulk of them are also concerned about the city and – unlike their country cousins – most Dubliners feel that it receives too little attention from the Government.

According to the poll, the main attraction of Dublin – in descending order of importance – are its history, people, shops, parks and rivers, friendliness, theatres and pubs. On the blacker side, the city's main problems – again in descending order – are perceived as unemployment, lawlessness, poverty, untidiness, housing, road and prices.

The Lord Mayor emerges from the poll as more popular than any of the party leaders, not just in Dublin but throughout the country. And because she is an independent, her popularity cuts right across party lines, with significant majorities among supporters of Fianna Fáil, Fine Gael, Labour and the Progressive Democrats favouring her re-election.

On being informed of the poll findings yesterday, Mrs Hederman said she was delighted 'I've put a lot of work into promoting the

city and the Millennium and it's very heartening to learn that so
many people think that I've done a good job. However, what will
count in the end is whether my colleagues on the City Council
share this view, because it's really up to them to decide to give me
another run at it.'

No Dublin Lord Mayor has been re-elected for a second term
since Mr Eugene Timmons, the former Fianna Fáil TD, over 21
years ago. Since then the view taken by many councillors is that
the post, which brings with it a large amount of publicity, should
be "rotated" every year.

Despite her upper middle-class background, the poll shows
that Mrs Hederman, has won the support of people from all classes
and age-groups. Everyone seems to admire her strong commitment
to Dublin and the fact that she has proved to be an articulate
ambassador for the city. Some people, indeed, believe that she is
the best Lord Mayor Dublin has had since the legendary Alfie Byrne,
who was re-elected no fewer than eight times during the 1930s.

FRANK McDONALD
from *The Irish Times* (1988)

Buying Winkles

My mother would spare me sixpence and say,
'Hurry up now and don't be talking to strange
men on the way.' I'd dash from the ghosts
on the stairs where the bulb had blown
out into Gardiner Street, all relief.
A bonus if the moon was in the strip of sky
between the tall houses, or stars out,
but even in rain I was happy – the winkles
would be wet and glisten blue like little
night skies themselves. I'd hold the tanner tight
and jump every crack in the pavement,
I'd wave up to women at sills or those
lingering in doorways and weave a glad path through
men heading out for the night.

She'd be sitting outside the Rosebowl Bar
on an orange-crate, a pram loaded
with pails of winkles before her.
When the bar doors swung open they'd leak
the smell of men together with drink
and I'd see light in gold mirrors.
I envied each soul in the hot interior.

I'd ask her again to show me the right way
to do *it*. She'd take a pin from her shawl –
'Open the eyelid. So. Stick it in
till you feel a grip, then slither him out.
Gently, mind.' The sweetest extra winkle
that brought the sea to me.
'Tell yer Ma I picked them fresh this morning.'

I'd bear the newspaper twists
bulging fat with winkles
proudly home, like torches.

PAULA MEEHAN
from *The Man who was Marked by Winter* (1991)

Dancing Feet

'Jesus, Mary and Joseph, he'll kill me poor child!' Mother cried, rushing over and tugging the child from his arms, rocking it upon her breast, hushing its frightened cries.

'I'm as sober as a judge, missus, word of honour,' said Father, swaying back on his heels. 'Wouldn't you know just be looking at me? Ah, me poor woman!' he said with sudden desperate remorse, awkwardly rubbing her face with his thumb and forefinger, his eyes misting over. 'You've been through the mill, haven't you?' He turned to his son. 'If you've got yourself half as fine a bargain as I did thirty-odd years ago, you'll be doing bloody all right, me bucko!' he said, then turned back to Mother and put his arm around her shoulder. 'She stood by me through thick and thin and never begrudged me the price of a pint if it was in it. She has a heart of

pure bloody gold, that woman, and none of yous appreciate it!
Ungrateful buggers. Ah, me poor woman!' he sighed, nuzzling his
face against hers and singing out in a soft unsteady voice:

Let the great big world keep turning
never mind what may come through
for I only know that I love you so
and there's no one else but you...

I'll make the tea,' said Mother, edging away, a little embarrassed
in front of the girl and her grown sons. 'Sit down and rest your feet.'

'Me feet!' he said with swift nostalgia, looking down at them
fondly, lifting one then the other slowly and carefully in the air;
through the day-long cement-dust and muck the boot-polish still
shone hard. 'I once had the best pair of dancing feet in Dublin,
boys,' he said to his sons, eyes bright as pale cherries under a frosty
moon. 'Ask your mother! Isn't that right, missus?' he said, grabbing
her cardigan sleeve. 'Wasn't it me dancing feet that made you be
me mot? D'yeh remember when we used to dance to the Magazine
Waltz up beyant in the oul Round Rooms of the Rotunda?' He
started to whistle the tune of that far-gone unclouded time, catching
hold of her hands and swirling her into the dance. 'I'm not beat
yet bejasus!' he roared exultantly, twirling her round and round in
ever-widening circles, whistling madly all the time, his face shining
and wild, sandy hair bushy and erect, heedless of her protests,
something of summer alive in him still.

'You'll break something!' Mother gasped, trying desperately to
keep her feet as he swept her faster. 'For God's sake...'

'He's mad,' whispered the fat eldest son, awed and scared. 'Stone
mad.'

'He'd better stop it,' muttered the other tensely, clenching his
fists; the girl held on to his arm tightly.

'Nineteen-eighteen...the Ancient Concert Rooms they were called
then... Parnell Square...' Father's voice, ragged but rough with
reviving memories, broke through the rhythm of his wild whistling,
mounting to a shrill crescendo, his boots twinkling, beating out an
erratic yet insistent drumming upon the floor, her hair tumbling
and flying about her tense flushed face. 'You wore...a white dress
...red ribbons in your hair...little black shoes...O Jesus, we were
young...'

The Christmas tree toppled over on its side as they inexorably
crashed into it, falling with a bang and hiss of crackling exploding
fairy lights, its gay little glass globes rolling over the floor, the box
of clay splitting and spilling out; the bottle of sherry went over as

somebody bumped against the table; the room plummeted into sudden darkness save for the weird red radiance from the little oil lamp on the altar; the children whimpered and began to cry as their toys were stepped on in the sudden chaos of frantic feet and muttered curses, which was followed by a strange and baffled silence.

'Jesus,' said Father softly, hoarsely, sprawled amid the ruins of the festive tree, passing a trembling hand over his forehead.

The carol singers were closer now, almost outside the front gate, clear voices rising in the cold brilliant night air, singing 'Adeste Fidelis'.

CHRISTY BROWN
from *Down All The Days* (1970)

Most Susceptible

The north side of Dublin was then noted for the escapades of vaga-bonds who played malign tricks on unoffending citizens. Party feeling ran high in those days. Lever's schoolfellows, who all represented families with unpopular sympathies, were more than once pelted as they passed. The roughs found allies in the pupils of another school in Grenville Street – one of inferior social caste. These boys were under the able generalship of a stripling not undistinguished in after life. Skirmishes took place, and at last it was agreed that a regular pitched battle should be fought in Mountjoy Fields, then a piece of waste ground on which Gardiner Street Church and Convent have since been built. Lever helped to organize the tiny troops. The little army had its companies, commander-in-chief, its outlying pickets, reserves, and even its sappers and miners. Mr Robert Mallet, a subsequent eminent engineer and F.R.S., first showed his talents by mining the ground on which the enemy were to be next day engaged. A small mine was worked, and some pounds of blasting powder laid. The opposite faction mustered at length in great force, and opened the fight by a brisk discharge of sharp stones, which was returned by Mr Wright's boys with shouts of defiance, and a fire of miniature cannon. A charge forward was then made by the roughs, some of whom were provided with blackthorns, which, if applied to the skulls of the juvenile army, would have inflicted serious subsequent loss on letters, law, science, physic, and divinity. Dr Biggar is now almost the only survivor who took part in this conflict. He held a high rank in the command, and just as the enemy was about to fall upon them like an avalanche, word was given to fire the mine, which a lighted cigar promptly accomplished. The explosion scattered dismay, and inflicted some slight bodily wounds. Lever's company suffered quite as much as the enemy; the faces on both sides were scorched and scratched. The army of the north retreated in disorder, leaving Mr Wright's pupils in possession of the field – only to be scared, however, by the rapid approach of the police, who, with their glazed caps and side arms, the uniform of that day, entered Mountjoy Fields at every point.

Marlborough Street Police Office exhibited a scene of some excitement when the case came on next day. Hanging was still the penalty for incendiarism; and terrible forebodings of the gibbet or Botany Bay smote the small prisoners brought up before Mr Magrath, who, in his occasional ebullitions of temper, resembled Mr Fang, Oliver Twist's stern judge: and Fang, we know, was a veritable portrait. Some fussy matrons were in attendance to testify that the north side had been all but blown into the southern division by the shock, while the weak police seem to have regarded the whole affair very much as a god-send. The boy prisoners, including Edward Dix, afterwards police magistrate, are described by Dr Biggar as tongue-tied. Mr Magrath said it was a bad case, and scowled. The police shook their heads, and a pin might be heard to drop.

At last a boy came forward as spokesman, and appealed to the bench. The magistrate declared that they were before him on a charge of riot and outrage, which it behoved him to suppress with a firm hand. Lever submitted that the provocation they received from a lawless gang justified them in inflicting condign punishment: that the vagabonds were the first aggressors; that self-defence was the first law of nature, and that a war of juveniles was not worse in principle than war waged by wiser heads.

MR MAGRATH. – 'But you are not to take the law into your own hands. Moreover, you use firearms and introduce gunpowder into a mine previously prepared, and with malice prepense.'

MASTER LEVER. – 'All sound and smoke, sir; our cannon were only toy-guns, and the mine a mimic mine. Most of us may take up arms yet in defence of our king and country; and might we not be worse employed than in learning the science at the most susceptible period of our lives?'

Mr Magrath's attitude of hostility relaxed: without complimenting

Lever on his eloquence, he certainly seemed struck by it; and he brought the case to a close by imposing sundry small fines, which would suffice, he said, to satisfy offended justice.

This magistrate was himself soon after arraigned for much graver offences. He was proved guilty of embezzlement and banished. As for Master Biggar – the juvenile commander-in-chief – he was flogged five successive days because of the determination with which he refused to divulge the spot where Mallet had concealed his mining powder.

W.J. FITZPATRICK
from *The Life of Charles Lever* (1884)

A Challenge

David Garrick put an arm around her shoulder and she gave him a brilliant smile, practised, sweet, the kind I bestow on the bucks in the Playhouse, she told herself and was ashamed. Bells were pealing over the city, announcing the Sabbath. Christ Church shrill and impatient, St Patrick's sonorous and the sweet silvery bells of St Bride's. 'I was born to the sound of the bells. Even when I am far away I remember them–and the street vendors.' She threw back her head and sang out. 'Cockles and mussels. Dublin bay herrings. Knives, combs or ink horns. Fresh river water. Fresh gingerbread.'

He laughed. 'What a good mimic you are.'

'I'm a Dubliner, born and bred.'

He held her close. 'Oh, Peg, it's like reaching journey's end. We'll show Dublin what the theatre should be. It will be a challenge.'

How rash you are,' she said lightly. 'Dubliners can be very critical.' She thought, particularly of one of themselves. What was it the Good Book said: 'A prophet is not without honour, save in his own country.'

BRID MAHON
from *A Time to Love: The Life of Peg Woffington* (1992)

Sweeties and Tweedies

The ingredients were the same; the stream of hackneys and motor cars on their way to the grounds of the Royal Dublin Society, the foreign visitors, the military, the strings of horses, the riders in black caps and scarlet coats and tightly cut breeches. The ladies as usual engaged his special interest. Most of them were at their best; fashionable and feminine and agreeably pretty. A hefty and horselike few displeased him. That was as usual too. He had once described the ladies of the Dublin Horse Show as a mixture of Sweeties and Tweedies.

JAMES PLUNKETT
from *Strumpet City* (1969)

Mad and Desperate

They were settting up food kitchens for the women and children in Liberty Hall. The Countess Markievicz was going to serve the meals with her own hands. He asked Rashers if he had ever heard of her. Rashers grunted. She was one of them high class oul wans that were sticking their noses into a hundred and one things nowadays. Troublemakers. Like Madame Despard and Maud Gonne. Acting the hooligan about votes for women when they should be at home looking after their husbands and their unfortunate children. Mad Gonne and Mrs Desperate, the people were calling them. No wonder the city was starving.

JAMES PLUNKETT
from *Strumpet City* (1969)

A Gang of Mates

Acne and bristles and cigarettes. Johnny rarely stays at home now. Each evening he merges into a gang of mates, shouting from the open platforms of dark green buses. In *The Astor*, they wolf-whistle Brigitte Bardot in *A Very Private Affair*. In the *Bohemian, Rock Around the Clock* is being revived. They spend hours sharpening the tips of steel combs to rip out the seats during the theme song. In the twisting streets around Stonybatter, small pubs welcome the scrum of underage boys. At weekends they would spend most of their wages there and queue in the greasy fish and chip shops of Phibsborough before strutting the two miles out by the cemetery with catcalls at the couples walking home from dances. They piss in front gardens, ring doorbells and empty dustbins along the main road.

DERMOT BOLGER
from *The Woman's Daughter* (1987)

Odour of Corruption

I do not think that any writer has yet presented Dublin to the world. It has been a capital of Europe for thousands of years, it is supposed to be the second city of the British Empire and it is nearly three times as big as Venice. Moreover, on account of many circumstances which I cannot detail here, the expression Dubliner seems to me to bear some meaning and I doubt whether the same can be said for such words as 'Londoner' and 'Parisian' both of which have been used by writers as titles. From time to time I see in publishers' lists announcements of books on Irish subjects, so that I think people might be willing to pay for the special odour of corruption which, I hope, floats over my stories.

JAMES JOYCE
Letter to Grant Richards (15 October 1905)

Genteel Dastards

I suppose they were great days – I was younger anyway – and even if I had no money there were people in the literary pubs in the vicinity of Grafton Street that would give me an odd pint of porter or a glass of malt betimes, as long as I could listen respectfully enough to the old chat about Angst. A generation or so ago they were arsing around the bog, and a bowl of stirabout and a couple of platefuls of spuds would have cured all the Angst from here back to Norway; but since the change-over in 1922, when they got well down to the porridge-pot, there was no holding them. It started off with top-hats and white ties and getting into the gentry and then to chatting about the servant problem with the Anglo-Irish Horse-Protestants (who at least were reared to it) and it went from that to late dinner and now it's Angst, no less.

Not that the Horse-Protestants were any better, but they were longer at it. They are just as ignorant except that their ill-manners are sharpened by time. Sheridan was a peasant's grandson, Yeats an artist's son, Wilde a doctor's son, Parnell was the grandson of an American sea-captain, Robert Emmet a doctor's son, Bernard Shaw a clerk. The myth of the Anglo-Irish, and the attempt to drag Irish writers (particularly those who happened to be Protestants) after the fox-hunt and the royalist inanity, would have us believe that the most rapacious rack-renting landlord-class in Europe were really lamps of culture in a bog of darkness, doing good by stealth and shoving copies of *Horizon* under the half-doors of the peasantry after dark and making wedding presents to the cottagers of Ganymede Press reproductions of Gauguin.

There is, of course, no such thing as an Anglo-Irishman, as Shaw pointed out in the preface to *John Bull's Other Island* – except as a class distinction. Even all Protestant genius is not nobbled for the stableboys and girls. It must, at least, wear a collar and tie. Sean O'Casey is not claimed as an Anglo-Irish writer because he had no land except what a window-box would hold on the window-sill of a tenement. The Belfast industrial workers, who are the thickest concentration of royalism and pro-Britishism in Ireland, are never claimed as Anglo-Irish. The whole thing nowadays is a middle-class myth. One thing about Dublin which is indicative of this is that the middle classes are inflicted with a desire to ride. They have their daughters going bandy taking riding lessons out there in Stillorgan and competing at the Horse Show. When Yeats said about Dublin: 'Great hatred, little room,' he was referring to the middle and so-called upper classes. Joyce described the same crowd as 'the centre of paralysis'. John Mitchell, a rebel leader of 1848, was being transported to Van Diemen's Land and, passing in the ship the villas on Killiney Hill on the south side of the bay, he described it as 'a city of genteel dastards and bellowing slaves'. I remember once saying to my father: 'I suppose he really said bastards but they changed it to dastards for reasons of respectability.' 'No,' said my father, 'It's nobody's fault to be a bastard but to be a dastard you have to work at it.'

BRENDAN BEHAN
from *Brendan Behan's Island: An Irish Sketch-book* (1962)

4. TOUCHSTONES

All Change

Poblacht na hEireann:
The Provisional Government of the Irish Republic
to the people of Ireland, 1916

Irishmen and Irishwomen: In the name of God and of the dead generations from which she receives her old tradition of nationhood, Ireland, through us, summons her children to her flag and strikes for her freedom.

Having organised and trained her manhood through her secret revolutionary organisation, the Irish Republican Brotherhood, and through her open military organisations, the Irish Volunteers and the Irish Citizen Army, having patiently perfected her discipline, having resolutely waited for the right moment to reveal itself, she now seizes that moment, and, supported by her exiled children in America and by gallant allies in Europe, but relying in the first on her own strength, she strikes in full confidence of victory.

We declare the right of the people of Ireland to the ownership of Ireland, and to the unfettered control of Irish destinies, to be sovereign and indefeasible. The long usurpation of that right by a foreign people and government has not extinguished the right, nor can it ever be extinguished except by the destruction of the Irish people. In every generation the Irish people have asserted their right to national freedom and sovereignty; six times during the past three hundred years they have asserted it in arms. Standing on that fundamental right and again asserting it in arms in the face of the world, we hereby proclaim the Irish Republic as a Sovereign Independent State, and we pledge our lives and the lives of our comrades-in-arms to the cause of its freedom, of its welfare, and of its exaltation among the nations.

The Irish Republic is entitled to, and hereby claims, the allegiance of every Irishman and Irishwoman. The Republic guarantees religious and civil liberty, equal rights and equal opportunities to all its citizens, and declares its resolve to pursue the happiness and prosperity of the whole nation and of all its parts, cherishing all the children of the nation equally, and oblivious of the differences carefully fostered by an alien government, which have divided a minority from the majority in the past.

Until our arms have brought the opportune moment for the establishment of a permanent National Government, representative of the whole people of Ireland and elected by the suffrages of all men and women, the Provisional Government, hereby constituted, will administer the civil and military affairs of the Republic in trust for the people.

We place the cause of the Irish Republic under the protection of the Most High God, Whose blessing we invoke upon our arms, and we pray that no one who serves that cause will dishonour it by cowardice, inhumanity, or rapine. In this supreme hour the Irish nation must, by its valour and discipline and by the readiness of its children to sacrifice themselves for the common good, prove itself worthy of the august destiny to which it is called.

Signed on Behalf of the Provisional Government

Thomas J. Clarke

Sean Mac Diarmada	*Thomas Mac Donagh*
P.H. Pearse	*Eamonn Ceannt*
James Connolly	*Joseph Plunkett*

Rough Beasts

The mass of Dubliners hated the Rising. They insulted and abused the insurgents; in Moore Street, the market women threw vegetables and chamberpots at them. They blamed Pearse's men for the destruction and deaths and, if there were outcries against atrocities committed by one British regiment, the sympathies were with the British. The awful slums of Dublin poured out their looters. The mob smashed into shops, crowds of children went after the toys, and near Parnell's monument the mob lit a bonfire and danced round it, while the shooting went on, and the ambulances went by.

V.S. PRITCHETT
from *Dublin* (1991)

No Enemy But Time

When she left for Ireland later that week, the platform was crowded with fans singing 'The Soldier's Song' which was fast becoming the hymn of the republic. As they finished, Con, like a true prima donna, scattered her bouquet of roses among them. On the boat, the ex-convict turned hero was feted with smiles and grapes and peaches. Her arrival in Dublin was triumphant: 'The Countess entered Dublin in the midst of a long procession with banner after banner and brass band after brass band; with riders on horseback; with running boys waving branches; with lumbering floats drawn by slow-footed good-natured Clydesdale horses', ragged urchins, public figures in uniform, trades guilds. Some of it was orchestrated by the thriving post-1916 movement, and much of it was a spontaneous display of the love and respect she had inspired among the people. It was a love she would not lose.

ANNE HAVERTY
from *Constance Markievicz: Irish Revolutionary* (1993)

GPO in Peril

Last night the city was rife with rumours that the GPO was under attack by the SSDG (Semi-State Destructive Group). It is understood that many developers believe that the building is not only an eyesore but also an occasion of sin for many Irish people.

The Minister for Post and Telegraphs, Dr O'Brien, acted swiftly and sent a battalion of the new army SAS to surround the building in case of its seizure. He declined the help of all ten wings of the Republican Movement to defend the building.

At least a quarter of a million Irish people last night signed a petition against the destruction of the GPO. All claimed to have intimate association with the building. One man said that he taken part in the building of the GPO. Another said that it was there he always drew his father's British Army pension in the old days. An old woman said she bought stamps in the GPO on Easter Monday, 1916. Some group of thugs were attacking it.

DONAL FOLEY
from *Man Bites Dog*

Paper Boy

Only thirty-three years had elapsed between the foundation of the paper and my arrival – and thirty-three years in the history of a national newspaper is but the tick of a clock. That morning I was woefully ignorant of that or indeed any history. I did not then appreciate how recent were the euphoric days when the great founder stalked the building, supervising everyone, criticising the leaders, delegating nothing. More importantly, I did not then understand how close we were to many of the powerful myths which the founder's 'great enterprise' (as he liked to call it) has helped to generate. I did not know then that many of our boasts were hollow and were leading us into a territory hostile and dangerous enough to threaten our very existence.

Like many youngsters of peasant origin, I had grown up with the *Irish Press*. My grandfather, Michael O'Toole, revered Eamon de Valera. He saw him as the leader who would liberate the poor man from his hovel and his ignorance and create some Celtic Shangri-La where dwelt the comely maidens and their camán-wielding swains. If my grandfather was sitting by his wireless on St Patrick's Day, 1943, listening to his hero inviting him to share his dream of 'a land whose countryside would be bright with...the laughter of comely maidens', I have no doubt but that he had tears in his eyes.

While I would have known the paper since I started to read Captain Mac's column at the age of four or thereabouts, my first clear memory of its bold news-laden front page dates from Saturday, 11 January, 1952. That was the day after the crash of the Aer Lingus DC-3 *St Kevin* in Snowdonia, and I can still vividly remember walking out of Mitchell's shop in Hospital with that direful front page in my hands. In those pre-TV days the impact of a dramatic black-and-white photograph and well-presented news story was infinitely greater than now when our minds have become jaded and numbed from the constant bombardment of images and words.

A few images of that first morning in Burgh Quay remain vivid: I was struck by the dinginess of the big room with its long custom-made reporter's table, the telephone wires dropping from the ceiling, the horseshoe-shaped table where the sub-editors sat. The deadline for the first edition of the *Evening Press* was approaching and there was a *frisson* in the air that I hadn't experienced elsewhere. Tony Gallagher, a tough ex-Fleet Street man and the senior reporter on the *Evening Press* cadre, was working on the lead story and in a voice that might be heard on O'Connell Bridge he was trying to extract details from some lethargic country correspondent. Now he was upbraiding this unwilling correspondent demanding, 'What the hell does it matter if the parish priest won't like it?' and 'You had better make up your mind as to whether you want to be a press correspondent or the parish priest's self-appointed censor.'

MICHAEL O'TOOLE
from *More Kicks Than Pence* (1992)

No Hoops or Swords

The greatest event in the musical history of Dublin was the visit that Handel had paid there in 1741-42. He had previously been living in London, where his concerts were becoming neglected owing to dissensions in the musical world which had spread to fashionable circles. It was probably this which led him to accept the Duke of Devonshire's invitation to visit Dublin, and try out his fortunes in a new scene. To the Lord-Lieutenant's invitation was added that of the Fishamble Street Musical Society and those of a number of benevolent institutions who hoped to secure his services for their charities. He was willing to give the performances asked for, and is said to have composed his Messiah only a few weeks before his arrival in Dublin on November 18, 1741, expressly for this purpose. The first concert that he gave is described in Faulkner's *Journal* as follows:

> Last Wednesday, (23rd December) Mr Handel had his first Oratorio at Mr Neal's Musick Hall in Fishamble Street, which was crowded with a more numerous and polite Audience than ever was seen upon the like Occasion. The Performance was superior to anything of the kind in the Kingdom before; and our Nobility and Gentry, to shew their Taste for all kinds of Genius, expressed their great Satisfaction, and have already given all imaginable Encouragement to this grand Musick.

Handel himself gives a fuller account of this, his first reception by a Dublin audience, in a letter to his friend Charles Jennens, of Gopsall Hall, in Leicestershire, who had written for him the words of *The Messiah*:

> The Nobility did me the honour to make amongst themselves a sub-
> scription for six Nights, which did fill a Room of six hundred Persons,
> so that I needed not sell one single ticket at the Door, and without Vanity
> the Performance was received with a general Approbation. Signora
> Avoglio, which [sic] I brought with me from London, pleases extra-
> ordinary. I have formed [found?] another Tenor Voice which gives great
> Satisfaction, the Basses and Counter Tenors are very good, and the
> rest of the Chorus Singers (by my Direction) do exceeding well; as for
> the Instruments, they are really excellent, Mr Dubourgh being at the
> Head of them – and the Musick sounds delightfully in this charming
> Room, which puts me in such Spirits (and my health being so good)
> that I exert myself on my Organ with more than usual success. I opened
> with the Allegro Penseroso and Moderato, and I assure you that the
> Words of the Moderato are vastly admired. The Audience being composed
> (besides the Flower of Ladies of Distinction, and other people of the
> greatest Quality) of so many Bishops, Deans, Heads of the Colledge,
> the most eminent People in the Law as the Chancellor, Auditor-General
> etc. etc., all which are very much taken with the Poetry, so that I am
> desired to perform it again the next time. I cannot sufficiently express
> the kind treatment I receive here; but the Politeness of this generous
> Nation cannot be unknown to you, so I let you judge of the satisfaction
> I enjoy, passing my time with Honour, Profit and Pleasure.

On January 13, 1742, Handel gave another performance for the
benefit of Mercer's Hospital and the Charitable Infirmary, and by
February 10 had given six concerts in all. He conducted these himself,
being always assisted by Dubourg, who was leader of the band.
Signora Avoglio and Mrs Cibber, who had already made her repu-
tation as singer and actress in London, were his chief vocalists, and
in the great performance of *The Messiah* which was to follow the
choirs of both cathedrals, St Patrick's and Christ Church, took part.
The first public rehearsal, which was given on April 8, was reported
by Faulkner's *Journal* as follows:

> Yesterday, Mr Handel's new Grand Sacred Oratorio, called *The Messiah*
> was rehearsed at the Musick Hall in Fishamble Street, to a most Grand,
> Polite, and Crowded Audience; and was performed so well, tht it gave
> universal Satisfaction to all present; and was allowed by the greatest
> Judges to be the finest Composition of Musick that ever was heard.

The first public performance took place on the 13th, when the
crowd expected was so large that the stewards of the Charitable
Musical Society published a request that ladies would come without
hoops and gentlemen without swords. The success of the concert, at
which some seven hundred people were present (£400 being collected
for charity) was complete. 'Words are wanting,' we read in the *Journal*,
'to express the exquisite Delight it afforded to the admiring crowded
Audience; the Sublime, the Grand, and the Tender, adapted to the

most elevated, majestick and moving Words, conspired to transport and charm the ravished Heart and Ear.'

CONSTANTIA MAXWELL
from *Dublin Under The Georges* (1979)

Bum's Rush

With regard to the disposal of these my body, mind and soul, I desire that they be burnt and placed in a paper bag and brought to the Abbey Theatre, Lr Abbey Street, Dublin, and without pause into what the great and good Lord Chesterfield calls the necessary house, where their happiest hours have been spent, on the right as one goes down into the pit, and I desire that the chain be there pulled upon them, if possible during the performance of a piece, the whole to be executed without ceremony or show of grief.

SAMUEL BECKETT
from *Murphy* (1938)

A Magic Thumb

Clare's father makes his way from the Customs House to O'Beirne's on the Quays, crosses the Liffey by means of a bridge, so sited as to add to the distance between the two buildings a length of nearly three hundred yards.

'If I could swim now, I'd be right.' He is a man much given to speaking aloud when company is absent, and to silence when the nicer of social obligations might urge him into speech. Those contributions he does make are as counterpoint to the sounds of liquid consumption only, the sweetest of which is the sound of a pint drawing creamily at the bar, a music only those born with the gift, or those who spend a minimum of three thousand hours acquiring the gift, can hear.

O'Donnel was doubly blessed. He was born with a magic thumb, the sucking of which enabled him to discern the music of a good pint from the discord of a bad, before a head had even begun to form; but being a man of diligence and application (those same qualities which, combined with tenacity, ensured his promotion to the rank of Under-Manager, Grade Two of Dublin Corporation, Sanitation Section, despite the vagaries of political influence, which was never behind him, the unenlightened reservations of his superiors, cognisant as they were of his talents, and thence careful of their own interests and tenure, and the constant, whingeing begrudgery of his fellow workers, craven in the envy of a magnitude only the true culchie could muster, with the smell of dung still clinging to their boots, the stripes of the diocesan fathers still stinging their palms and the sly post-colonialism still giving the edge of flattery to every utterance of a personal nature that crossed their lips), he distrusted the gifts of nature and concentrated the subtle power of his intelligence on discerning, without the aid of his cool, Fenian thumb, that crystalline hum, that black, creamy noise, of a pint just waiting to be drunk.

*   *   *

'There will be peace in the valley,' he assures her and all the other backs now interrupting his view of her, as a benediction, then turns to square himself against the tide.

'I wouldn't spit now,' he says, 'at a pint. If it was handed to me.' He was a man who could not abide spit.

O'Donnel avoids the snug in O'Beirne's, likely as it is to contain Elements. He takes his place with the dockers at the bar.

'Stevedores.'

There is no need for another word, his order is known. The brown suit strains tightly against the yoke of his back as he places the elbows, long stained with old porter, carefully on two beer-mats equidistant from the apex of his nose. His head is loosely cupped in two large hands.

'There's one for the drip,' says the barman, slapping a mat under the point of his snout. O'Donnel stares at the wood of the counter, his feet broadly placed on the brass rail. His air could be interpreted as one of dignified rebuke.

'Larry,' he says, from the cavern of his crouched torso, 'would you ever hinge that elbow in the way God intended.' And not wishing to disturb the barman by his tone, he adds the phrase, 'he says', to allow a proper distance from the remark.

'Does he so?' says Larry, and places a small preliminary Bushmills
on the central mat.

After many hours of similar silences, the air is punctuated by
the single word 'Nevermore'.

The barman gives the wink to a man in the snug, the long-suffering
recipient of countless memos on the subject of parking meters: the
cleaning thereof, embellished in O'Donnel's hand by the appropriate
quotations from the Latin.

'So they finally gave the old codger the push, eh?' The final
syllable is terse, sympathetic, way-of-the-worldish; harsh, without
interrogative cadence or function.

'Resigned, Larry. For God's sake, the word is "resigned".' He
salutes the barman with his pint, and with one finger he taps, three
times, on the interstice of his left nostril.

ANNE ENRIGHT
from *The Portable Virgin & Other Stories* (1991)

Willie and the Taypot

Before I came to Dublin I had never met a great or famous person,
though I had once seen G.K. Chesterton fast asleep over a bottle
of wine in a London restaurant. Dublin had many great men and
was full of people who knew them familiarly; this is one of the
characteristics of the easy-going city. I had the ineffable experience
of seeing the beautiful Mrs Yeats riding a bicycle in St Stephen's
Green, of seeing the large, tweeded, bearded figure of AE going
next door but one to the Yeats's, up the stairs to the offices of the
Irish Statesman, squeezing a bunch of wallflowers in his big hands.
To me these persons seemed to be beings from another world, and
over forty years later I still have this impression of certain Irish
people. They are real enough, yet have the faculty of vanishing into
their own eyes. Yeats was famous for studiously creating a vanishing
effect. Tall, with thick soft grey hair finely rumpled, a dandy with
negligence in collar and tie and with the black ribbon dangling from
the glasses on a short, pale and prescient nose – not long enough
to be Roman, not sharp enough to be a beak – he came to meet
one, a big ring on his finger, and the nearer he got the further away

he seemed to float. His air was bird-like, suggesting at once one of the notable swans of Coole and an exalted blindness.

What did he say? I have scarcely any recollection at all. I have a memory of high windows, tall candles, books, and of a bullet hole in the window. I heard a deliberate, fervent, intoning voice which flowed over me as he walked up and down. We were in the middle of the Celtic revival. Suddenly he remembered tea. He had already had tea, but now he must make a new pot. The problem was where to empty the old tea leaves. It was a beautiful pot and he walked about the room with his short, aesthete's steps, carrying it in his hand. It came spout foremost towards me, retired to the book cases, waved in the air. I invented the belief that it was Rockingham and I was alarmed for it. Suddenly he went to the Georgian window, opened it and swooshed the tea leaves into Merrion Square, for all I knew on the heads of Gogarty, AE, Lady Gregory, James Stephens – who might have popped over from the Library or the Museum. They were China tea leaves, scented.

V.S. PRITCHETT
from *Dublin* (1991)

The Pigeon House

I went there with a man
The water black like a silent sound
The stars were dancing all around us and he held my hand
And said 'I want to be inside you, do you mind?'
I said 'If you don't, I'll kill you.'
Oh Jesus love, I love you
What am I going to do without you?
I was laughing afterward
Wiping the footprints off the dashboard
So that no one would notice
Then we had a pint of Guinness
And then he had to leave
Early 'cos it was Christmas Eve.

SINÉAD O'CONNOR

Social Boozing

But anyway Dublin in the late nineteen-forties was an odd and, in many respects, unhappy place. The malaise that seems to have affected everywhere in the aftermath of war took strange forms there, perhaps for the reason that the war itself had been a sort of ghastly unreality. Neutrality had left a wound, set up complexes in many, including myself, which the post-war did little to cure.

Nor were there then concourses of young poets to associate with, such as exist to keep each other company today. Most of the elder ones, known to local fame, were respectable Gaelic revivalists, in orthodox employment in the civil service or the radio station. Left becalmed in the wake of genius, they sat, it seemed, nightly in the Pearl or the Palace, comforting themselves with large whiskeys, reminiscences of F.R. Higgins and discussions of assonance, before going home to the suburbs. One recognised their life-style as the *vie de lettres* locally accepted and approved. It was not somehow attractive, nor probably attainable, but of course one felt the lack of confrères. Except for one or two who had been student poets along with me, and were now busy bracing themselves for the serious business of getting on in the world, I had none. I disliked, as I say, my childish, snobbish, bar contemporaries. I knew no girls; could not be bothered to go through the motions necessary to pick one sort up in dancehalls, nor make the arrangements involved in taking another to the middle-class dress and supper dances in the Gresham and the Metropole which appeared to provide my contemporaries with a large part of their social and, such as it was, their sex life. What I needed, I obscurely felt, was a bohemia of some kind, but I did not know where to find one.

Then things suddenly took a turn for the better. I got thrown out of digs and met an acquaintance to whom I explained my problem, which was really that I could not afford ordinary digs and do my drinking at the same time. He told me he knew about a place where I might get to stay pretty cheaply and told me the name of the pub where I might find the owner. The pub was McDaid's; and the place was the since-famous Catacombs. I did not know it then, but my feet had been happily set upon the downward path, and there was to be no looking back.

McDaid's is in Harry Street, off Grafton Street, Dublin's main boulevard of chance and converse. It has an extraordinarily high ceiling and high, almost Gothic, windows in the front wall, with stained glass borders. The general effect is church-like or tomb-like, according to mood: indeed indigenous folklore has it that it once was a meeting-house for a resurrection sect who liked high ceilings in their places of resort because the best thing of all would be for the end of the world to come during religious service and in that case you would need room to get up steam.

The type of customer who awaited the resurrection and the life to come has varied a little over the years, but in spite of rather weak-minded attempts to make it so, McDaid's was never merely a literary pub. Its strength was always in variety, of talent, class, caste and estate. The divisions between writer and non-writer, bohemian and artist, informer and revolutionary, male and female, were never rigorously enforced; and nearly everybody, gurriers included, was ready for elevation, to Parnassus, the scaffold or wherever.

At the time of which I speak the company was very various. There was a number of painters and sculptors, few of them serious, fewer to last. There were some Americans, ex-servicemen who had come to Ireland originally to be Trinity students under the GI Bill and remained on when its bounty was exhausted, among them J.P. Donleavy, then supposed to be a painter but meditating a big book about Ireland to be called, I seem to remember, *Under the Stone*; and Gainor Crist, who was to provide the original for that book, subsequently *The Ginger Man* (a curiously transformed and lessened portrait) and to die, in appalling circumstances, in the Canary Islands in the early sixties.

Originally perhaps because of the association of Desmond Mac-Namara, a sculptor who had a studio nearby, with the late 'Pope' O'Mahoney and the Republican Prisoners' Aid Fund, there were numbers of former prisoners, variously in need of aid of diverse kinds (some of it highly unorthodox) and fairly recently released from various gaols and internment camps in Britain and Ireland. In fact if the prevailing atmosphere in McDaid's at this time could have been described, bohemian-revolutionary might have been the phrase.

*   *   *

Most of this company assembled in McDaid's every day under the benevolent aegis of one of the great barmen of all time, Paddy O'Brien, and almost every night the entire assemblage moved on to the Catacombs [...] The Catacombs had once been the basement, composed of kitchen, pantries and wine-cellar, with presumably also a servant's bedroom or two and their attendant corridors, of one of those high Georgian mansions that are the pride of Dublin. One went down the area steps and through a pantry into the kitchen, which was large, low-ceilinged and vaulted, with a flagged floor. The whole place smelt of damp, decaying plaster and brickwork, that smell of money gone which was once so prevalent in Ireland. Off the corridor leading out of the kitchen were various dark little rooms. Mine had, I think, once been the wine-cellar. There was hardly space for a bed in it, and none for anything else except a few bottles and books.

The other rooms were variously occupied and people came and went according to need and circumstance, but our host was a great stickler for the rent, so one had to preserve some sort of affluence or go. There was never any difficulty about gatherings, however, for he lived partly on the proceeds of the bottles that the revellers brought and left behind. He was rumoured by outsiders – who rumoured much in those days about both McDaid's and the Catacombs – to have another source of income; but, although once in the watches of the night I heard him ejecting some young lout who had apparently accompanied him home under a misapprehension with the angry declaration that he was not accustomed to pay but to be paid for whatever it was, as far as my observation went anyway the charge was unfounded, and what he was saying was a mere boast.

Ireland has changed somewhat since, and I suppose the existence of our little enclave had something to do with the change, but so holy was Ireland then and so strangely afraid that I still hear lurid descriptions of our goings on, descriptions echoed with a delightful innocence recently in Mr Ulick O'Connor's book. Alas, no. When asked, *'Qu'as tu fait de ta jeunesse?'* I can truthfully answer: 'Even with this part of it, not enough, not nearly enough.'

Most of what went on in the Catacombs was in fact ordinary social boozing.

ANTHONY CRONIN
from *Dead As Doornails* (1976)

Anna Livia

O

tell me all about

Anna Livia! I want to hear all

about Anna Livia! I want to hear all about Anna Livia. Well, you
know Anna Livia? Yes, of course, we all know Anna Livia. Tell me
all. Tell me now. You'll die when you hear. Well, you know, when
the old cheb went futt and did what you know. Yes, I know, go on.
Wash quit and don't be dabbling Tuck up your sleeves and loosen
your talk-tapes. And don't butt me – hike! – when you bend. Or
whatever it was they threed to make out he thried to two in the
Fiendish park. He's an awful old reppe. Look at the shirt of him!
Look at the dirt of it! He has all my water black on me. And it
steeping and stuping since this time last wik. How many goes is it
I wonder I washed it? I know by heart the places he likes to saale,
duddurty devil! Scorching my hand and starving my famine to make
his private linen public. Wallop it well with your battle and clean
it. My wrists are wrusty rubbing the mouldaw stains. And the
dneepers of wet and the gangres of sin in it! What was it he did a
tail at all on Animal Sendai? And how long was he under loch and
neagh? It was put in the newses what he did, nicies and priers,
the King fierceas Humphrey, with illysus distilling, exploits and
all. But toms will till. I know he well. Temp untamed will hist for
no man. As you spring so shall you neap. O, the roughty old rappe!
Minxing marrage and making loof.

*   *   *

I'm dying down off my iodine feet until I lerryn Anna Livia's cushin-
gloo, that was writ by one and rede by two and trouved by a poule
in the parco! I can see that, I see you are. How does it tummel?
Listen now. Are you listening? Yes, yes! Idneed I am! Tarn your
ore ouse! Essonne inne!

   *By earth and the cloudy but I badly want a brandnew bankside,
bedamp and I do, and a plumper at that!*

   *For the putty affair I have is wore out, so it is, sitting, yaping and
waiting for my old Dane hodder dodderer, my life in death companion,
my frugal key of our larder, my much-altered camel's hump, my joint-
spoiler, my maymoon's honey, my fool to the last Decemberer, to wake
himself out of his winter's doze and bore me down like he used to.*

   Is there irwell a lord of the manor or a knight of the shire at strike,

*I wonder, that'd dip me a dace or two in cash for washing and darning
his worshipful socks for him now we're run out of horsebrose and milk?*

*Only for my short Brittas bed made's as snug as it smells it's's our
I'd lep and off with me to the slobs della Tolka or the plage au Clontarf
to feale the gay aire of my salt troublin bay and the race of the saywint
up me ambushure.*

Onon! Onon! tell me more. Tell me every tiny teign. I want to
know every single ingul. Down to what made the potters fly into
jagsthole. And why were the vesles vet. That homa fever's winning
me wome. If a mahun of the horse but hard me! We'd be bundukiboi
meet askarigal. Well, now comes the hazel-hatchery part. After
Clondalkin the Kings's Inns. We'll soon be there with the freshet.
How many aleveens had she in tool? I can't rightly rede you that.
Close only knows. Some say she had three figures to fill and confined
herself to a hundred eleven, wan bywan bywan, making meanacumin-
amoyas. Olaph lamm et, all that pack? We won't have room in the
kirkeyaard. She can't remember half of the cradlenames she smacked
on them by the grace of her boxing bishop's infallible slipper, the
cane for Kund and abbles for Eyolf and ayther nayther for Yakov Yea.
A hundred and how? They did well to rechristien her Pluhurabelle.

* * *

She was just a young thin pale soft shy slim slip of a thing then,
sauntering, by silvamoonlake and he was a heavy trudging lurching
lieabroad of a Curraghman, making his hay for whose sun to shine
on, as tough as the oaktrees (peats be with them!) used to rustle that
time down by the dykes of killing Kildare for forstfellfoss with a
plash across her. She thought she's sankh neathe the ground with
nymphant shame when he gave her the tigris eye! O happy fault!
Me wish it was he! You're wrong there corribly wrong! Tisn't only
tonight you're anacheronistic! It was ages behind that when nullahs
were nowhere, in county Wickenlow, garden of Erin, before she ever
dreamt she'd lave Kilbride and go foaming under Horsepass bridge,
with the great southerwestern windstorming her traces and the mid-
land's grainwaster asarch for her track, to wend her ways byandby,
robecca or worse, to spin and to grind, to swab and to thrash, for
all her golden lifey in the barleyfields and pennylotts of Humphrey's
fordofhurdlestown and lie with a landleaper, wellingtonorseher. Alesse,
the lagos of girly days! For the dove of the dunas! Wasut? Izod?

JAMES JOYCE
from *Finnegans Wake* (1939)

The Stones of Dublin

Four Courts and Custom House must be considered together, for they stand for the two aspects of Gandon's mind. The Four Courts is masculine in feeling, built on a cubical if not vertical theme: the Custom House is feminine and predominantly horizontal. The active and the contemplative phases are complementary. This antinomy runs through every aspect of these two buildings: materials and colour (grey granite versus white Portland in the main fronts), texture (roughness and baroque 'movement' versus smoothness and the purest Palladian clarity), mass (the seventy-six-foot diameter drum-tower as against the thirty-one feet of the Custom House). In the Four Courts drum and dome we see one of those dream-palaces of Poussin or Piranesi in all their Roman grandeur. In that of the Custom House the elements are taken straight from Wren's twin towers at Greenwich, but with the proportions and detail so subtly adjusted as to seem a feminine version of the theme.

The same contrast runs through the use of the orders. In the Four Courts Gandon uses a robust Roman Corinthian, breaking his cornice out over coupled and clustered pilasters to give the bold rich modelling of which that orders is capable. In the Custom House he is more daring and uses a Roman Doric, which one might suppose to be the very embodiment of male sturdiness. Yet the effect, by some strange alchemy, is one of grace at least as much as of strength.

*   *   *

When George IV came to Ireland in 1821, the first British monarch to land here on a peaceful mission, he was expected to pass through Lucan on his way to the Curragh, and it was believed that the King intended to confer a knighthood on Gandon. The old man was wheeled down to the road in his Bath chair by some friends, but for some reason the royal route was changed, and he was wheeled up the hill again to dinner. Two years later a deputation including Francis Johnston, went out to see him and ask him to become a foundation member of the new Royal Hibernian Academy. He refused on the score of age and infirmity, but kept Johnston and the others entertained with the sketches and designs with which he had been amusing himself; and all the way back to town Johnston could talk of nothing but the old man's liveliness and generosity. The ministers of his peace during his last days were his sketch-

book and his Bible. When he died later in the same year his neigh-
bours and tenants followed him to Drumcondra, many of them
walking the sixteen miles there and back and refusing to accept
any conveyance. In 1942, on the two-hundredth anniversity of his
birth, the Royal Institute of Architects of Ireland erected a plaque
to his memory in the church. He was a man, in the words of his
biographer, 'whose urbanity of heart and blandness of manner
converted acquaintances into friends, rendering a long-protracted
life one continued exercise of benevolence and affection'. But even
these private virtues are as nothing beside his services to architecture
and to Dublin.

MAURICE CRAIG
from *Dublin 1660–1860* (1980)

Dear Dirty Dublin

DEAR DIRTY DUBLIN

Dubliners.
– Two Dublin vestals, Stephen said, elderly and pious, have lived
fifty and fiftythree years in Fumbally's lane.
– Where is that? the professor asked.
– Off Blackpitts.
Damp night reeking of hungry dough. Against the wall. Face
glistening tallow under her fustian shawl. Frantic hearts. Akasic
records. Quicker, darlint !
On now. Dare it. Let there be life.
– They want to see the views of Dublin from the top of Nelson's
pillar. They save up three and tenpence in a red tin letterbox money-
box. They shake out the threepennybits and a sixpence and coax
out the pennies with the blade of a knife. Two and three in silver
and one and seven in coppers. They put on their bonnets and
best clothes and take their umbrellas for fear it may come on to
rain.
– Wise virgins, professor MacHugh said.

LIFE ON THE RAW

– They buy one and fourpenceworth of brawn and four slices of panloaf at the north city dining rooms in Marlborough street from Miss Kate Collins, proprietress...They purchase four and twenty ripe plums from a girl at the foot of Nelson's pillar to take off the thirst of the brawn. They give two threepenny bits to the gentleman at the turnstile and begin to waddle slowly up the winding staircase, grunting, encouraging each other, afraid of the dark, panting, one asking the other have you the brawn, praising God and the Blessed Virgin, threatening to come down, peeping at the airslits. Glory be to God. They had no idea it was that high.

Their names are Anne Kearns and Florence MacCabe. Anne Kearns has the lumbago for which she rubs on Lourdes water given her by a lady who got a bottleful from a passionist father. Florence MacCabe takes a crubeen and a bottle of double X for supper every Saturday.

RAISING THE WIND

– When they have eaten the brawn and the bread and wiped their twenty fingers in the paper the bread was wrapped in, they go nearer to the railings.

– Something for you, the professor explained to Myles Crawford. Two old Dublin women on the top of Nelson's pillar.

SOME COLUMN!–
THAT'S WHAT WADDLER ONE SAID

– That's new, Myles Crawford said. That's copy. Out for the waxies' Dargle. Two old trickies, what?

– But they are afraid the pillar will fall, Stephen went on. They see the roofs and argue about where the different churches are: Rathmines' blue dome, Adam and Eve's, saint Laurence O'Toole's. But it makes them giddy to look so they pull up their skirts...

THOSE SLIGHTLY RAMBUNCTIOUS FEMALES

– Easy all, Myles Crawford said, no poetic licence. We're in the archdiocese here.

– And settle down on their striped petticoats, peering up at the statue of the onehandled adulterer.

– Onehandled adulterer! the professor cried. I like that. I see the idea. I see what you mean.

DAMES DONATE DUBLIN'S CITS SPEEDPILLS
VELOCITOUS AEROLITHS, BELIEF

– It gives them a crick in their necks, Stephen said, and they
are too tired to look up or down or to speak. They put the bag of
plums between them and eat the plums out of it one after another,
wiping off with their handkerchiefs the plumjuice that dribbles out
of their mouths and spitting the plumstones slowly out between
the railings.

He gave a sudden loud young laugh as a close. Lenehan and Mr
O'Madden Burke, hearing, turned, beckoned and led on across
towards Mooney's.

– Finished? Myles Crawford said. So long as they do no worse.

JAMES JOYCE
from *Ulysses* (1922)

Pub Crawl

In the past, just as today, the tavern and now the pub was a meeting
place for Dubliners, most of whom are a gregarious and talkative
people. In the eighteenth and nineteenth centuries the tavern was
a social rendezvous. Readers of Gilbert's *History of Dublin* must
be amazed not only at the number of taverns but at the variety of
names and purposes for which they were used. Within the narrow
confines of the city and before the movement of the population to
the north and south side of the Liffey, many well-known taverns
were listed in contemporary memoirs.

One of the principal city streets now more or less completely
levelled, and stretching from Christ Church Cathedral to the quays,
was appropriately named Winetavern Street and appears as early
as the fourteenth century in the records as '*Vicus tabernariorum
vini*'. Here some of the best-known taverns were located. The area
directly under the Castle walls and now called Castle Street, boasted
a number of taverns which catered for the nobles, officials and
better-off citizens. One of the oldest of these taverns was the 'Feathern
Tavern' established in the time of Charles II. Other taverns were
'The Garter', 'Duke's Head', 'The Thatched House', 'Rose Tavern',
a noted meeting place for Freemason Lodges as were also the 'Hen
and Chicken', 'Two Blue Posts' and the 'Ring of the Bells'. Most,

if not all, of the taverns in Castle Street disappeared when the Wide Street Commission widened the approaches to the Castle.

Winetavern Street retained its character well into the nineteenth century, and was from the twelfth the centre of the wine trade of Dublin. Barnaby Rich's description of Dublin and Winetavern Street, written in 1610, gives a fair description of conditions that maintained well into the last century: 'I am nowe to speake of a certaine kind of commodity, that outstretcheth all that I have hitherto spoken of, and that is the selling of ale in Dublin, a quotidian commodity that hath vent in every house in the towne, every day in the weeke, at every houre in the day, and in every minute in the houre: There is no merchandise so vendible, it is the very marrow of the common wealth in Dublin. The whole profit of the towne stands upon ale-houses, and selling of ale, but yet the cittizens a little to dignifie the title, as they use to call every pedlar a merchant, so they use to call every ale-house a taverne, whereof there are such plentie, that there are whole streates of tavernes, and it is as rare a thing to finde a house in Dubline without a taverne, as to find a taverne without a strumpet. This free mart of ale selling in Dublyne is prohibited to none, but that it is lawfull for every woman (be she better or be she worse) either to brewe or else to sell ale.'

Rich mentions the number of people brewing beer in the seventeenth century, but even in the early part of the last century there were over 200 breweries in Dublin.

A brief pub-crawl in the eighteenth century would reveal such curious names as the 'Dog and Duck', owned by a notorious informer Francis Magan in what was known as 'Pudding Row', an alley off Winetavern Street and Wood Quay. The 'Old Scots Hole', despite its name, was a respectable eating tavern near the former Custom House on Essex Quay, and not far from Smock Alley Theatre. It was patronised by merchants, and boasted the best ale and beef-steaks in the city. It was a popular place too, even though Threlford, the owner, would never give credit 'even to the best company'. This tavern appears to have existed for more than 50 years, and only sank into oblivion when the old Custom House gave way to Cassels' imposing building a mile down the river.

While the majority of taverns were poor and squalid, others offered a higher standard and were patronised by the nobility, free-masons and members of numerous clubs mainly of a political hue. The 'Rose and Bottle' in Dame Street, for instance, was patronised by the business community, while the 'Eagle Tavern' on Cork Hill, directly opposite Christ Church Cathedral, was a haunt of the profligate young aristocrats who established, under the tutelage of the Earl of Rosse, a Hellfire Club, modelled on the lines of similar institutions in England; and the members who gathered in the 'Eagle Tavern' were heavy drinkers, gamblers and womanisers. For more convivial and bucolic entertainment the rakes repaired to Speaker Conolly's lodge on Montpelier Hill at the foot of the Dublin mountains the ruins of which are still known as the 'Hell-Fire Club'. The 'Eagle Tavern' was certainly respectable in 1755 when the beautiful Elizabeth Gunning, then duchess of Hamilton, was constrained to seek its safety when the roads were blocked with throngs of admiring citizens, intent on seeing her.

Either beside or part of the 'Eagle Tavern' was the 'Eagle Cock-pit Royal', considered an elite cockpit, of which there were many in the city; for this, with cards, dice and rat-baiting, was one of the prime amusements of not only the upper and middle classes, but of the labouring poor who were inveterate gamblers, hence the popularity of various lotteries which were so much part of the daily life of the citizens. The stakes wagered at the 'Eagle Cock-pit Royal' were large, and the average prize money was 40 guineas, with as much as 500 guineas for the main fight.

All the old taverns, 'The Golden Sugar Loaf', 'Tom of Lincoln', 'The Cock Robin', 'The Rose and Bottle' where the Sportsman's Club met to arrange the races at the Curragh, 'Jacob's Ladder', 'The Cock and Punchbowl', 'The Hop', to mention a few, have long since disappeared; and though many public houses in Dublin are more than 100 years old, the only surviving tavern of Augustan and pre-Augustan Dublin is the 'Brazen Head' standing in one of the narrow laneways which still bears the name of Bridge Street and housed such distinguished residents in the seventeenth century as the Marquis of Antrim, the Duke of Marlborough's father, Sir Winston Churchill, and Sir Hercules Langford. 'The Brazen Head', more an inn than a tavern, was established in 1668. 130 years later this was the meeting place of the United Irishmen, the first political group whose aim was the establishment of an independent Irish republic.

In 'The Brazen Head' the wealthy wool merchant, Oliver Bond, Napper Tandy, the Honourable Simon Butler, the first president of the organisation and a son of Lord Mountgarret, Lord Edward Fitzgerald and other leaders met, unaware that one of their members, a well-to-do land owner named Thomas Reynolds, was an informer who conveyed their plans to the Government. One day in 1797 troops moved into 'The Brazen Head' and arrested most of the leaders of the United Irishmen. Those who escaped the net were later rounded up, so when the insurrection of 1798 broke out it had little support from Dublin. Some years later 'The Brazen Head' was a meeting place for the ill-fated Robert Emmet, whose abortive rising in 1803 was marked by the murder of the humane judge, Lord Kilwarden, and the subsequent excecution of young Emmet and some of his followers.

DESMOND CLARKE
from *Dublin* (1977)

Men of Standing

After meeting Mr Black with his two front teeth in his hand, and his mouth bleeding, he had gone to the nightclub and arrested Mr White, the guard told District Justice Good in Dublin District Court 6.

Mr Black took the stand. He was dressed in a nondescript grey suit, with a striped tie and a cardigan. His eyes were soft and brown, his hair waved just a little over the collar of his shirt.

In the dock sat Mr White. He wore a close-fitting three-piece pin-striped suit, with a thick gold chain across the breast. His hair was short and tight against his head, his eyes sharp blue.

Mr Black's barrister had requested that the case finish after the morning's adjournment, because his client was due to go abroad on the morrow.

'It appears,' said the Justice to Mr Black, 'that there was some litigation between you and Mr White. There had been proceedings in the High Court that day.'

'Yes,' said Mr Black. 'Mr White took an action against me for breach of partnership. The case was fought, and we won, with costs. I adjourned to the bar of the Four Courts, where I had an orange. I don't drink too much. I was with my solicitor, and we met two leading members of the Bar there, and we went on to Dublin's leading Watering Spot for lunch, where we had two bottles of wine. Then the four of us went for a drive into Wicklow, where we had tea at a well-known place. After that we returned to the Watering Spot. I had not seen Mr White since the case finished that morning.

'He was in the Watering Spot and he shouted across to my table: "There is Black, the lying, perjuring bastard. You bought off Judge

X—— X—— is a lying hack. He is your puppet. I'll go to jail before I pay costs." We left the Watering Spot, despite the fact that we had ordered fresh drinks, and went off to Dublin's Latest Night Club for a meal. I am ignorant of the place, myself, Justice – but we went there with the two leading members of the Bar. They stayed with us. My solicitor, as you know Justice, is very amusing company. In the night club, we had one bottle of wine and a great talk, and we danced. One of the Bar members has a great interest in classical music – '

'Who are your trying to impress?' broke in Mr White's solicitor.

'Mr White then entered the night club,' continued Mr Black, unperturbed, 'and said the same things that he had said two hours earlier, except that he added, to one of my lady guests, "You're the perjurer's bitch," but that's only a minor detail.'

Mr Black's solicitor had told him that Mr White was possibly acting in contempt, and the solicitor approached Mr White to warn him of this. Mr Black went off to get his party's coats.

At that stage they were grouped in the night club 'around a sort of pool, about 10 feet by five...no, it's not a swimming pool, Justice, but they have women dancing around in it, very scantily-dressed ladies.'

'Women dancing in the swimming pool?' asked the surprised Justice.

'Staff only, not the guests,' smiled Mr Black, 'Anyway, Mr White spoke to the owner of the night club and – '

He produced three photographs from a file. They were colour pictures of his gaping mouth, showing lips drawn back from upper and lower teeth. There was a gap in the upper set of molars. The pictures were reminiscent of the stills from *Jaws*.

'I'm objecting to these photographs,' said Mr White's solicitor, stretching across Mr Black's barrister and slapping the photographs face down onto the witness stand. Mr Black held them up again. Mr White's solicitor pushed them down.

'I'm in charge of this case. Please keep yourself under control,' the Justice rebuked the solicitor.

Mr White had struck him, continued Mr Black 'and my natural teeth broke and fell into my hand. He then tried to knee me. I turned around to avoid this blow; luckily I was sober, for if I had been drunk I would have been too slow. I had my hand in my pocket, and his knee broke my key ring and my fingernail.' He held up his thumb.

The next morning the manager of the Watering Spot 'managed

to get me one of the better dentists in Dublin. He's the top dentist, actually, Justice, and the manager got him to cancel all his appointments for that day, and I spent the whole day with him.'

'They don't look too bad on you,' the Justice smiled.

'But they are not my natural teeth. You can see the difference in colour,' Mr Black smiled back, revealing his two new front teeth. 'And may I just add one or two things, Justice...four days later I was eating in an inexpensive restaurant in Grafton Street.' He named the latest restaurant.

'I wouldn't know the expensive restaurants,' smiled the Justice.

'It was an inexpensive restaurant,' Mr Black enunciated clearly, 'and my car was parked in a street opposite to the window of the restaurant. I looked out and saw someone who appeared to be interfering with my car. I thought it was being stolen, and I raced out. I was groggy after my session with the top dentist, and I stopped near my car and shouted, 'Mr White,' for it was he, 'this is ridiculous. You must not interfere with my car.' Then I ran back – yes, away from the scene, Justice – hoping to get a guard. He ran after me, caught up with me at the jeweller's, repeated his remarks concerning the Judge and me, and took a swipe at me, to use the expression. I moved aside and he hit the shutters, but as a result my two new dentures loosened, and I had to get them fixed by my own dentist in the country.'

NELL McCAFFERTY
from *In the Eyes of the Law* (1981)

Her Number's Up

The lottery-hall was in Capel Street, which was every day choked up by the crowds of adventurers eager to hear their fate. The multitude of those unhappy beings, and the anxiety and distraction they displayed, was sometimes appalling. All industry was suspended; a number was to be insured at any risk, though the means were secured by pawning, selling, or robbery; every faculty seemed absorbed in watching the chance of the number when procured; all the excesses that have been attributed to gambling in a few of the upper classes, were here displayed by the whole population; the scenes that shock an observer in the privacy of a gaming-house were of common occurrence in the public streets – the cheer of success and the groan of ruin, the wildness of exultation and the frenzy of despair, were daily to be witnessed. The man who was honest before became a thief that he might have the means of insuring. The very beggars allocated their alms to this fascinating pursuit. A poor blind creature used to beg in Sackville Street, and attracted the notice of passengers by her silent and unobtrusive manners and cleanly appearance. She had a little basket with articles for sale, covered with a net, and received more alms than an ordinary beggar. She dreamed of a number that was to make her fortune; and next day was led to a lottery-office, and insured it. It was not drawn, and she lost; but convinced that it was to make her fortune she still persevered in insuring it. Her little store was soon exhausted; she sold her clothes, and pledged her basket; but her number still stuck in the wheel, and when she had nothing left she was obliged to desist. She still, however, inquired after the number, and found it had been drawn the very day she ceased to insure it. She groped her way to the Royal Canal, and threw herself into it.

JOHN EDWARD WALSH
from *Rakes & Ruffians* (1979)

Dazzly Dublin

December now was spent in lovely dazzly Dublin. Joseph travelled in and out of the city on the train. His dad hurtled along bringing his son all the magic and music, hullabaloo and razzmatazz of Christmas in the capital of Ireland. The crowds made way for the boy in the wheelchair, the waitresses put extra cream in his coffee, the shopkeepers beautifully looked pleased with his choice of presents, while the porters helped him board his train at the vantage point for him. For lonely youth he gave not a fig, here he was now watching people's faces, smiling at times as street dealers raucously bellowed, 'Buy your Christmas wrapping paper...Lovely balloons...Christmas decorations...Get your fairy lights...Look son, lovely Christmas crackers last two boxes.' Never offended if passed by, they just revved up and bellowed again. Seeing but not believing, the boy loved the burly busy streets. Great chains of fairy lights mimicked magic for his lost chances. In multicolour Henry Street and back-in-time Moore Street he listened to the daughters of Molly Malone still wheeling

and dealing from their barrows, 'Lovely juicy oranges...Ripe bananas
...Buy your brussels sprouts – look mam, lovely and fresh...Fresh
musharooms.' Moidered by brash niceness of sounds, healed by
being part of the scene, warmed by the rosy-cheeked women clutch-
ing their mugs of pure unlaced tea, he nodded to his father, hinting
that his frame was filled and that it was time to move on.

Joseph always cutchied down inside his scarf as his father wheeled
him across the Liffey. Glancing through the bridge balusters his
eyes buttonholed glimpses of the sombre, neon-marbled looking
glass beneath. Seconds away from O'Connell Bridge was D'Olier
Street. Frantic rushing traffic snaked along, but Matthew steered
his bus in and out through the convoyed, belching streams. Then
with a prayer and a promise, the man and boy dropped into the
chapel in D'Olier Street. Theirs would be but a fleeting visit, in
one door and out the other they hurried, yet taking just long enough
to salute Christ in the Blessed Sacrament. Then leaving the gentle
silence of the oratory behind them, they trundled around the corner
at Trinity College. Joseph would busy himself glancing from the
colonnaded old parliament house to the mullioned windows of the
ancient university. A hasty look at Dame Street was all he ever
needed – he would have his eye hurtling on towards the street of
his dreams. As though not to fail him, Grafton Street always laid
on burly surprises for boys bleary chastened. Buskers rippled their
music on the frosty cold air, choirs of carol singers nested the
opulence of the stores in the manger at Bethlehem while goggle-eyed
children asked thousands of questions to parcel-laden parents about
the moving animals in Switzer's shop windows.

Joseph always loved the special feeling of suppressed excitement
in glamorous Grafton Street. His face might be blue-cold but inside
he would feel comfortable and cosy. He always watched and secretly
examined folk as they paraded themselves up and down the fashion-
able street. He felt zoo-caged and wished he wasn't, but on his
visits to Grafton Street he always noted that the street was but a
busy cat walk where not only the beautiful people, but punks, rockers,
Jesus-freaks and beggars strutted, stumbled, posed or minced, all
wanting to be noticed, all searching for something. But at Christmas
time the cat walk glittered and winked at the passer by, for now it
carried the ordinary folk, each of them hell-bent on getting a special
gift for a certain someone.

CHRISTOPHER NOLAN
from *Under the Eye of the Clock* (1987)

Hellish Drinkers

Sir Jonah Barrington's descriptions of Irish 'gentlemen' having what they thought was a good time would make any sensible person prefer the lowest circle of hell as an alternative. In Dublin there was no lack of entrepreneurs to provide facilities for the whoring, drinking and gambling. Clubs and taverns abounded, some sited in odd places: for example, the crypt of Christchurch cathedral.

The degradation of the cathedral began in 1548 with the leasing by its authorities to Arland Ussher, a relation of two Archbishops of Armagh, of part of the crypt which had been turned into a tavern. The practice of sepulchral boozing flourished. By 1633 the Lord Deputy, Thomas Strafford, Earl of Wentworth, complained to Archbishop Laud in London that the entire crypt was now given over to the sale of drink and tobacco 'where they are pouring either in or out their drink offerings and incense whilst we above are serving the high God'. He had therefore ordered the removal of the shops, making the Archbishops of Armagh, Dublin and Tuam, or any two of them, responsible for seeing the orders were carried out. He was obliged to issue another ordinance: 'that no person presume to make urine aginst the walls of the said church'.

It can be mentioned here that pubs and tobacconists weren't the only intrusions into this house of God. Strafford also told Laud that secular buildings had been erected right up against the cathedral walls. He wasn't able to get rid of these, perhaps because they were mostly connected with the law, and indeed housed the law courts themselves. The entrance to the buildings was known as hell. It was a partly arched and gloomy passage some ten feet below the level of the cathedral's present floor, with, over the arch, a horned figure carved in black oak and said to be the devil. The fame of this 'hell' reached Robert Burns:

> But this I am gaun to tell
> Which lately on a night befell,
> Is just as true as the deil's in hell
>   Or Dublin city.

The Christchurch hell was lined with taverns and snuggeries which, being convenient to the courts, were much patronised by lawyers. Above the taverns were apartments for single men, which were once memorably advertised: 'To be let, furnished apartments in hell. N.B. They are well suited to a lawyer.'

JOHN O'DONOVAN
from *Life by the Liffey: A Kaleidoscope of Dubliners* (1986)

Jailhouse Blues

The new prison was designed by Thomas Cooley, who also designed the Royal Exchange, now City Hall; it was three storeys tall with a round tower at each corner and was entirely built of black calp except for a pediment and centre break of granite. An apparatus for hanging was situated above the main door and was used for public executions. This helped to give a macabre, almost theatrical, air to the prison. Public executions were indeed great occasions at Little Green. Coffins for the bodies of those to be executed were sent into the prison a day or two before the event. The condemned man, who often sold his body to the surgeons, would celebrate his last night by having a party with his friends and 'the widow to be', using it was said his coffin as a table for drinks and cards. The next morning the hangman would arrive, his face covered by a mask and a wooden bowl forming a hump on his back to fend off the missiles with which the crowd invariably assailed him.

It was hoped that the new prison would be secure, comfortable and would prevent the spread of contagious diseases. The choice of the site did not favour the fulfilment of these hopes: Little Green was low-lying, and thus there were immediate difficulties in the construction of proper drains; it was an environment that naturally facilitated the spread of disease. The major problem with the 'new' Newgate however, was mismanagement. Only a year after the completion of the prison, John Howard, the English reformer, claimed that it was 'the very reverse of every idea that he can form of a perfect and well regulated jail'. According to a parliamentary report in 1782, it was already dirty and crowded, and prisoners were being crammed into underground cells with men, women and children sharing the same quarters. There was neither straw nor bedding and drunkenness was prevalent among the prisoners. It is not surprising that within a decade there were public calls that Newgate should be abandoned and a more hygienic and secure prison be built.

The 'new' Newgate was the recipient of a range of criminal offenders, from vagrants to those convicted of high treason. In 1798, two of the leading United Irishmen, Oliver Bond and Lord Edward Fitzgerald were held there, both dying within its walls. Newgate also held some debtors, but its main function was as the collection centre for those awaiting transportation from the northern half of the country. The building of the new prison had coincided with a change in transportation policy, for the old destination of the convicts, the American colonies, were no longer available after 1776. Under the acts of 17 & 18 Geo. III, c.9, three to ten years of hard labour on harbour improvements in Dublin port became a substitute for transportation. Many difficulties arose with this scheme in the later stages of the American war and after, not least because Newgate could barely house all those supposedly working in the port. By the end of the 1780s large-scale transportation was revived, with a new destination introduced, Australia.

Newgate offered two types of accommodation: the common hall, which possibly housed the majority of prisoners and the 'private' rooms, for which they had to pay. Those who could afford it paid for the private rooms – often through fear of the common hall where they would be stripped and their clothes sold for alcohol by fellow-prisoners. They would also be at greater risk of infection there, since vagabonds and strolling beggars cluttered the hall. Drunkenness and fighting were common features of the overcrowded life. Deaths from alcoholic poisoning and from wounds inflicted by other prisoners were quite common, even murders were occasionally committed. The common hall did not have windows but slits in the wall through which prisoners suspended alms bags to the street below, the proceeds of which went to pay various necessary expenses such as food and drink. In this way professional beggars could continue to ply their trade from within the prison walls. The hall was heated by a fire in the centre of the room which was 'encircled by desperados' who excluded the weak and the feeble. A hierarchy existed in the hall, with favoured prisoners often monopolising the meagre space for their own diversions. The men's common hall measured 20 feet by 17 feet. On 18 January 1788 the prison contained 212 prisoners, of which 52 were women. We have no figure for the proportion then living in the common hall but if we assume that a quarter of the men could not afford private accommodation then the number of prisoners sharing the 20 feet by 17 feet was about 40. This would mean that each prisoner had a mere eight square feet of living space. Prisoners in the common hall also had access to a yard which measured 54 feet by 43 feet.

*   *   *

Medical attention was available in the prison although the service was sporadic. Conditions were, however, difficult. In 1788 four women were reportedly in the 'hospital' lying on the ground with no covering, and nothing but water to drink; the hospital area was filthy, and excrement was infrequently removed, which greatly hampered the recovery of the sick. The provision of medical facilities was prompted by two factors, the desire to help the sick and dying prisoners, and the anxiety to prevent gaol fever spreading outside the prison, especially to the nearby courts. The lack of systematic medical care in Newgate, according to the 1782 report, 'endangers the lives of those respectable characters whose duty it is to attend the Courts of Justice as has been fatally evinced in many recent instances'. But the normal conditions of life, at least in the common hall, cancelled out medical provision: the 'deaths of many and the decrepit state of others arise from the want of necessary sustenance, clothing and proper linen'. Although some prisoners were given bread, it was not enough to help those who were too ill to recover, nor to keep healthy those who had to endure such appalling conditions.

BERNADETTE DOORLEY
from *The Gorgeous Mask: Dublin 1700-1850*
edited by David Dickson (1987)

Heggelomayell!

The Catholic sympathies of *Freeman's* left the Protestant badly in need of daily journalistic reassurance at the breakfast table. The need was met to some extent by the venerable and dull *Saunders News Letter* and respectable and dull *Daily Express*. The afternoon sustenance required to fill the gap between one morning and another was provided by the Dublin *Evening Mail*. Of the three the Mail was to last the longest, achieving a century of existence as a grand old institution which shared with the *Irish Times* the reputation of keeping two headlines permanently in type: SERIOUS CHARGE AGAINST CLERGYMAN and SCOUTMASTER ON SERIOUS CHARGE. But whereas the *Times* contrived to print such items with an air of doing a painful duty, the *Mail* was clearly offering them as interesting items in their own right, and did not shrink from including details which the *Times*, blushing, dropped in the waste-paper basket. In due course the *Mail* enlarged its repertoire to include WOMAN PATIENT ACCUSES DOCTOR: according generous space to what the *Times* dismissed in a paragraph.

The man who set the *Mail* on the path it was to follow through three generations was Dr Henry Maunsell. Born in the heart of Dublin 1806, a son of the general manager of the Grand Canal Company, Maunsell trained as a surgeon. In 1839 he started, with another doctor, the *Dublin Medical Press*, a weekly crammed with trade advertisements which rapidly made him his fortune. In 1860 he bought the *Mail*, printed whatever local news was cheaply available and topped up the remaining space with matter lifted without payment from British and foreign papers.

Maunsell's political policy was simple. He adopted the provincial papers' practice of printing speeches by candidates at election time at a charge of so many pence per line. Editorial praise of a candidate cost a shilling a line. In my youth I was told by veterans of the press that this practice, which obviously had to be hush-hush, was continued by the *Mail* long after other big papers had dropped it, and that an extra guinea or two could be picked up by *Mail* men able to guarantee prominent positioning of the puffs.

Older Dubliners will have vivid memories of a once famous newsboy cry: 'Heggelomayell! Heggelomayell!' This, interpreted, signified, '*Herald* or *Mail*', the *Herald* being the *Mail's* more strait-laced rival, which resolutely averted its puritan gaze from serious charges and women patients' accusations. For many years Dubliners carried outward and visible signs of their religious affiliations. Soft hats, coloured shirts, imperfectly cleaned footwear and the *Irish Independent* and *Evening Herald* proclaimed the Roman. Bowler hats, white shirts, brown leather gloves, rolled umbrellas, gleaming foot-wear and the *Irish Times* and *Evening Mail* denoted membership of the Anglican communion.

JOHN O'DONOVAN
from *Life by the Liffey: A Kaleidoscope of Dubliners* (1986)

In a Café

The café was in a back street. Mary's ankles ached and she was glad Maudie had not got there before her. She sat down at a table near the door.

It was a place she had only recently found, and she dropped in often, whenever she came up to Dublin. She hated to go anywhere else now. For one thing, she knew that she would be unlikely ever to have set foot in it if Richard were still alive. And this knowledge helped to give her back a semblance of the identity she lost willingly in marriage, but lost doubly, and unwillingly, in widowhood.

Not that Richard would have disliked the café. It was the kind of place they went to when they were students. Too much water had gone under the bridge since those days, though. Say what you liked, there was something faintly snobby about a farm in Meath, and together she and Richard would have been out of place here. But it was a different matter to come here alone. There could be nothing – oh, nothing – snobby about a widow. Just by being one, she fitted into this kind of café. It was an unusual little place. She looked around.

The walls were distempered red above and the lower part was boarded, with the boards painted white. It was probably the boarded walls that gave it the peculiarly functional look you get in the snuggery of a public house or in the confessional of a small and poor parish church. For furniture there were only deal tables and chairs, with black-and-white checked tablecloths that were either unironed or badly ironed. But there was a decided feeling that money was not so much in short supply as dedicated to other purposes – as witness the paintings on the walls, and a notice over the fire-grate to say that there were others on view in a studio overhead, in rather the same way as pictures in an exhibition. The paintings were for the most part experimental in their technique.

The café was run by two students from the Art College. They often went out and left the place quite empty – as now – while they had a cup of coffee in another café – across the street. Regular clients sometimes helped themselves to coffee from the pot on the gas-ring, behind a curtain at the back; or, if they only came in for company and found none, merely warmed themselves at the big fire always blazing in the little black grate that was the original grate when the café was a warehouse office. Today, the fire was banked up with coke. The coffee was spitting on the gas-ring.

MARY LAVIN
from 'In a Café', *The Stories of Mary Lavin* (1976)

Least Insignificant City

No other city, said Dubliners, possessed so many splendid buildings, and they rattled off the familiar list like so many Hail Marys in a decade of the Rosary: the Custom House, the Four Courts, Trinity College, the Old Parliament House (made redundant by the Act of Union and re-employed as head office of the Bank of Ireland), the Rotunda, the General Post Office, Charlemont House, the Casino at Marino, The Lodge, the Castle, and that typical example of Irish *embarras de richesse*, two cathedrals of the same denomination.

In Dublin Castle, citizens will tell you, there was a large apartment, St Patrick's Hall, which was assuredly the largest and most magnificent in the British Isles, an opinion which used to stagger incoming ducal viceroys to whom it would have appeared hardly larger than their own diningrooms at home. Visitors hearing of 'The Lodge' and asking what and where it was, were pitied for their ignorance. Didn't the whole world know that The Lodge was the Viceregal Lodge in the Park?

The Park?

Good heavens, man, the Phoenix Park, the largest park in the world. Look at Sackville (O'Connell) Street, the widest in Europe. The best English was spoken in Dublin. Dublin wit was celebrated...

In a word, nineteenth-century Dublin hadn't yet grasped that it was only the least insignificant city in an island off an island off mainland Europe. Nor did it yet realise that it was a century behind the times in its appearance, and two in its ideas. But it did have the advantage of being cheap enough for persons of narrow means to cut a dash in.

JOHN O'DONOVAN
from *Life by the Liffey: A Kaleidoscope of Dubliners* (1986)

Love in Old Dublin – 1928

To Burdock's chip shop for my one-and-one,
I put them in my chest to keep warm
Coming down Bride Street I met my new fellow
Hair all peroxide, a buttercup yellow.

To Stickfoot for a bowl of soup
He had sixpence he was a duke
I turned at the door and felt getting sick
I thought of old Stickfoot stirring the pot with his stick.

At my halldoor which was nearby
His kisses and squeezes made me cry
The chips are now burning right into my chest
Now flattening out all over my breast

A few loose chips fell onto my foot
Along came Bang Bang and started to shoot
At the last kiss and squeeze he said 'You're very hot,
The Maro tomorrow at eight on the dot.'

Charles Farrell and Janet Gaynor kissed in the scene
While we kissed and cuddled behind the Woodbine smokescreen
Coming out of the pictures a smell in the air
Hot pigs' feet, sixpence a pair.

The crubeens in newspaper were roasting hot
But we ate them and licked them and spent the lot
We kissed and cuddled all the way home
Still licking and sucking the very last bone
There was no talk of sex or anything like that
A kiss and a cuddle but we'd no more do that.

ROSE O'DRISCOLL
from *Rose of Cabra* (1990)

Talking Shop

The first Irish Parliament after the Restoration of Charles II met
in Chichester House in May 1661. This venue was not ideal and
by the 1720s the advanced decay of the house convinced the members
to demolish it and order a new structure of some magnificence to
replace it.

Edward Lovett Pearce was appointed architect and the foundation
stone was laid in 1728. In attendance were Pearce, the Lords Justice,
nobility, Members of Parliament, Yeomen of the Guard and detach-

ments of dragoons and foot. A purse with 21 guineas was placed on top of the stone which 'the architect distributed among the crafts-men to drink towards the health of their Majesties'. A decade passed before work was completed.

The new building was the world's first to be designed specifically as a two-chamber legislature. The octagonal-shaped House of Com-mons was crowned by a lofty dome and the proceedings could be watched by up to 700 spectators in the upper galleries.

The Lords and Members also had their priorities right and provided themselves with ample kitchens equipped 'with a large apparatus for good eating'. In the dining rooms 'all distinctions as to Government or opposing parties were totally laid aside; harmony, wit, wine and good humour reigning triumphant'.

A further effort to increase their creature comforts backfired when a newly installed but defective heating system caused a fire which destroyed the Commons Chamber in 1792. By the time it was rebuilt the Parliament had less than four years to run before it was dissolved by the Act of Union in 1800.

Three of Dublin's greatest architects were involved in expanding or re-adapting the building; James Gandon (East portico 1785), Robert Parke (Foster Place portico 1797) and Francis Johnston (curving screen wall and armoury in Foster Place and major interior alterations 1803). Edward Smyth carved the statues of Fidelity, Hibernia and Commerce.

[Former Houses of Parliament, now Bank of Ireland, College Green.]

PAT LIDDY
from *Temple Bar* (1992)

House Rules

Advice to playwrights who are sending plays to the Abbey, Dublin:

The Abbey Theatre is a subsidised theatre with an educational object. It will, therefore, be useless as a rule to send it plays intended as popular entertainments and that alone, or originally written for per-formance by some popular actor at the popular theatres. A play to be suitable for performance at the Abbey should contain some criticism of life, founded on the experience or personal observation of the writer, or some vision of life, of Irish life by preference, important from its beauty or from some excellence of style; and this intellectual quality is not more necessary to tragedy than to the gayest comedy.

We do not desire propagandist plays, nor plays written mainly to serve some obvious moral purpose; for art seldom concerns itself with those interests or opinions that can be defended by argument, but with realities of emotion and character that become self-evident when made vivid to the imagination.

The dramatist should also banish from his mind the thought that there are some ingredients, the love-making of the popular stage for instance, especially fitted to give dramatic pleasure; for any knot of events, where there is passionate emotion and clash of will, can be made the subject matter of a play, and the less like a play it is at the first sight the better play may come of it in the end. Young writers should remember that they must get all their effects from the logical expression of their subject, and not by the addition of extraneous incidents; and that a work of art can have but one subject. A work of art, though it must have the effect of nature, is art because it is not nature, as Goethe said: and it must possess a unity unlike the accidental profusion of nature.

The Abbey Theatre is continually sent plays which show that their writers have not understood that the attainment of this unity by what is usually a long shaping and reshaping of the plot, is the principal labour of the dramatist, and not the writing of the dialogue.

Before sending plays of any length, writers would often save themselves some trouble by sending a 'Scenario', or scheme of the plot, together with one completely written act and getting the opinion of the Reading Committee as to its suitability before writing the whole play.

W.B. YEATS
from *Our Irish Theatre* by Lady Gregory (1913)

Abbey Theatre Fire

Pride made of Yeats a rhetorician.
He would have called them knave or clown,
The playwright, poet, politician,
Who pull his Abbey Theatre down.

Scene-dock and wardrobe choked with rage,
When warriors in helmets saved
The auditorium and stage.
Forgetting our age, he waved and raved
Of Art and thought her Memory's daughter.
Those firemen might have spared their water.

AUSTIN CLARKE
from *Too Great a Vine* (1957)

Morning on Grafton Street

Grafton Street is yawning, waking
limb by limb; jewellers' steel
shutters clatter upwards, the sweet
doughy smells from hot-bread

shops steam the frosty morning,
warm our passing; disc-stores'
sudden rhythms blare an introit,
launch the busy liturgy of day.

Look! Two breakfast wooers
fallen in love with farewells
smooch, soul-kiss on the kerb.
Gently, my street puts on her face.

Grafton Street, witness of my time,
seer, watcher of every mood,
traps me the grandeur, the melancholy,
ever-new carnival of man.

Walk here alone in broodiness,
inwoven, anonymous, swept along;
stroll here infatuated, self-communing,
lost in the lyric flow of street.

MICHEAL O'SIADHAIL
from *The Image Wheel* (1985)

Dublin Funerals

Boyhood takes its fun where it finds it, without looking beneath
the surface; and, since society chose to dispose of its dead with a
grotesque pageant out of which farcical incidents sprang naturally
and inevitably at every turn, it is not to be wondered at that funerals
made me laugh when I was a boy nearly as much as they disgust
me now that I am older, and have had glimpses from behind the
scenes of the horrors of what a sentimental public likes to hear
described as 'God's acre'.

BERNARD SHAW
from *Music in London* (1931)

Death Duties

They were followed by some neighbours who came to help to carry
the coffin down.

– We'll miss her, Sean, said one of them; and the kids will too
– badly. A great oul' woman gone west – th' light o' heaven to her!

– There y'are said the leading hearseman, handing an envelope
to Sean; that's for you – th' bill.

– The bill? Oh, righto, said Sean carelessly, thrusting the envelope
into his pocket. You can start to screw her down now.

– There'll be no screwin' down, nor no effin' funeral here till
th' money's paid, said the hearseman harshly. Right, Bill? he added,
turning to his mate.

– The bill'll be paid, said Sean, as soon as a cheque I have is
cashed – your manager knows about it.

– I'm tellin' you no funeral'll leave here till th' money's paid,
repeated the hearseman fiercely; we want no tricks with cheques.

– Aw, murmured one of the neighbours, you couldn't leave th'
poor woman sthranded like that; th' money'll be paid.

– Sthranded or no, said the hearseman, if th' money owed, four
pound nineteen shillings, an' sixpence, isn't in them two hands –
stretching them out – in ten minutes' time, we sail off, an' you can
do what you like with th' stiff; an' them's th' last words!

Sean jumped down the stairs, rushed along the road, darted into
a side street, and burst into Murphy's to splutter out the way things

were, pleading for God's sake to let him have enough to pay the
bill for coffin and hearse.

– Wait, now, said Murphy slowly; for it never does to rush money
matthers. Cheque passed awright, couple o' days ago; so we're all
serene. Had I known you were in a hurry, I'd a had things ready.
I don't know there's as much as you want in the till – th' days young
yet. He stuck a hand into the till, raking forward some coins, and
fingering gently a few pound notes. Wait till I see. One, two, three,
four – there's four o'them, anyway for a start; an' five, ten, fifteen
shillin's in half-crowns – for a funeral you should ha' warned me
beforehand – sixteen, seventeen, eighteen – if I hadda known, I'd
ha' had everything ready – nineteen; now which'll you have – two
thrupenny bits, or six coppers?

– When'll I get the rest due to me? asked Sean, swiftly gathering
up the notes and coins as they were handed out to him.

– Aw, sometime at th' end o' of the week, when I've taken what's
mine, an' when th' till's flush. If I hadda known you were in a
hurry, I'd ha' had things ready; but Sean heard only the beginning
of the sentence, for he was racing back, breathless, to where his
mother patiently lay, waiting to be laid to rest. He handed the money
to the hearseman who signed the receipt, the lid of the coffin was
screwed down, and then the hearseman gestured to the neighbours
to bear the box below.

– The burial docket? he asked of Sean, and carefully put it into
a breast pocket. We'll have t'hurry, Bill, he said to his mate, if we're
to get to th' cemetery in time to settle th' old lady properly.

SEAN O'CASEY
from *Inishfallen, Fare Thee Well* (1949)

Viking Ground

Cathedral on the Viking ground. The crypt
contains the arid quiet of a hiding-place.

Pigsqueals in the slaughterhouse.
Brickdust trickling down.
Black railings gird the gaping emptiness
of the park in February.

The foodbringer fetches bread
still cooling
still luminous with heat from the ovens.
The timber merchant's men
are busy judging and splitting tree-trunks.

Chimneys. Church bells.
Pigeons test the sharpness of a roof's apex.

The rows of houses have their secret thoughts.
Breath from inside the rooms
keeps appearing on windows swollen with frost.

GERARD SMYTH
from *Painting the Pink Roses Black* (1986)

Going to the Gaiety

I thought of you as the hard man
ruling a house through the bottle
but when the opera opened
we climbed as one
up a hundred steps
and sat, dreamy from song
and the height of the gods,
to hear sad Traviata
peer down at Mimi in damson
Othello in saffron damask
and were lost in the lustre
of gaud and strut
as the scent of the heated crowd
rose in our faces like opium
and I squeezed close to your old serge
with its years of tobacco,
feeling emotion swell
with the taut of the long sweet note

releasing you
to be the father I loved
who wandered home

through the gold lit dark of Dublin
arm in arm with his daughter,
whistling the tune of your man
the Italian tenor.

SHEILA O'HAGAN
from *The Peacock's Eye* (1992)

Bewley's Oriental Café, Westmoreland Street

When she asked me to keep an eye on her things
I told her I'd be glad to keep an eye on her things.
While she breakdanced off to the ladies' loo
I concentrated on keeping an eye on her things.
What are you doing? – a Security Guard growled,
His moustache gnawing at the beak of his peaked cap.
When I told him that a young woman whom I did not know
Had asked me to keep an eye on her things, he barked:
Instead of keeping an eye on the things
Of a young woman whom you do not know,
Keep an eye on your own things.
I put my two hands on his hips and squeezed him:
Look – for me the equivalent of the Easter Rising
Is to be accosted by a woman whom I do not know
And asked by her to keep an eye on her things;
On her medieval backpack and on her spaceage Walkman;
Calm down and cast aside your peaked cap
And take down your trousers and take off your shoes
And I will keep an eye on your things also.
Do we not cherish all the children of the nation equally?
That woman does not know the joy she has given me
By asking me if I would keep an eye on her things;
I feel as if I am on a Dart to Bray,
Keeping an eye on her things;
More radical than being on the pig's back,
Keeping an eye on nothing.
The Security Guard made a heap on the floor
Of his pants and shoes,
Sailing his peaked cap across the café like a frisbee.
His moustache sipped at a glass of milk.

It is as chivalrous as it is transcendental
To be sitting in Bewley's Oriental Café
With a naked Security Guard,
Keeping an eye on his things
And on old ladies
With thousands of loaves of brown bread under their palaeolithic
      oxters.

PAUL DURCAN
from *The Berlin Wall Café* (1985)

Dicey Reilly

Ah poor old Dicey Reilly, she has taken to the sup,
And poor old Dicey Reilly she will never give it up,
It's off each morning to the pop then she goes in for another little
      drop,
But the heart of the rowl is Dicey Reilly.

She will walk along Fitzgibbon Street with an independent air
And then it's down by Summerhill, and as the people stare
She'll say, 'It's nearly half past one, time I went in for another little
      one.'
But the heart of the rowl is Dicey Reilly.

Now at two, pubs close and out she goes as happy as a lark
She'll find a bench to sleep it off down in St Patrick's Park.
She'll wake at five feeling in the pink and say 'Tis time for another
      drink.'
But the heart of the rowl is Dicey Reilly.

Now she'll travel far to a dockside bar to have another round
And after one or two or three she doesn't feel quite sound
And after four she's a bit unstable; after five underneath the table
The heart of the rowl is Dicey Reilly.

Oh they carry her home at twelve o'clock as they do every night
Bring her inside, put her on the bed and then turn out the light.
Next morning she'll get out of bed and look for a curer for her head
But the heart of the rowl is Dicey Reilly.

Ah poor oul Dicey Reilly she has taken to the sup
And poor oul Dicey Reilly she will never give it up.
It's off each morning to the pop then she goes in for another little
      drop
But the heart of the rowl is Dicey Reilly.

ANONYMOUS

Objects of Relief

In Dublin the scale of metropolitan "distress", to use the contem-
porary euphemism, can be seen by the extraordinary number of
charitable organisations which were exclusively concerned with the
poor of the metropolis. The fact that these organisations were often
completely dependent on the generosity of the city's inhabitants
reveals something of the charitable ethos of the society: 'few capitals
in Europe have in proportion to their population more charitable
foundations than Dublin has at present', wrote Warburton and
Whitelaw in 1818, and contemporary sources add weight to this
claim. The *Dublin Gazette* of July 1822 reported that among the
beneficiaries cited in the will of Henry Downing esquire of Dublin
City were the Female Orphan House, Circular Road; the Old Man's
Asylum, Russell Place; the Strangers' Friend Society; the Seminary
for the Instruction of Deaf and Dumb Children; the Mendicity
Institution; and four different hospitals.

It has been claimed that the proliferation of these philanthropic
institutions in Ireland was part of the general European trend towards
a more humanitarian response to the wretched condition of the poor
and also, that it was associated with the evangelical revival in Ire-
land. The truth of these claims can only be tested through an invest-
igation of individual charities. The Sick and Indigent Room-keepers'
Society was one of the most successful and certainly the most en-
during of the charities founded in this period. The history of its
origins and development, while in many ways unusual, gives some
general insights into the phenomenon of pre-Victorian Irish charities.

The origins and early history of the Sick and Indigent Room-
keepers' Society has been well-recorded despite the absence of the
Society's early archives. Warburton and Whitelaw stated that

> a few individuals in the middle ranks of life, inhabiting a part of the town
> where the population was poor and crowded, had daily opportunities of

> knowing that many poor creatures who were unable to dig and ashamed to beg expired of want and were often found dead in the sequestered garrets and cellars to which they had silently returned; they resolved therefore to form a society for the purpose of searching out those solitary objects.

The 'part of town' referred to was the area of Charles Street (West) behind Ormond Quay and, although sources differ regarding the individuals involved, all include the following six men among the names of the Society's founders: Samuel Rosborough, wholesale linen draper, 24 Charles Street (West); Patrick Magin, grocer, 14 Charles Street (West); Timothy Nowlan, pawnbroker, 14 Greek Street; Philip Shea, carpenter, 64 Little Mary Street; Peter Fleming, fruitman, 5 Mountrath Street; and Laurence Toole, schoolmaster, Mary's Lane (the latter being appointed first secretary of the Society). These men, and possibly others, met in Mountrath Street on 15 March 1790 and resolved that

> as a charitable feeling for the relief of our fellow creatures must be pleasing to Almighty God we...have resolved unanimously to form a Society, to be called the Charitable Society for the Relief of Sick and Indigent Roomkeepers of all Religious Persuasions in the City of Dublin.

A subscription was set – a minimum of 2d. per week or 8s.8d. per annum. Members would be entitled to recommend 'known and deserving persons' to be given relief by the Society. It was laid down that the objects of relief

> shall be poor roomkeepers who never begged abroad and who by unfore-seen misfortune, sickness, death of friends, or other dispensations of Providence, have been reduced to indigence, and that such persons must be of good character, for sobriety and general good conduct.

It was also stated as a general principle that 'no political or religious subjects shall be introduced or allowed to be discussed at any of the meetings of the Society'.

For its first three years the Society confined its activities to the poorer households in the Charles Street, Mountrath Street and Ormond market area, and gave relief in the form of potatoes, meal, bread, straw, fuel or money, as the circumstances of the roomkeeper dictated. In 1790, the Society received £20.2s.4½d. in contribu-tions, and spent £17.9s.8½d. in the relief of 129 families (516 persons altogether). However, according to Warburton and Whitelaw's account a quarter century later, 'the obvious utility of the charity soon attracted public notice and support', and in the course of 1793 the Society had received £300.14s.11d. which enabled them to give relief to 2957 families (7785 persons).

DEIRDRE LINDSAY
from *The Gorgeous Mask: Dublin 1700–1850*, ed. David Dickson (1987)

Like It or Lump It

The Fianna Fáil Government had brought in the Health Act of 1947 as the basis of a badly-needed health service. Being particularly concerned by the high rate of infant mortality in Ireland at this time, Dr Browne decided to introduce maternity treatment and medical attention for children up to the age of sixteen, free of charge and without any means test. This was essentially what the Mother and Child scheme was about.

For anyone who wishes to understand fully the various complications, inconsistencies and misunderstandings surrounding this first public confrontation between Church and State (not forgetting, as is frequently the case, the vested medical interest), Professor J.G. Whyte's book, *Church and State in Modern Itreland: 1923-1979*, traces its background and development with scholarly detachment but in the manner of a well-constructed political thriller.

He has also brought to light an interesting point about the initial public health legislation in 1945. This was handled by Dr Con Ward for the Fianna Fáil Government and was attacked in the Dáil on the grounds that it contravened Christian principles and that it would not meet with the approval of the Catholic hierarchy. The main attack came from Deputies Costello, McGilligan and Mulcahy of Fine Gael and seemed to be part of a growing tendency in Dáil Eireann to put party political advantage ahead of every other consideration. Fine Gael were far from being the only offenders but in this instance the issues they raised came back to haunt them.

These attacks caused Dr Ward, who was a religious man, to approach the Archbishop of Dublin, Dr McQuaid, privately for advice. In the second of two letters to the Parliamentary Secretary the Archbishop described the proposed legislation as 'substantially good'. However, this public health bill, which the Irish Medical Association found little fault with, never became law. Fate, in the shape of the Monaghan bacon factory, intervened and a justifiably disgruntled Dr Ward left public life.

Dr Jim Ryan, the Irish politician who brought the practice of inarticulation to the level of an art form, took over the handling of a new health bill which was essentially the same as Dr Ward's, particularly in the provision for a mother and child scheme. Now, however, Fine Gael seemed happy with the proposals (Fianna Fáil folklore has it that it was an exceptionally busy time in the courts and the lawyers were otherwise occupied) but the doctors were unhappy and the Hierarchy registered an official protest against the proposals for a mother and child scheme.

Although the 1947 proposals were essentially the same as those of 1945 the Church seemed to detect a move towards undue state intervention in family medical matters: one of the Church's main spheres of influence. The war was over and the world was returning to normal and Ireland would again be susceptible to disturbing trends from abroad.

It is the considered opinion of two generations of begrudgers that the medical profession alerted the Church to dangers, moral in both instances, but in one instance the morality had distinct financial attributes. One was spoken, the other unspoken. It was another example of the organised lay Catholics getting out there and putting pressure on the Church to put pressure on the politicians, on the doctors and on the laity, who would in turn... it would take a clever and exceedingly alert person to tell his arse from his elbow in that kind of scrimmage. Poor Noel Browne!

James Dillon challenged certain proposals in the legislation, concerning compulsory medical examination, in the courts on the grounds of their unconstitutionality; and there are neither gold watches nor free holidays in Butlins for those who guess who got places on his legal team. James Dillon, to his credit, was against compulsion in all matters; although older begrudgers recall that the live-in apprentices in Monica Duff's were expected to say the Rosary aloud each night. And good enough for them too, if they were!

His intervention enabled de Valera to reply to the Bishops' complaint by saying that the constitutionality of the legislation was now in question. At this stage the February 1948 election was over and the ball was heading for the Coalition's court. But the obvious point is that it was exceedingly strange that the confrontation with the bishops and the doctors, when it came, seems to have taken so many people who ought to have been fully aware of the pitfalls so badly on the wrong foot. It is, perhaps, as well to note that the Coalition was not brought down by the Dr Browne resignation, although that romantic gloss has crept into history. The government fell when some rural Independents turned their backs on it for failing to increase the price of milk.

Before he knew what really hit him, Dr Browne was in conflict with the Irish Medical Association (always regarded as a posse of not so silent and not holy Knights), the Bishops, all his fellow-ministers and his Taoiseach; not forgetting his party leader who was eventually asked by the Taoiseach to request his Minister for Health's resignation: a trick which obviously slipped Garret FitzGerald's mind when he tried to shift his Minister for Health in 1986.

Any one of these opponents was heavyweight eliminator material; not even Cassius Clay in his heyday could have hoped to handle two out of four and win. But in defeat Noel Browne had one glorious round which won him his permanent place in the record books. For the first time in the history of the state, anyone who could read and who had the price of a newspaper got the inside story of what happened when the Church set out to bend politicians to its will. It was all there because Browne had made the necessary arrangements with the editor of the *Irish Times* that all the other papers carried the correspondence also.

It has been said frequently about that episode that Dr Browne was raw and inexperienced in negotiations, that he was vain, that he fought on too many different fronts, that he was incapable of responding to party or cabinet discipline except by displays of petulance and that only by agreeing that he was always right, even when he was contradicting something he had earlier asserted, could anyone get on with him.

It is just because he lacked the so-called virtues these deficiencies seem to indicate that he succeeded in doing what he did: break the rules of the Lodge and emerge screaming that the Emperor had not a stitch between him and his maker.

This has got nothing to do with the rights and wrongs of the case; it has everything to do with the manner in which the business of the state was conducted. He provided the evidence to support what every thinking citizen in the country suspected: that we had a Catholic Constitution for a people who could either like it or lump it. All pressure groups have equal rights when it comes to exercising what political muscle they possess; the problem was that in this respect the Catholic Church was much more equal than others.

BREANDÁN Ó hEITHIR
from *The Begrudger's Guide to Irish Politics* (1986)

Daily Bread

This morning, the sky cleared to reveal Spring.
I went to the bakery hard by the markets,
and the streets were vital in the fresh light.
A woman pushed a pram, her son holding on,
and she was happy to be with her children.

We dodged Japanese forklifts shifting oranges
from Jaffa, apples from Spain, potatoes from Rush.
With her sunglasses on, a driver reclined,
enjoying the breeze in the hold of her van.
The district was thronged, and juggernaut drivers
edged their way through on roads made for horses.
I heard some slagging, and a man with a moustache
studied his racing page, brooding on luck
as nearby a drayhorse relished abandoned cabbage.
I bought my two loaves of brown, and on my way home
the glasses were gone, as she loaded her van.

PHILIP CASEY
from *The Year of the Knife* (1991)

On Raglan Road
(Air: *The Dawning of the Day*)

On Raglan Road on an autumn day I met her first and knew
That her dark hair would weave a snare that I might one day rue;
I saw the danger, yet I walked along the enchanted way,
And I said, let grief be a fallen leaf at the dawning of the day.

On Grafton Street in November we tripped lightly along the ledge
Of the deep ravine where can be seen the worth of passion's pledge,
The Queen of Hearts still making tarts and I not making hay –
O I loved too much and by such by such is happiness thrown away.

I gave her gifts of the mind I gave her the secret sign that's known
To the artists who have known the true gods of sound and stone
And word and tint. I did not stint for I gave her poems to say.
With her own name there and her own dark hair like clouds over
        fields of May.

On a quiet street where old ghosts meet I see her walking now
Away from me so hurriedly my reason must allow
That I had wooed not as I should a creature made of clay –
When the angel wooes the clay he'd lose his wings at the dawn of day.

PATRICK KAVANAGH
from *Collected Poems* (1964)

Sketch from the Great Bull Wall

He paints the sand when a tide has gone
and an arm of pier as ever out in water
lit clean yellow by a late-going sun.
His hand runs and taps at the rim of his hat
with a long-sticked brush among his fingers.
Green time sits on the tips of stakes
stiff to a hundred tides. Lined and
lined to the lighthouse at the end
cut stone goes in sleepered shape all warm with day
even in stretching shadow where the sun at some hour lay.

He paints a thin shimmer of the backing sea,
a dull fire tracing four serpent miles
from Bull Wall to Monkstown. Bulls
thud in herds along its back in autumn,
they spring like waves from the open sea
on leafless mornings. Tonight,
a tide will slop over the smooth wall
with water from the inner bay
oiled by entered ships.

              O sweet
is the oil in Dublin harbour,
sweet is the song of the sewerage plant,
sweet O sweeter is the fine dust of coalyards,
but sweetest of all the tall wind
ruffling buds of the heavy seaweed
near where he paints the untided sand.

SEBASTIAN BARRY
from *The Water-Colourist* (1983)

Viking Dublin: Trial Pieces

I

It could be a jaw-bone
or a rib or a portion cut
from something sturdier:
anyhow, a small outline

was incised, a cage
or trellis to conjure in.
Like a child's tongue
following the toils

of his calligraphy,
like an eel swallowed
in a basket of eels,
the line amazes itself

eluding the hand
that fed it,
a bill in flight,
a swimming nostril.

II

These are trial pieces,
the craft's mystery
improvised on bone:
foliage, bestiaries,

interlacings elaborate
as the netted routes
of ancestry and trade.
That have to be

magnified on display
so that the nostril
is a migrant prow
sniffing the Liffey,

swanning it up to the ford,
dissembling itself
in antler combs, bone pins,
coins, weights, scale-pans.

III

Like a long sword
sheathed in its moisting
burial clays,
the keel stuck fast

in the slip of the bank,
its clinker-built hull
spined and plosive
as *Dublin*.

And now we reach in
for shards of the vertebrae,
the ribs of hurdle,
the mother-wet caches –

and for this trial piece
incised by a child,
a longship, a buoyant
migrant line.

IV

That enters my longhand,
turns cursive, unscarfing
a zoomorphic wake,
a worm of thought

I follow into the mud.
I am Hamlet the Dane,
skull-handler, parablist,
smeller of rot

in the state, infused
with its poisons,
pinioned by ghosts
and affections,

murders and pieties,
coming to consciousness
by jumping in graves,
dithering, blathering.

V

Come fly with me,
come sniff the wind
with the expertise
of the Vikings –

neighbourly, scoretaking
killers, haggers
and hagglers, gombeen-men,
hoarders of grudges and gain.

With a butcher's aplomb
they spread out your lungs
and made you warm wings
for your shoulders.

Old fathers, be with us.
Old cunning assessors
of feuds and of sites
for ambush or town.

VI

'Did you ever hear tell,'
said Jimmy Farrell,
'of the skulls they have
in the city of Dublin?

White skulls and black skulls
and yellow skulls, and some
with full teeth, and some
haven't only but one,'

and compounded history
in the pan of 'an old Dane,
maybe, was drowned
in the Flood.'

My words lick around
cobbled quays, go hunting
lightly as pampooties
over the skull-capped ground.

SEAMUS HEANEY
from *North* (1975)

Home

The next morning I stood on deck while the boat came into Dún Laoghaire, and looked at the sun struggling out over the hills; and the city all around the Bay.

> ...and I will make my journey, if life and health but stand,
> Unto that pleasant country, that fresh and fragrant strand,
> And leave your boasted braveries, your wealth and high command.
> For the fair hills of Holy Ireland...

There they were, as if I'd never left them; in their sweet and stately order round the Bay – Bray Head, the Sugarloaf, the Two Rock, the Three Rock, Kippure, the king of them all, rising his threatening head behind and over their shoulders till they sloped down to the city. I counted the spires, from Rathmines fat dome on one side of St George's spire on the north, and in the centre, Christchurch. Among the smaller ones, just on the docks, I could pick out, even in the haze of morning, the ones I knew best; St Laurence O'Toole's and St Barnabas; I had them all counted, present and correct and the chimneys of the Pigeon House, and the framing circle of the road along the edge of the Bay, Dún Laoghaire, Blackrock, Sandy-mount Tower, Ringsend and the city; then the other half circle, Fairview, Marino, Clontarf, Raheny, Kilbarrack, Baldoyle, to the height of Howth Head.

I couldn't really see Kilbarrack or Baldoyle, but it was only that I knew they were there. So many belonging to me lay buried in Kilbarrack, the healthiest graveyard in Ireland, they said, because it was so near the sea, and I thought I could see the tricolour waving over Dan Head's grave, which I could not from ten miles over the Bay. And I could see Baldoyle, there, because it was the races.

'Passport, travel permit or identity document, please,' said the immigration man beside me.

I handed him the expulsion order.

He read it, looked at it and handed it back to me. He had a long educated countryman's sad face, like a teacher, and took my hand.

'Céad míle fáilte sa bhaile romhat.'

A hundred thousand welcomes home to you.

I smiled and said, 'Go raibh maith agat.'

Thanks.

He looked very serious, and tenderly enquired, 'Caithfidh go bhuil sé go hiontach bheith saor.'

'Caithfidh go bhuil.'

'It must be wonderful to be free.'

'It must,' said I, walked down the gangway, past a detective, and got on the train for Dublin.

BRENDAN BEHAN
from *Borstal Boy* (1958)

5. INSIDERS & OUTSIDERS

Do not enquire if a man be a heretic, if he be a
Quaker, or a Jew, or a heathen, but if he be a
virtuous man, if he love liberty and truth, if he
wish the happiness and peace of human kind. If a
man be ever so much a believer, and love not these
things, he is a heartless hypocrite, a rascal, and a
knave. Despise and hate him as ye despise a tyrant
and a villain. Oh! Ireland! thou emerald of the
ocean, whose sons are generous and brave, whose
daughters are honourable and frank and fair, thou
art the isle on whose green shores I have desired to
see the standard of liberty erected – a flag of fire –
a beacon at which the world shall light the
torch of Freedom!

PERCY BYSSHE SHELLEY

An Address to the Irish People

Fellowmen, I am not an Irishman, yet I can feel for you. I hope there are none among you who will read this address with prejudice or levity, because it is made by an Englishman; indeed, I believe there are not. The Irish are a brave nation. They have a heart of liberty in their breasts, but they are much mistaken if they fancy that a stranger cannot have as warm a one. Those are my brothers and my countrymen who are unfortunate. I should like to know what there is in a man being an Englishman, a Spaniard, or a Frenchman that makes him worse or better than he really is. He was born in one town, you in another, but that is no reason why he should not feel for you, desire your benefit, or be willing to give you some advice which may make you more capable of knowing your own interest, or acting so as to secure it. There are many Englishmen who cry down the Irish and think it answers their ends to revile all that belongs to Ireland; but it is not because these men are Englishmen that they maintain such opinions, but because they wish to get money, and titles, and power. They would act in this manner to whatever country they might belong, until mankind is much altered for the better, which reform, I hope, will one day be effected. I address you, then, as my brothers and my fellowmen, for I should wish to see the Irishman who, if England was persecuted as Ireland is; who, if France was persecuted as Ireland is; who if any set of men that helped to do a public service were prevented from enjoying its benefits as Irishmen are – I should like to see the man, I say, who would see these misfortunes and not attempt to succour the sufferers when he could, just that I might tell him that he was no Irishman, but some bastard mongrel bred up in a court, or some coward fool who was a democrat to all above him, and an aristocrat to all below him. I think there are few true Irishmen who would not be ashamed of such a character, still fewer who possess it. I know that there are some – not among you, my friends, but among your enemies – who seeing the title of this piece will take it up with a sort of hope that it may recommend violent measures and thereby disgrace the cause of freedom, that the warmth of an heart desirous that liberty should be possessed equally by all will vent itself in abuse on the enemies of liberty, bad men who deserve the contempt of the good, and ought not to excite their indignation to the harm of their cause. But these men will be disappointed – I know the warm feelings of an Irishman sometimes carries him beyond the point of prudence. I do not desire to root out, but to moderate this honourable warmth. This will disappoint the pioneers of oppression, and they will be sorry that through this address nothing will occur which can be twisted into any other meaning but what is calculated to fill you with that moderation which they have not, and make you give them that toleration which they refuse to grant to you. You profess the Roman Catholic religion, which your fathers professed before you. Whether it is the best religion or not, I will not here enquire; all religions are good which make men good; and the way that a person ought to prove that his method of worshipping God is best is for himself to be better than all other men. But we will consider what your religion was in old times and what it is now; you may say it is not a fair way for me to proceed as a Protestant, but I am not a Protestant nor am I a Catholic, and therefore not being a follower of either of these religions, I am better able to judge between them. A Protestant is my brother, and a Catholic is my brother. I am happy when I can do either of them a service, and no pleasure is so great to me than that which I should feel if my advice could make men of any professions of faith, wiser, better, and happier.

The Roman Catholics once persecuted the Protestants; the Protestants now persecute the Roman Catholics. Should we think that one is as bad as the other? No, you are not answerable for the faults of your fathers any more than the Protestants are good for the goodness of their fathers. I must judge of people as I see them; the Irish Catholics are badly used. I will not endeavour to hide from them their wretchedness; they would think that I mocked at them if I should make the attempt. The Irish Catholics now demand for themselves and profess for others unlimited toleration, and the sensible part among them which I am willing to think constitutes a very large portion of their body, know that the gates of Heaven are open to people of every religion, provided they are good. But the Protestants, although they may think so in their hearts, which certainly, if they think at all, they must seem to act as if they thought that God was better pleased with them than with you; they trust the reins of earthly government only to the hands of their own sect. In spite of this I never found one of them impudent enough to say that a Roman Catholic, or a Quaker, or a Jew, or a Mahometan, if he was a virtuous man and did all the good in his power, would go to Heaven a bit the slower for not subscribing to the thirty-nine articles – and if he should say so, how ridiculous in a foppish courtier not six feet high to direct the spirit of universal harmony in what manner to conduct the affairs of the universe!

The Protestants say that there was a time when the Roman Catholics burned and murdered people of different sentiments, and that their religious tenets are now as they were then. This is all very true. You certainly worship God in the same way that you did when these barbarities took place, but is that any reason that you should now be barbarous? There is as much reason to suppose it as to suppose that because a man's great-grandfather, who was a Jew, had been hung for sheep-stealing, that I, by believing the same religion as he did, must certainly commit the same crime. Let us see then what the Roman Catholic religion has been. No one knows much of the early times of the Christian religion until about three hundred years after its beginning; two great Churches, called the Roman and the Greek Churches, divided the opinions of men. They fought for a very long time, a great many words were wasted, and a great deal of blood shed.

*   *   *

The folly of persecuting men for their religion will appear if we examine it. Why do we persecute them? To make them believe as we do. Can anything be more barbarous or foolish. For, although we may make them say they believe as we do, they will not in their hearts do any such thing – indeed they cannot; this devilish method can only make them false hypocrites. For what is belief? We cannot believe just what we like, but only what we think to be true; for you cannot alter a man's opinion by beating or burning, but by persuading him that what you think is right, and this can only be done by fair words and reason. It is ridiculous to call a man a heretic because he thinks differently from you; he might as well call you one. In the same sense the word orthodox is used; it signifies 'to think rightly', and what can be more vain and presumptuous in any man or any set of men, to put themselves so out of the ordinary course of things as to say, 'What we think is right; no other people throughout the world have opinions anything like equal to ours.' Anything short of unlimited toleration and complete charity with all men, on which you will recollect that Jesus Christ principally insisted, is wrong, and for this reason, What makes a man to be a good man? Not his religion, or else there could be no good men in any religion but one, when yet we find that all ages, countries, and opinions have produced them. Virtue and wisdom always so far as they went produced liberty or happiness long before any of the religions now in the world had ever been heard of. The only use of a religion that ever I could see is to make men wiser and better; so far as it does this, it is a good one.

*   *   *

There is no doubt but that the world is going wrong, or rather that it is very capable of being much improved. What I mean by this improvement is the inducement of a more equal and general diffusion of happiness and liberty. Many people are very rich and many are very poor. Which do you think are happiest? I can tell you that neither are happy so far as their station is concerned. Nature never intended that there should be such a thing as a poor man or a rich one. Being put in an unnatural situation, they can neither of them be happy, so far as their situation is concerned. The poor man is born to obey the rich man, though they both come into the world equally helpless and equally naked. But the poor man does the rich no service by obeying him – the rich man does the poor no good by commanding him. It would be much better if they could be prevailed upon to live equally like brothers – they would ultimately both be happier. But this can be done neither today nor tomorrow; much as such a change is to be desired, it is quite impossible. Violence and folly in this, as in the other case, would only put off the period of its event. Mildness, sobriety, and reason are the effectual methods of forwarding the ends of liberty and happiness.

*   *   *

Can you conceive, O Irishmen! a happy state of society, conceive men of every way of thinking living together like brothers? The descendant of the greatest prince would then be entitled to no more respect than the son of a peasant. There would be no pomp and no parade; but that which the rich now keep to themselves would then be distributed among the people. None would be in magnificence, but the superfluities then taken from the rich would be sufficient when spread abroad to make every one comfortable. No lover would then be false to his mistress, no mistress could desert her lover. No friend would play false; no rents, no debts, no taxes, no frauds of any kind would disturb the general happiness; good as they would be, wise as they would be, they would be daily getting better and wiser. No beggars would exist, nor any of those wretched women who are now reduced to a state of the most horrible misery and vice by men whose wealth makes them villainous and hardened; no thieves or murderers, because poverty would never drive men to take away comforts from another when he had enough for himself. Vice and misery, pomp and poverty, power and obedience would then be banished altogether. It is for such a state as this, Irishmen, that I exhort you to prepare. 'A camel shall as soon pass through the eye of a needle, as a rich man enter the kingdom of heaven.'

This is not to be understood literally. Jesus Christ appears to me only to have meant that riches have generally the effect of hardening and vitiating the heart; so has poverty. I think those people then are very silly, and cannot see one inch beyond their noses, who say that human nature is depraved; when at the same time wealth and poverty, those two great sources of crime, fall to the lot of a great majority of people; and when they see that people in moderate circumstances are always most wise and good. People say that poverty is no evil; they have never felt it, or they would not think so; that wealth is necessary to encourage the arts – but are not the arts very inferior things to virtue and happiness? – the man would be very dead to all generous feelings who would rather see pretty pictures and statues than a million free and happy men.

*   *   *

It is my intention to observe the effect on your minds, O Irishmen, which this Address, dictated by the fervency of my love and hope, will produce. I have come to this country to spare no pains where expenditure may purchase you real benefit. The present is a crisis which of all others is the most valuable for fixing the fluctuation of public feeling; as far as my poor efforts may have succeeded in fixing it to virtue, Irishmen, so far shall I esteem myself happy. I intend this Address as introductory to another. The organisation of a society whose institution shall serve as a bond to its members for the purposes of virtue, happiness, liberty, and wisdom, by the means of intellectual opposition to grievances, would probably be useful. For the formation of such society I avow myself anxious.

Adieu, my friends! May every sun that shines on your green island see the annihilation of an abuse and the birth of an embryon of melioration! Your own hearts may they become the shrines of purity and freedom, and never may smoke to the Mammon of unrighteousness ascend from the unpolluted altar of their devotion!

Postscript

I have now been a week in Dublin, during which time I have endeavored to make myself more accurately acquainted with the state of the public mind on those great topics of grievances which induced me to select Ireland as a theatre, the widest and fairest, for the operations of the determined friend of religious and political freedom.

The result of my observations has determined me to propose an association for the purposes of restoring Ireland to the prosperity which she possessed before the Union Act, and the religious freedom

which the involuntariness of faith ought to have taught all monopo-
lists of Heaven long, long ago, that every one had a right to possess.

For the purpose of obtaining the emancipation of the Catholics
from the penal laws that the aggrieve them, and a repeal of the
Legislative Union Act, and grounding upon the remission of the
church-craft and oppression which caused these grievances: *a plan
of amendment and regeneration in the moral and political state of society,
on a comprehensive and systematic philanthropy which shall be sure
though slow in its projects; and as it is without the rapidity and danger
of revolution, so will it be devoid of the time-servingness of temporising
reform* – which in its deliberate capacity, having investigated the
state of the government of England, shall oppose those parts of it
by intellectual force which will not bear the touch-stone of reason.

For information respecting the principles which I possess, and
the nature and spirit of the association which I propose, I refer the
reader to a small pamphlet, which I shall publish on the subject in
the course of a few days.

I have published in the above Address (written in England) in
the cheapest possible form, and have taken pains that the remarks
which it contains should be intelligible to the most uneducated minds.
Men are not slaves and brutes because they are poor; it has been
the policy of the thoughtless or wicked of the higher ranks (as a
proof of the decay of which policy I am happy to see the rapid
success of a comparatively enlightened system of education) to conceal
from the poor the truths which I have endeavoured to teach them.
In doing so I have but translated my thoughts into another language;
and, as language is only useful as it communicates ideas, I shall
think my style so far good as it is successful as a means to bring
about the end which I desire on any occasion to accomplish.

A Limerick paper, which I suppose professes to support certain
loyal and *John Bullish* principles of freedom, has in an essay for
advocating the Liberty of the Press, the following clause: 'For lawless
licence of discussion never did we advocate, nor do we now.' What
is lawless license of discussion? Is it not as indefinite as the words
contumely, reproach, defamation, that allow at present such latitude
to the outrages that are committed on the free expression of individual
sentiment? Can they not see that what is rational will stand by its
reason, and what is true stand by its truth, as all that is foolish will
fall by its folly, and all that is false be controverted by its own false-
hood? Liberty gains nothing by the reform of politicians of this
stamp, any more than it gains from a change of Ministers in London.
What at present is contumely and defamation would at the period

of this Limerick amendment be 'lawless licence of discussion', and such would be the mighty advantage which this doughty champion of liberty proposes to effect.

I conclude with the words of Lafayette, a name endeared by its peerless bearer to every lover of the human race, 'For a nation to love Liberty it is sufficient that she knows it; to be free, it is sufficient that she will it.'

PERCY BYSSHE SHELLEY
from *An Address to the Irish People* (1812)

Last Words, 1803

I have been charged with that importance in the emancipation of my country as to be considered the keystone of the combination of Irishmen; or, as your lordship expressed it, 'the life and blood of the conspiracy'. You do me honour overmuch; you have given to the subaltern all the credit of a superior. There are men engaged in this conspiracy who are not only superior to me, but even to your own conceptions of yourself, my lord-men before the splendour of whose genius and virtues I should bow with respectful deference, and who would think themselves disgraced by shaking your blood-stained hand.

What, my lord, shall you tell me, on the passage to the scaffold, which that tyranny (of which you are only the intermediary executioner) has erected for my murder, that I am accountable for all the blood that has and will be shed in this struggle of the oppressed against the oppressor – shall you tell me this, and must I be so very a slave as not to repel it? I do not fear to approach the Omnipotent Judge to answer for the conduct of my whole life; and am I to be appalled and falsified by a mere remnant of mortality here? By you, too, although if it were possible to collect all the innocent blood that you have shed in your unhallowed ministry in one great reservior, your lordship might swim in it...

[*Here Lord Norbury told Emmet that his sentiments and language disgraced his family and his education, and that his late father would not have countenanced such views.*]

If the spirits of the illustrious dead participate in the concerns and cares of those who were dear to them in this transitory life, oh! ever dear and venerated shade of my departed father, look down with scrutiny upon the conduct of your suffering son, and see if I have even for a moment deviated from those principles of morality and patriotism which it was your care to instil into my youthful mind, and for which I am now about to offer up my life. My lords, you are impatient for the sacrifice. The blood which you seek is not congealed by the artificial terrors which surround your victim – it circulates warmly and unruffled through the channels which God created for noble purposes, but which you are now bent to destroy, for purposes so grievous that they cry to heaven. Be yet patient! I have but a few more words to say – I am going to my cold and silent grave – my lamp of life is nearly extinguished – my race is run – the grave opens to receive me, and I sink into its bosom. I have but one request to make at my departure from this world, it is – the charity of its silence. Let no man write my epitaph; for as no man, who knows my motives, dare now vindicate them, let not prejudice or ignorance asperse them. Let them rest in obscurity and peace! Let my memory be left in oblivion, and my tomb remain uninscribed, until other times and other men can do justice to my character. When my country takes her place among the nations of the earth, *then*, and *not till then*, let my epitaph be written. I have done.

ROBERT EMMET (1803)

A Life-Long Duel

Dubliners are still shocked by the wickedness of England and go there for a holiday from virtue. The fact is that it is very much a city caught by anxieties, for it is half way between an old way of life and a new one. It is crowded with country people who bring with them the obduracy, the gossipy pleasures of small-town life. Shop assistants gather in corners excitedly whispering, and if an impatient customer calls to them, they turn with offended astonishment at him, wondering who 'the stranger' is as all country girls do, and then turn round and go on whispering. Shops, in the country, are meeting places. Before anything else Dublin is dedicated to gregariousness, to meeting people, to welcome, to the longing to hear who they are and what they will say. As you walk down St Stephen's Green past the Shelbourne or the clubs, indeed as you walk down any street, in the wealthy quarters or the poor, you see the man or woman who is coming towards you pause for a second. They gaze at you perplexedly, search your face, even smile to convey that they wished they knew you, and not knowing you, are puzzled by this break in the natural order. They ache for acquaintance; and if they don't find out who you are they will invent it. This instant *accueil* is part of the charm of Dublin which glows with promises and with promises to mend broken promises, which sparkles with guesses, which loves to agree and reserves the private pleasure of not really agreeing at all. You are in fact walking among the preliminaries of a life-long duel.

V.S. PRITCHETT
from *Dublin* (1991)

Split Loyalties

I think I was about nine or ten when we went to live in Kimmage. The reason for this was, I suspect, that it was safer there than being beside the canal. But I'm not sure why.

Life was a little more difficult for me there because, and I have to say this, on my Jewish side they never made such a fuss about my Catholic side, but the Catholics made an awful fuss about my Jewish side. They would torment me, asking me what I was eating. Of course in the Jewish school they would ask if you ate bacon or did you eat ham, which was a terrible sin. But you got it more on the other side.

Growing up I had two sets of festivals, Passover and Easter, Christmas and Hanukkah, which sounds festive and a great feast, but I always had to keep one set of festivals secret from one part of my friends. So if I was with Jewish friends I couldn't admit that Santa had come to our house because he didn't go to Jewish houses. And if I were with Christian kids I couldn't admit that we celebrated Passover. After all it didn't go down well mentioning Jewish festivals as the Jews had killed Christ.

The result was that growing up in Dublin, after I left my nanny's in Pembroke Road, I was always full of anxiety, of not knowing, of not belonging. So reading Joyce, even though he wasn't recognised, was great in my eyes since he understood what the outcast feels like. The outcast who hasn't done anything. Poor old Bloom! What did he ever do? He didn't do anything but he felt out of it. It's a marvellous portrayal of how people feel when we don't accept them because they're a bit different or they come from a different place.

This is why the women's movement meant so much to me when I was still torn by all that conflict. It was only in the 70s I realised that my people weren't Jews and they weren't Catholics. They were women. This was for me the resolution of that conflict.

JUNE LEVINE
from *Alive, Alive O!* edited by Mairín Johnston (1988)

Paper Tiger

When Adam next took up his place by the Shelbourne Hotel he was warned off by the porter and driven across Kildare Street. And two days after that, striving to establish himself outside one of the clubs nearer Grafton Street, he was challenged by a constable, who demanded a sight of his wares. Though conscious of no guilt, he turned a deaf ear and fled down Dawson Street, only to run into the arms of an inspector, who cuffed him with professional cunning that put to shame the mere heavy-handed violence of his father, and confiscated his whole stock. St Stephen's Green was no longer tenable.

'You done wrong to quarrel with O'Toole!' Mrs Macfadden had a proper pleasure in telling her husband commenting on this catastrophe: 'I warned you that he had the Castle behind him.'

'Castlemiyelbo!' was that strong man's undaunted answer. 'Rutland Square's as good as Saint Stephen's Green any day, and maybe the Gresham Hotel is grander than the Shelbourne if the truth was known...And talking of truth, there the Cat'lic Truth Company second next door to it you might say, where I'd feel a young lad like Adam would be a deal safer selling his papers outside of, than among that bastard O'Toole's fine Prodestan friends on the south side.'

CONAL O'RIORDAN
from *Adam of Dublin* (1920)

A Free Hand

Recruiting Con Houlihan was one of Ward's major contributions to the *Evening Press*. Con has become something of a legend and, as far as the paper is concerned, a big commercial asset. Recruiting him wasn't difficult – the two men met in the Silver Swan – and Ward reckoned quite rightly that if Houlihan could write about sport as he talked about it the result should be interesting. The difficulty lay in keeping him.

Con is a prima donna. Like all performers, he loves adulation. And I suspect that he is heir to a fine legacy of the doubts and insecurities that bedevil even the most brilliant and most successful writers. From the very beginning he was a huge success and within a short time he had the statutory retinue of fans, genuine *aficionados* and hangers-on. The public image has been as carefully cultivated as that of Bernard Shaw. His costume is simple and serviceable – the anorak being *de rigueur* even when working in tropical conditions. Irish sports journalists have (with some justification) been described as 'fans with typewriters'. Con has no typewriter – he has consistently refused to recognise the invention. His copy is handwritten, a single paragraph to the page.

As with all celebrities, there is a gulf between the public and private person. Con's public image is of a wild, dishevelled and highly disorganised man. Dishevelled he sometimes may be – wild and disorganised he certainly is not. Few journalists are as disciplined or as single-minded as Con. Unlike most newspaper journalists he corrects his own proofs, working meticulously through the computer print-outs and threatening resignation if the slightest corrections are not immediately attended to. His prose can be as spare as Hemingway's and like all great professionals, he makes the finished product look simple and effortless.

He has made an enormous contribution to the *Evening Press* – and not only in terms of attracting and holding on to readers. Like his hero William Hazlitt, he is the common man blessed with extraordinary powers of perception and expression. His wide learning and love of literature have rubbed off on many a colleague. Like many of those who are 'come of Kerry clay and rock' there is a roughish side to him. In the early days he was prone to tantrums, particularly around the time his contract came up for renewal. On those occasions he would insist that the call to the bog or to the potato field was too strong to resist. At the oddest of hours he would phone the editor

at home and announce that he was on his way to Castle Island
and that he wouldn't be back. Fortunately for the *Evening Press*
and for all of us who work there, Con hasn't carried out his threat.

MICHAEL O'TOOLE
from *More Kicks Than Pence* (1992)

Elegy for Jim Larkin
Died February 1947

Not with public words can his greatness
Be told to children, for he was more
Than labour agitator, mob orator
The flashing fiery sword merely was witness
To the sun rising. Cried Larkin: Look!
The fields are producing for you and the trees;
And beyond are not the serf stockland, but seas
Rolling excitement in God's Poetry Book.
When the full moon's in the river the ghost of bread
Must not be in all your weary trudgings home.
The masts of once black galleys will become
Fir forests under the North's glittering Plough,
And the rusty gantries, the heroic ahead
With man the magician whom the gods endow.
It was thus I heard Jim Larkin shout above
The crowd who would have him turn aside
From the day's shocking reality. Their morphine pride
Hid in the fogs of unhope and would not move –
The smoke and the drug of the newspaper story;
And with mouths open they were glad to stare
Not at a blackbird, but a millionaire
Whose two-year olds ran off with all their worry –
Though battoned by policemen into Dublin's garbage.
Jim Larkin opened a window wide
And wings flew out and offered to slow rising things
A lift onto high altars with proud carriage.
And they swayed above the city in young knowledge
And they ate the loaf that nourishes great kings.

PATRICK KAVANAGH
from *Complete Poems* (1972)

The Failure of Jim Larkin

Big Jim is not among the makers of modern Ireland. And if his ghost
stalks – as in one sense or another it will always continue to stalk
– the streets of Dublin, it must be at least as much a disconsolate
and forlorn as a triumphant or a happy spirit.

In saying this of course one can hardly be other than aware that
a building called 'Liberty Hall' dominates the skyline; that trade
union membership is in the region of 400,000; that the standard
of living of manual workers (and of a great many other people too)
bears no relationship to that of 1907 or 1913; that the old tenement
slums, which in the year of his death still encroached on Stephen's
Green, have been abolished; and that the power of organised union-
ism is felt in every branch of industry.

*　　*　　*

There is no question of course but that he would be pleased with
the changes in material conditions such as they are, and whatever
their degree of absoluteness or relativity. That he had himself a
firm grasp of the economic side of unionism is indubitable: indeed
it was in this firm grasp of the difference between betterment and
the status quo ante that much of his great greatness lies. And as
far as the other things are concerned, nothing that his enemies said
of him was truer than that when he sought a wider application of
his vision he almost invariably turned out to be both disruptive
and destructive. Not only was it true that he was rather an inept
politician; but it was also very obviously the case that, like many a
socialist before and since, he had no clear grasp of how, or by what
means, a transition to socialism was to be managed. R.M. Fox said
he 'belonged to the English school of Socialism' in the sense that
he 'always had a disregard for social theory', and, indeed, though
almost every utterance that Big Jim ever made proves that he under-
stood quite clearly and passionately what socialism was, almost
every other utterance proves that he had likewise only very hazy
ideas as to how it might come about.

*　　*　　*

Trade union leadership is on the whole, in a way that would have
shocked Larkin, content with things as they are; nor does it ever
seriously envisage the weapons in its armoury as weapons to bring
about a complete transformation of society along socialist lines.

No less than does its equivalent in Britain, established Irish trade union leadership would, by all the signs, retreat from the brink if the brink ever appeared in view; and in the sense that the organisations that sprang from his living word do not share his living vision, Jim Larkin is a failure.

But the failure, whether it is primarily a matter of union leadership or not, goes deeper. Larkin himself did not want a trade union leadership which would drag its organised members into a struggle for change which would only distract from its immediate betterment or lead to the collapse of its immediate hopes. He was never guilty of playing with the working class in the sense which the common contemporary description of him as an agitator would suggest, or the way in which certain middle-class socialists who look upon it unrealistically as a weapon of their individual dreams would like to do. But every time he brought workers out for better wages he was at pains to emphasise that their action was bringing an end of the wages system itself a day or two nearer. Every time he spoke of class betterment he spoke also of liberation from the chains of class itself. The strike may have been a primary weapon; but the primary object remained an awakening which would go beyond the immediate causes of the strike or the immediate conditions of its settlement. That awakening, for whatever reason, has not come about, and though ultimately conservative theorists may continue to suggest that revolutionary aspirations will always vanish when the Hondas and the coloured television sets come within people's grasp, to say that that happens in any country where it does happen (and it must be emphasised over and over again that it does not happen universally or even in countries near at hand) may be simple to put the blame more squarely where it lies: with the leadership of the working class, whether trade union or parliamentary.

That leadership has certainly on balance failed Larkin and failed in what used to be called Larkinism. The causes of the failure may be many and, as far as the leadership is concerned, they may reside in part at least in the tangled history of the splits which Big Jim had his part in creating. But it exists nonetheless, and the consciousness of it should be present – no less than his ghost itself – in this city at this time. Big Jim was a socialist; and while it may be true that reasons other than a growth in the revolutionary consciousness of the working class may help to bring socialism about; it cannot come about without it or in spite of its absence. The extent of its absence may or may not be the measure of the degree to which, even with their access to the media, their educative activities and everything else, his successors have failed him; but to that extent anyway, he has had little or no influence on the making of modern Ireland.

ANTHONY CRONIN
from *An Irish Eye* (1985)

Quakers

The Religious Society of Friends was introduced into Ireland in 1654. Most of the early adherents came over from Britain with the various waves of Protestant settlers. These Quakers were mainly tradesmen, merchants and farmers.

Down the centuries the Friends took an active role in the commercial and philanthropic life of Ireland and some Quaker families, including those of Pim, Jacob, Bewley, Walpole, Webb and Haughton, became household names in Dublin.

During the Great Hunger of 1846/7 a group of Quakers formed a Central Relief Committee and soup kitchens were opened throughout the country. To help the starving poor to become more self sufficient, the committee also distributed tons of seeds to farmers and grant-aid to fishermen.

The Dublin Quakers, obliged by the Penal Laws not to open any meeting house on a main street, first met in Bride's Alley (beside St Nicholas Street), moved to Wormwood Gate (near Bridge St), next to Cole's Alley (Meath Street) and finally to Sycamore Alley in 1692.

In 1705 they purchased a plot on the developing Eustace Street and over the next one hundred and fifty years they merged and expanded the buildings between Sycamore and Eustace Streets. About ten years ago the Quakers relinquished Number 6 and moved their meetings next door.

Imaginatively restored and adapted, Number 6 now houses the Irish Film Centre which opened on the 27 September 1992. Contained within are: two cinemas, the Irish Film Archive, ten film organisations, educational and conference facilities and a film library. The design is by architects O'Donnell and Twomey and the main contractors were Cleary and Doyle.

PAT LIDDY
from *Temple Bar* (1992)

A Tolerant City

Oliver Cromwell had received an enthusiastic reception because he had been cheered into a Protestant city. Ormonde's departure in 1647 had initiated a pogrom in which Catholics were expelled. In 1651 Colonel John Hewson observed that Dublin had formerly swarmed with Papists, but now 'I know none there but one who is a surgeon and a peaceable man'. The policy of expulsion continued under the Commonwealth. An edict of 1650 declared that 'all Papists are to be turned out of this city; and for the Jesuits, priests, friars, monks and nuns, £20 will be given to anyone that can bring certain intelligence where any of them are'. A few priests took on disguise, but Catholics who stayed risked death, like Edward Hetherington who was tried by court martial in St Patrick's Cathedral in 1655 and hanged with placards on his breast and back which read: 'for not transplanting'. However, nothing could keep people from outside coming into the city, and edicts forbidding them to approach within two miles of any walled town or garrison soon proved impracti-cable. For a time they were registered – name, age, and appearance were noted – and issued with licences that allowed them to stay in the city up to twenty days. But such policies proved ineffective. In October 1656 there were instructions that 'all Popish shoemakers to be searched for by the Mayor and Sheriffs of Dublin and not to be allowed to inhabit Dublin and its suburbs'. Six months later Protestant coopers complained that Irish coopers were still present in the city. By then ancient complaints were being repeated in the Assembly Rolls which noted that 'there is Irish commonlie and usuallie spoken and the Irish Habbit worne not onlye in the streetes and by such as live in the countrie and come to this cittie...which is highly provoking of God which may justly cause the plague and other judgements to seize upon this cittie'.

Quakers were also persecuted from the time their meetings were first held in 1655 in the house of a tailor named George Lathan. Many were imprisoned like John Perrot who in 1656 wrote from his prison in Dublin to Henry Cromwell complaining of 'my share of suffering and persecution I have & doe under goe as well by beating, threatenings and Cruell mockings & scoffings as by imprisonment & tryalls and hallings before Rulers and Magistrates but all being for the Lord's sake'. His pleas did him little good; later he suffered another spell of imprisonment in the 'Common Gaole of the fower Courtes, Dublin'. It was Henry Cromwell who first advocated sending undesirables as slaves to Jamaica. In 1659 instructions were given to beadles and constables 'to imprison all beggars, idle women and maidens sellinge apples and oranges, and all regraters, all idle boys...others trafficked in eggs, hens and various commodities'. They were enclosed in a large cage in the Cornmarket for examination and punishment – in many cases deportation to the West Indian plantations.

PETER SOMERVILLE-LARGE
from *Dublin, The First 1000 Years* (1988)

The Life of Riley

Lord Cloncurry wrote from his recollections of Dublin before the Union that it was

> one of the most agreeable places of residence in Europe. There were no conveniences belonging to a capital in these days which it did not possess. Society in the upper classes was as brilliant and polished as that of Paris in its best days, while social intercourse was conducted with a conviviality that could not be equalled in France.

People in upper-class society in Ireland in the eighteenth century were really very much the same as elsewhere. 'There are great numbers of the principal people residing in Ireland,' wrote Arthur Young, 'who are as liberal in their ideas as any people in Europe... a man may go into a vast variety of families which he will find actuated by no other principles than those of the most cultivated politeness and the most liberal urbanity.' And Mrs Delany, writing of Dublin earlier in the century, says, 'As for the generality of people that I meet with here, they are much the same as in England – a mixture of good and bad; all that I have met with behave themselves very decently, according to their rank, now and then an oddity breaks out, but none so extraordinary but that I can match them in England.' She was especially struck, however, by the 'great sociableness' of the people she came across. 'There is a heartiness among them,' she says, 'is more like *Cornwall* than any I have known.' Every one who has left a record of a visit to Dublin during the period seems to have been of the same opinion. All were impressed by the air of gaiety in the houses of the well-to-do which went with a peculiarly splendid way of living – a multiplicity of servants, great profusion of dishes on the table, abundant wine.

Bishop Berkeley noticed that while in England many gentlemen with a thousand a year never drank wine in their houses, in Ireland this could hardly be said of any who had but a hundred a year, and he demands in *The Querist* 'whether any kingdom in Europe be so good a customer at Bordeaux as Ireland?'

*   *   *

Indulgence in claret and port was not the only symptom of that extravagance which brought the descendants of so many Irish gentry of the period into the Incumbered Estates Court, for their meals also were so prodigious that one marvels at their digestive capacity. 'High Living is too much the fashion here,' wrote Mrs Delany from Delville, her villa near Dublin, in 1752. 'You are not invited to dinner to any private gentleman of £1000 a year or less, that does not give you seven dishes at one course, and Burgundy and Champagne; and these dinners they give once or twice a week.' She and her husband entertained a great deal, and often had as many as twenty persons to dinner, but, although she complains on several occasions of lack of means, her own menus as given in her memoirs are quite remarkable. For four guests – Primate Stone and his sister and the Bishop of Derry and his wife – she provided as follows. The first course consisted of 'Fish – beefsteaks – soup – rabbits and onions – Fillet Veal.' In the second course was included 'Turkey Pout – salmon grilde – pickled salmon – quails – little Terrene Peas – Cream – Mushrooms – Apple Pye – Crab – Leveret – Cheese-cakes'. For the 'Dessert' they had 'Blamange – Cherries – Dutch Cheese – Raspberries and Cream – sweetmeats and jelly – strawberries and cream – almond cream – currants and gooseberries – Orange Butter'. Another menu detailed in a letter from Delville (6 October 1764) for twelve persons, including the Delanys themselves, was as follows: 'Turbot and Soles, remove Ham; Force meat etc; two partridges and two grouse; rabbits and onions; Pies, sweetbreads and crumbs; Salmigundi; Soup; Boiled chicken; Collop veal and olives; pease; Cream Pudding; Plumb Crocant; Chine of Mutton; Turkey in jelly; Hare; Lobster Fricassée.' The items here are not divided into "courses", but there is a note under 'Dessert': 'Nine things – six of them fruit out of our own garden, and a plate of fine Alpine Strawberries.'

CONSTANTIA MAXWELL
from *Dublin Under The Georges* (1979)

Dublin Country

Every dairy shop in Dublin was like a little bit of the country. The smell of fresh buttermilk, the big white bowls of milk with muslin cloths to keep out the Dublin house flies, the 56 pound blocks of butter and the wooden butter knives standing in a tall delph jug with ice cool water. The marble top counters and shelves and the cat sipping in the window. The sign of the cat was the sign of fresh milk and a decent dairy woman. It was like magic, the way the butter knives cut into the big blocks of butter and took out the right amount and weighed it on the round white marble scales with shining brass weights. Then the butter was slapped about with the knives and made into the shape of a square box. The final touch came when the little lines of the butter knives left their mark on the butter. Every dairy had, at least, three dairy boys, the boys were over seventy years of age. They milked the cows and delivered the milk on bicycles. The dairy girls were a few years younger. Mary Gartlin was a dairy girl, she milked the cows in Goldenbridge Farm and delivered the milk all around Inchicore and Kilmainham. She'd fly down the Emmet Road like Stanley Woods, the motor bike racer, with three big cans of milk on the handle bars of her bike. She never needed a bell as the pint, half pint, and tilly measures rattled against the milk cans. The tilly was a little extra free milk, a sup for the cat.

I suppose, too, the country in Dublin, was in the form of the Church, the bank, the law, canal horses, Guiney's and education. Our parish priest was from County Kildare, the bank manager, not that we needed him, was a Sligo man, the local sergeant of police was a Mayo man. The canal horses always looked happier when they were heading towards the country than when they were coming into Dublin.

EAMONN MACTHOMÁIS
from *Janey Mack Me Shirt Is Black* (1982)

A Tolerant City II

– Mendelssohn was a jew and Karl Marx and Mercadante and
Spinoza. And the Saviour was a jew and his father was a jew. Your
God.

– He had no father, says Martin. That'll do now. Drive ahead.

– Whose God? says the citizen.

– Well, his uncle was a jew, says he. Your God was a jew. Christ
was a jew like me.

Gob, the citizen made a plunge back into the shop.

– By Jesus, says he, I'll brain that bloody jewman for using the
holy name. By Jesus, I'll crucify him so I will. Give us that biscuit-
box here.

– Stop! Stop! says Joe.

JAMES JOYCE
from *Ulysses* (1922)

Dublin Made Me

Dublin made me and no little town
With the country closing in on its streets,
The cattle walking proudly on its pavements,
The jobbers, the gombeenmen and the cheats

Devouring the Fair Day between them,
A public-house to half a hundred men,
And the teacher, the solicitor and the bank-clerk
In the hotel bar, drinking for ten.

Dublin made me, not the secret poteen still,
The raw and hungry hills of the West,
The lean road flung over profitless bog
Where only a snipe could nest,

Where the sea takes its tithe of every boat.
Bawneen and curragh have no allegiance of mine,
Nor the cute, self-deceiving talkers of the South
Who look to the East for a sign.

The soft and dreary midlands with their tame canals
Wallow between sea and sea, remote from adventure,
And Northward a far and fortified province
Crouches under the lash of arid censure.

I disclaim all fertile meadows, all tilled land,
The evil that grows from it, and the good,
But the Dublin of old statutes, this arrogant city,
Stirs proudly and secretly in my blood.

DONAGH MacDONAGH
from *The Hungry Grass* (1947)

Dublin

Grey brick upon brick,
Declamatory bronze
On sombre pedestals –
O'Connell, Grattan, Moore –
And the brewery tugs and the swans
On the balustraded stream
And the bare bones of a fanlight
Over a hungry door
And the air soft on the cheek
And porter running from the taps
With a head of yellow cream
And Nelson on his pillar
Watching his world collapse.

This was never my town,
I was not born nor bred
Nor schooled here and she will not
Have me alive or dead
But yet she holds my mind
With her seedy elegance,
With her gentle veils of rain
And all her ghosts that walk
And all that hide behind
Her Georgian façades –
The catcalls and the pain,

The glamour of her squalor,
The bravado of her talk.

The lights jig in the river
With a concertina movement
And the sun comes up in the morning
Like barley-sugar on the water
And the mist on the Wicklow hills
Is close, as close
As the peasantry were to the landlord,
As the Irish to the Anglo-Irish,
As the killer is close one moment
To the man he kills,
Or as the moment itself
Is close to the next moment.

She is not an Irish town
And she is not English,
Historic with guns and vermin
And the cold renown
Of a fragment of Church latin,
Of an oratorical phrase.
But oh the days are soft,
Soft enough to forget
The lesson better learnt,
The bullet on the wet
Streets, the crooked deal,
The steel behind the laugh,
The Four Courts burnt.

Fort of the Dane,
Garrison of the Saxon,
Augustan capital
Of a Gaelic nation,
Appropriating all
The alien brought,
You give me time for thought
And by a juggler's trick
You poise the toppling hour –
O greyness run to flower,
Grey stone, grey water,
And brick upon grey brick.

LOUIS MacNEICE
from 'The Closing Album' (August–September 1939)

The Ecstasy of Pity

I remember coming out of St Patrick's, Sunday after Sunday, strained almost to torture by the music, and walking out through the slums of Harold's Cross as the lamps were being lit. Hordes of wild children used to play around the cathedral of St Patrick and I remember there was something appalling – a proximity of emotions as conflicting as the perversions of the Black Mass – in coming out suddenly from the white harmonies of the Passion according to St Matthew among this blasphemy of childhood. The boys and girls were always in groups by themselves, for the utterly wild boy seems to regard a woman with the instinct of barbarians. I often stood for hours in a shadow to watch their manoeuvres and extraordinarily passionate quarrels...

If we find in Bach an agreeable vibration of some portion of the brain and in the study of these children the vibration of another portion a little inferior – the attitude of science – we loose in the music our transcendent admiration, and in the slums the ecstasy of pity and with it the thin relish of delightful sympathy with the wildness of evil which all feel but few acknowledge even to themselves. The man who feels most exquisitely the joy of contact with what is perfect in art and nature is the man who from the width and power of his thought hides the greatest number of Satanic or barbarous sympathies. His opposite is the narrow churchman or reformer who knows no ecstasy and is shocked chiefly by the material discomforts of earth or Hell...

J.M. SYNGE
from *Autobiography* (1896-1907)

Inside Out

Cathleen originally comes from Finglas in Dublin and married Pat when she was seventeen. They had five children in as many years, once of whom died. She was twenty-three when he was arrested in 1985. She visited her husband in prison in England for five years after his arrest but eventually it all became too much for her, and she stopped visiting and formed another relationship. 'I'll still support him any way I can,' she said 'He's still my husband. I still care about him a lot.'

'The visits were terrible. I went once on the boat with the kids and I was ready for a nervous breakdown when I got back. Then I had to get a doctor's letter to get the money for the plane from the brew. They ask you, "Are you sure you're taking the kids over?" You go down with the doctor's letter to the brew, then to the travel agent, then arrange transport to Belfast to get the plane. I always took two children, and the four at Christmas. The kids would be crying.'

'The last few visits were not very good. Every year I was bringing some bad news; there were deaths in the family or something. God knows how he feels.' The relationship was not very strong anyway. 'We were only seventeen when we married. He didn't understand me, I had a kid every year. I had five kids when I was twenty-two. He said to the kids once, "I don't know why I got married but I grew to love your mother".'

'It was my thirtieth birthday last year, and I didn't even get a card. The kids never got birthday cards, and it means so much to the kids. Things like that got me down. The wains were always upset around the visits. They didn't know whether they were coming or going. They'd be over in their granny's; they were always over and back. And all for what? To be depressed when you got back? With all the hassle, even if we had a good relationship I don't think I could have held out. I'd been on my own so long. You need a friend, you need someone to talk to. The kids were still being punished. They had no daddy to turn to and I had no one to help me with the kids.'

Then Cathleen formed another relationship and got pregnant. 'I was only six stone last Christmas, I lost that much weight with worry. I was five months pregnant. I was embarrassed all the time. People would be looking at the bump and saying, 'poor Pat, poor Pat.' But saying that, there's hardly anyone on the street didn't buy that child something when she was born. I was going to give her away, you know.' She turned to the six-month old baby asleep in the living room. 'I wouldn't swap you for the world. Even if I was split up she was the best thing ever happened.'

She told Pat, and he was prepared to accept the baby. 'He said, 'After all I did to you, it's the least I can do.' But by now her relationship with the baby's father was steady, and she told him that, though she is not sure what will happen in the future. 'I just want to be friends with Pat, be able to write to him and visit him as a friend, but Liam [her boyfriend] won't hear of it.

'I don't know what's around the corner for me, if this is a long-term relationship for me. My head's going round and round. I don't know where I am. Sometimes I feel I can't go on, that I'll do myself in; but you get the strength from somewhere. I don't know what's going to happen in the future. I get tired about everything sometimes. All I wanted was a good family and to love my kids and be happy.'

'I feel I've achieved nothing with my life. I've reared kids, kept a home and been a skivvy. That's what my life was about and at the end of the day I hope I'll be appreciated. I wasn't bright. I wanted them to be brighter than me, to do things. I hope to God they don't follow my footsteps. I put them off marriage. I say, "Don't waste your lives". I would dread it if Ciara [*her eldest*] came in and said she was pregnant. I'll never want her to get married even if that happens. She should live with the guy and see what she wants.'

'That baby feels like mine. I don't remember having the rest of them, I don't remember being pregnant. Now Ciara is more help with that baby than he was with them.'

CAROL COULTER
from *Web of Punishment* (1991)

Rags and Riches

There was a treatise written about nine years ago to persuade the people of Ireland to wear their own manufactures. This treatise had not one syllable in it of party or disaffection, but was wholly founded on the growing poverty of the nation, occasioned by the utter want of trade in every branch, except that ruinous importation of all foreign extravagancies from other countries. The treatise was presented, by the Grand-jury of the city and county of Dublin, as a scandalous, seditious, and factious pamphlets. I forget who was the foreman of the city Grand-jury, but the foreman for the county was one Doctor Seal, register to the Archbishop of Dublin, wherein he differed much from the sentiments of his Lord. The printer was tried before the late Mr Whitshed, that famous Lord Chief-Justice; who, on the bench, laying his hand on his heart, declared on his salvation that the author was a jacobite, and had a design to beget a quarrel between the two nations. In the midst of this prosecution, about 1500 weavers were forced to beg their bread, and had a general contribution made for their relief, which just served to make them drunk for a week; and then they were forced to turn rogues, or strolling beggars, or to leave the kingdom.

The Duke of Grafton, who was then Lieutenant, being perfectly ashamed of so infamous and unpopular a proceeding, obtained from England a *noli prosequi* for the printer. Yet the Grand-jury had solemn thanks given them from the secretary of State.

I mention this passage (perhaps too much forgotten) to show how dangerous it has been for the best-meaning person to write one syllable in the defence of his country, or complain of the miserable condition it is in.

JONATHAN SWIFT
from *A Proposal that all the Ladies... should appear constantly in Irish Manufacture* (1729)

Jobs for the Boys

The growth of the trade combinations in Dublin among skilled male artisans in the mid and late eighteenth century threatened women's access to workshop employment. Journeymen came to view their interests within a trade as distinct from those of the masters who flouted the apprenticeship conventions disappeared. The threat posed to skilled artisans by the growth of an unskilled labour force in the city caused many journeymen combinations to agitate against the employment of women and of outsiders in the same breath. Giving evidence to the Commons' Grand Committee of Trade in 1782 when it was investigting the activities of Irish combinations, one Dublin worsted manufacturer pointed out that combinations in that trade in the 1760s and after had caused all the city women to lose their jobs for no reason other than the fact that male journeymen felt 'the women had not a right to work at men's work, it was their inheritance'. The fact that the manufacturer in question felt that 'the women did most parts of the weaving better than the men, more diligently and cleaner', may have been a reason for the male employees' discontent. Did the well-entrenched male weavers see women workers, lacking the experience of assertive collective action, as too inclined to accept lower wages and poorer conditions? In 1820 journeymen tailors demanded from their employers a prohibition on the introduction of women or of 'unqualified' men into the trade. One master tailor noted in 1836 that 'the regulations among the

journeymen tailors prevent the employment of women in any branch
of that trade. There have been many times when the men would
strike in any shop which gave employment to women.' The evidence
of a shipbuilder in the same year echoed this: 'About fifteen years
ago I had a woman in my employ who had been threatened in
consequence of working at the trade – I found it necessary to escort
her to her lodgings.'

IMELDA BROPHY
from *The Gorgeous Mask: Dublin 1700-1850*
edited by David Dickson (1987)

Dublin 4 Thought

To be of Dublin 4 does not necessarily entail actually living in a
particular part of Dublin, or even, strictly speaking, living in Dublin
at all. To be a Dublin 4 'type' you require only to think in a particular
way, which essentially is to think only of yourself and your own
immediate interests. Dublin 4 types are left wing on social issues
but right wing on economic issues. Over the past decade, Dublin
4 has used these issues to provoke war after war with what it perceives
as the backward forces in Irish life. In reality it is conducting a war
among forces which it itself has created, which have little currency
outside its boundaries. In a sense, because Dublin 4 people are at
most one generation removed from the country, the war is waged
against the D4 type's own roots and background. They are people
embarrassed about not having emanated from a culture more in
keeping with their present position, and take their impatience out
on those they perceive to be too backward to climb the same ladder
as themselves. Everybody could be like them, they insist, just so
long as we agree to do things their way.

Inevitably, the Dublin 4 type is hated by the rest of the country,
with the result that, even when D4 occasionally comes up with
good ideas – as occasionally it does – the very fact of its sponsorship
ensures the roundest possible rejection by the population at large.

Dublin 4, however, has had one famous victory in recent years.
In the early 90s, it became the official sponsor of the drive to – as
the expression had it – 'reform the nation's finances'. As a result
of our troglodyte political practices, we were told, the country was
on the brink of bankruptcy. We had, in that famous phrase of the

time, been 'living beyond our means'. Through the medium of the Doheny & Nesbitt School of Economics, Dublin 4 succeeded in feeding its ideas about the economy intravenously into the political system. Fiscal rectitude became big in Irish politics, and close links were forged between politicians, economists and journalists, who between them succeeded in hijacking the entire political and social agenda and making it a vehicle for the views which, though they ensured the immediate survival of those who promoted them, had little to offer in terms of the long-term well-being of the country as a whole. Such was their power and influence, that no politician or political party seemed willing to break with this self-imposed consensus. Cutbacks became the order of the day and the catchcry of the time. Needless to say, most of the cutbacks occurred in places far removed from the habitats of Dublin 4. Ignoring the obvious contradictions under their very noses, these people insisted that all activity outside Dublin not just pay for itself, but be seen to pay for itself. They seemed wilfully blind to the obvious fact that, as an agricultural nation, we required, first and foremost, a vibrant rural life. Dublin may make a pretty cherry on top, but if there is no cake to hold it up, the cherry will roll off and end up in the dustbin.

JOHN WATERS
from 'Who's Afraid of Change? Irish Politics in the 1990s',
Letters from the New Island, edited by Dermot Bolger (1991)

Another World

The cellar was very spacious: I should think that the entrance into Dante's Inferno was paradise compared with it. I know and have known Dublin now for about half a century, better probably than any other man in it. I have lived in the Liberty and in every close and outlet in the City of the Panniers, driven by poverty to the most wretched of its localities, and I must confess that the scene which burst upon me that night stands beyond anything the highest flight of my imagination could have conceived without me having an opportunity of seeing it. Burns must have witnessed something of the sort, or he could never have written the most graphic and animated of all his productions – 'The Jolly Beggars'.

The inhabitants of Dublin, and even strangers, are in the habit of listening to the importunities of those irreclaimable beggars whom no law can keep from the streets of ballad-singers, strolling fiddlers, pipers, flute-players, and the very considerable variety of that class which even now, when we have to pay poor-rates, continue to infest our thoroughfares. What must not the city have been, however, before the enactment of poor-laws? Why, at that period, there existed in Dublin two distinct worlds, each as ignorant of the other – at least, in a particular point of view, and during certain portions of the day – as if they did not inhabit the same country. I have heard many a man of sense and intellect ask, before the establishment of poor-laws, where the vast crowds of paupers passed the night; I never heard the question satisfactorily answered. On that night, however, I found a solution of it, and ever since it has been no mystery to me.

When I got down to the cellar, and looked about me, I was struck, but only for an instant, by the blazing fire which glowed in the grate. My eyes then ran over the scene about me, but how to describe it is the difficulty. It resembled nothing I ever saw either before or since. The inmates were mostly in bed, both men and women, but still a good number of them were up, and indulging in liquors of every description, from strong whisky downwards. The beds were mostly what are called 'shakedowns' – that is, simple straw, sometimes with a rag of sheet, and sometimes with none. There were there the lame, the blind, the dumb, and all who suffered from actual and natural infirmity; but in addition to these, there was every variety of impostor about me – most of them stripped of their mechanical accessories of deceit, but by no means all. If not seen, the character of those assembled and their conduct could not possibly be believed. This was half a century ago, when Dublin was swarming with beggars and street impostors of every possible description. This, I understood afterwards, was one of the cellars to which these persons resorted at night, and there they flung off all the restraints imposed on them during the course of the day. I learned afterwards that there were upwards of two dozen such nightly haunts in the suburban parts of the city. Crutches, wooden legs, artificial cancers, scrofulous necks, artificial wens, sore legs, and a vast variety of similar complaints, were hung up upon the walls of the cellars, and made me reflect upon the degree of perverted talent and ingenuity that must have been necessary to sustain such a mighty mass of imposture. Had the same amount of intellect, thought I, been devoted to the exercise of honest and virtuous industry, how much advantage in the shape of energy and example might not society have derived from it. The songs and gestures were infamous, but if one thing puzzled me more than another, it was the fluency and originality of black-guardism as expressed in language. In fact these people possessed an indecent slang, which constituted a kind of language known only to themselves, and was never spoken except at such orgies as I am describing. Several offered me seats, and were very respectful; but I preferred standing, at least for a time, that I might have a better view of them. While I was in this position a couple of young vagabonds – pickpockets, of course – came and stood beside me. Instinct told me their object, but as I knew the amount in my purse – one penny – I felt little apprehension of having my pockets picked. On entering the cellar, I had to pay twopence for my bed, so that I had just one penny left.

How the night passed I need not say. Of course I never closed my eyes; but so soon as the first glimpse of anything like light appeared, I left the place, and went out on my solitary rambles through the city.

WILLIAM CARLETON
from *The Life of William Carleton* (1896)

From Monaghan to the Grand Canal

I have been thinking of making my grove on the banks of the Grand Canal near Baggot Street Bridge where in recent days I rediscovered my roots. My hegira was to the Grand Canal bank where again I saw the beauty of water and green grass and the magic of light. It was the same emotion as I had known when I stood on a sharp slope in Monaghan, where I imaginatively stand now, looking across to Slieve Gullion and South Armagh. An attractive landscape of small farms and a culture that hadn't changed in a thousand years. A hundred yards away from me I could observe primitive husbandry where Paddy Nugent was threshing oats with a flail in a barn. But something disturbs my imagination.

I am thinking of a term which was much in use in the early days of my life in Dublin. He has roots in the soil, they used to say. I was one of those who had an unchallenged right to claim roots in the soil, but I was an exception and the rooted in the soil theory gave birth to a vast amount of bogusry – in Ireland, writers like Michael McLaverty, and in England, H.E. Bates and indeed Thomas Hardy. Could any man be more remote from the simple, elemental folk of Wessex than Hardy?

Roots in the soil meant that you knew about people living close to nature, struggling for survival on the small farm, and you had a practical knowledge of animal breeding.

But of course roots in the soil have nothing to do with these things. What are our roots? What is our material?

Real roots lie in our capacity for love and its abandon. The material itself has no special value; it is what our imagination and our love does to it.

Lying at the heart of love we wander through its infinities.

*   *   *

When I came to Dublin the dregs of the Literary Revival were still stirrable. The Palace Bar was crowded with two or three dozen poets and their admirers. I do not wish now to be satirical about these men. I am speaking about them now as part of my literary pilgrimage. Here the Movement which I thought quite discredited was being talked about. When I came to Dublin, Yeats was dead. Yeats was a poet and he invented many writers. He invented Synge and Lady Gregory and he was largely responsible for F.R. Higgins. As George Moore wrote: 'The Irish Literary Movement began with Yeats and returned to him.'

During my early years in Dublin the virtue of being a peasant was much extolled. This peasant derived naturally from the roots in the soil theory. Knowing nothing better, I accepted it and flaunted my peasantry in their somewhat spivvier genealogies.

Poor Higgins tried hard to play the peasant with bad poems about blackthorn sticks. The ballad was the peasant's poetic form. I suffered sore at ballad-mongering sessions before I realised that this form of torture was no different from the self-expression of any bore from the golf bore to the architect and cricket bore. Ballad singing is all right for the singer, but will he ever stop and give the others an innings?

I was the established peasant poet. Far from the poet being a peasant – if there is such an article outside the Russian novel – he is the last word in sophistication. All his life's activities are towards the final fusion of all crudeness into a pure flame. The keynote of the poetic mind is an extreme subtlety.

All this stuff about roots in the soil, peasants and balladry was no doubt the degenerate family of the pre-Raphaelites, coupled, by the time I came to know them, with the left-wingery of the International Brigade of the Spanish Civil War. I cannot deny that I subscribed my quota of "working class" jargon. Somebody recently embarrassed me by reminding me of a poem I had printed in *Ireland Today* about a servant boy. Oh my goodness! Well, we live and sometimes learn.

With a small society lacking intensity like this, one needs a coarse formula, if we are to have any body of writing. And that is what we have had for the past fifty years.

I cannot help saying that as far as I can see and as far as I have experienced, there has never been a tradition of poetry in Ireland. One can feel this lack of belief all the time.

And now raising my eyes to the horizon I am again looking across the small fields of South Monaghan and South Armagh, and wondering did any of the Irish writers who claimed to bring realism instead of the old sentimentalities ever express the society that lies within my gaze, with the exception of my own small effort in *Tarry Flynn*?

I am not suggesting that being true to life in a realist way is the highest function of a writer. As I have pointed out already the highest function is the pure flame from the material.

The writers who wrote about Ireland in the new "truthful" way proved to be no truer than the popular sentimentalisers such as Kickham and Canon Sheehan; they all seemed off-truth. This is not surprising, for most men who attempt to write about a particular society are deluded as to their qualifications for the job. For example, Mr Peadar O'Donnell has written novels about Donegal. It seems at once *his* country, but is it? Similarly there is a group who write about Galway and another about Cork and another about Kerry. Yet another school believe that in Dublin with its unique *clichés* and way of life is a ready-built band wagon on which to ride to literary success. Any critic whether from Dublin or Soho can see that this stuff is just noisy emptiness, completely unfunny.

It took me many years to work myself free from that formula for literature which laid all the stress on whether it was Irish or not. For twenty years I wrote according to the dispensation of this Irish school. The appraisers of the school all agreed that I had my roots in the soil, was one of the people and that I was an authentic voice. I wrote, for example, a terrible piece about –

> My soul was an old horse
> Offered for sale in twenty fairs;
> I offered him to the Church, the buyers
> Were little men who feared his unusual airs.

One can at once see the embarrassing impertinence and weakness of it, the dissolute character whining. But it was the perfect Irish formula and English publishers loved it. Nothing would satisfy them but to put it first in the book. There has always been a big market in England for the synthetic Irish thing. Even Shaw who was a bogus Irishman had to do a bit of clowning.

Another villainous maw opened for things Irish-and-proud-of-it is the American literary market. The stuff that gets published as Irish in America is quite awful. One of the great, roaring successes of American publishing a couple of years ago was a novel by Brian Moore about some Irish girl who had a vast number of illegitimate children. In reviewing this book (and books of this kind) none leaned further back in referring to its compassion, its humour and its many other qualities than the Catholic papers. They seem terrified that they will be outdone in the liberal ethic race. A dreary dust of left-wingery, a formula which excludes all creative thought, lies over the vegetation. They feel, I suppose, that literary and thought politics, like all other politics, is the philosophy of the possible. What's the use in being different if you can't get your words printed? Still.

In Ireland one is up against the fact that very few care for or understand the creative spirit. You can come across by being specifically Irish in manner and spirit, but when you attempt to offer them the real thing it's no go.

When I started to write what I believe is the real thing there was not much response, except possibly from Stephen Spender who described it as 'violently beautiful'.

PATRICK KAVANAGH
from *Collected Pruse* (1967)

A Precipice

In the ball-room as in the forest, the female is most easily assailed when guarding her young, and nowhere in the whole animal kingdom is this fact so well exemplified as in Dublin Castle.

*   *   *

During the season in Dublin it is found convenient to give teas: the young ladies have to be introduced to the men they will meet afterwards at the Castle. These gatherings take place at five o'clock in the afternoon; and as Mrs Barton passed along the streets on her way to Lady Georgina's, she reflected on the appearance of the town. Its present animation she declared could not be taken as in the least representative of the normal condition of things. Once the Castle season ended, all would lapse into the usual state of torpor and indifference.

'I assure you, my dears, we are all on the brink of ruin, we are dancing on the edge of a precipice. In flying from Galway we thought we had fled from the Land League; but I was talking to Lord Dungory this morning, and he says that the city is undermined, that a network of conspiracy is spread all over the place. He says there are assassins waiting and watching night and day to kill the Lord Lieutenant, and that there are so many plots hatching for the blowing up of the Castle, that even now it is doubtful if it will be considered safe to hold a Drawing-room.'

'Oh! Mamma, I think I should die, if there were to be no Drawing-room.'

'Of course there'll be a Drawing-room; but it only shows what a terrible state things must be in that such rumours should be put forth. The shopkeepers are complaining dreadfully. Mrs Symond says she has to give three years' credit. You see lots of people have shut up their houses; I am afraid there will not be many parties; it is all the fault of that wicked Land League, and the Government won't put it down, nor yet the Pope. What's the use in our subscribing to his Church if he'll do nothing for us?'

GEORGE MOORE
from *A Drama in Muslin* (1886)

Skinners

City people can be very thick and ignorant. I got very annoyed once, Sharon. I went into the flats with Eddie to see Sally and we went into a pub. Billy, me son-in-law, took us. We had ourselves a drink and after, Sally left me at the bus with Eddie. And when I got on, didn't I walk up to the top and there was three skinhead fellas sitting there. They had their little bottle of cider and the three of them were sharing it. I sat down, lit me cigarette and I was smoking and taking no notice of them but I could hear them tittering. There was some girls with them and they were all grinning and laughing, 'Look at the knackers.'

'God!' I said to Eddie, letting them know I was getting annoyed about it. 'They're very happy now. They must have gettin' three bottles of cider instead of the one. Is today dole day? Cause it's only on dole day that they're able to get their cheap sup of cider, and they must think now that they're millionaries – the little pups.'

'You're only a knacker,' one of them said.

'Yes,' I said, 'thanks for calling me that. You're after making me very proud because a knacker has respect. If it was a few knacker young fellas up here in this bus tonight, they wouldn't make fun of an old person. They were better reared than that. Yous are the scruff of Dublin, it's yous that is half starved from one week to the other. Every shilling you get, you have to hand it down to the club man for your little suits. And just because you're a skinner, you think everyone is afraid of you.'

Well, there was a respectable aged man on the far side of the bus with his son and he said, 'Leave that woman alone.'

I got off the bus then and went home and told the boys about it. 'You're worse than them,' Michael said, 'an old woman giving sense to children.' But these skinners were no children, Sharon, they were from seventeen up to twenty-two years of age. They were grown up men.

SHARON GMELCH
from *Nan: The Life of an Irish Travelling Woman* (1986)

Street Poet

The city was as lively and loveable as ever. I walked over the Half-penny Bridge and went up Grafton Street. It was alive with a healthy assortment of buskers and street entertainers. The ducks still quacked in St Stephen's Green. One thing I saw that day, however, was a poignant reminder of both my own past and the underground reality of the city which few real tourists would see or believe. I was walking down Eustace Street and saw a woman kneeling down in the middle of the footpath outside the old Quaker Meeting House. Thinking that she must be facing Mecca or Jerusalem and deep in prayer I stepped out onto the road, walked around where she was and stepped back onto the path. I glanced back at her just as she was taking her face out of a plastic bag. Her face was pure white from the spray paint she had been sniffing. I walked back to her and asked if she was OK. She just looked at me with glazed eyes and stuck her face back into the bag. I walked away. I was disturbed but because of my own history of substance abuse I could understand her. I saw her around the city on and off for the following year or so and then she was not around anymore.

*   *   *

When I got back to Dublin I searched for work and signed on at the local labour exchange. I applied to join a FÁS training scheme but was told that I must be on the dole for a year to be eligible. What a stupid rule! I did not sit around doing nothing. I bought some 'remainder' books at Eason's bargain shop and sold them door to door from a little basket for a little profit. I published a collection of poems with the profits. I went on the Dublin Corporation housing list and in September was given a flat in Éamonn Ceannt Tower in Ballymun. I got very involved in the residents' association and am involved to this day. I did not forget my vow to do what I could to revive some semblance of the bardic tradition. I began selling sheets of my poems and ballads outside the GPO and also recited poems for those who wished to listen. I found reciting there to be difficult because of the noise of the traffic, so I moved on to Henry Street, where I was harassed by the Guards. I then moved operations to the Molly Malone statue on Nassau Street but found the noise of traffic and the pollution, particularly from the buses, to be a hindrance and a possible health hazard, so I ended up on Grafton Street, which turned out to be ideal in every respect. The street was pedestrianised and had a certain quaintness, with its narrow thoroughfare and replica turn-of-the-century street lamps. It was ideal for reciting poetry but for the first couple of months I was looked on with a mixture of curiosity and is-your-man-serious sort of amusement. Remember no one had done this type of thing on a Dublin Street since the turn of the century. I soon broke the barrier and crowds began to gather to hear me recite from memory the poems of W.B. Yeats, P.H. Pearse etc.

PAT TIERNEY
from *The Moon On My Back* (1993)

A Tearful Gaze

She stood for a time watching people thronging into the Gaiety Theatre. Some came in motor-cabs, others in carriages. Many hearse-like cabs deposited weighty and respectable solemnities under the glass-roofed vestibule. Swift outside cars buzzed on rubber tyres with gentlemen clad in evening dress, and ladies whose silken wraps blew gently from their shoulders, and, in addition, a constant pedestrian stream surged along the pathway. From the shelter of an opposite doorway Mary watched these gaily animated people. She envied them all innocently enough, and wondered would the big policeman ever ask her to to the theatre with him, and if he did, would her mother let her go. She thought her mother would refuse, but was dimly certain that in some way she would manage to get out if such a delightful invitation were given her. She was dreaming of the alterations she would make in her best frock in anticipation of such a treat when, half-consciously, she saw a big figure appear round the corner of Grafton Street and walk towards the theatre. It was he, and her heart jumped with delight. She prayed that he would not see her, and then she prayed that he would, and then, with a sudden, sickening coldness, she saw that he was not alone. A young, plump, rosy-cheeked girl was at his side. As they came nearer the girl put her arm into his and said something. He bent down to her and replied, and she flashed a laugh up at him. There was a swift interchange of sentences, and they both laughed together; then they disappeared into the half-crown door.

Mary shrank back into the shadow of the doorway. She had a strange notion that everybody was trying to look at her, and that they were all laughing maliciously. After a few moments she stepped out on the path and walked homewards quickly. She did not hear the noises of the streets, nor see the promenading crowds. Her face was bent down as she walked, and beneath the big brim of her straw hat her eyes were blinded with the bitterest tears she had ever shed.

JAMES STEPHENS
from *The Charwoman's Daughter* (1912)

Growing up in the Liberties

I was born in New Row. Everything was upside down when I was a kid because the Civil War wasn't over. There were these shell shocked soldiers (good types) standing on the pavements; and the atmosphere was slow and easy. It was mostly tradesmen living in the Liberties then and taking pride in it.

In New Row there was Keefe's the knackers and they had barley at the back. There were the dairies, the maltings, the knackers and breweries. Horses and carts everywhere, and barrels. It was the last row of the Huguenot houses, with a long bowsprit pole outside the windows. The families put clothes out on them to dry, and the quilts and sheets. Inside there was crowding; three or four families to a landing, very constricted.

But they kept up their little tricks for their respectability. My Granny, she lived in Brabazon Row; she had a squat door with bossed panels and an old knocker. But it wasn't a Huguenot house, it was a Georgian house. She had a shut hall door; and it was all oil lamps, no gas. And they weren't hanging off the ceiling but on a plate on the wall. There were the old casements still, and the floor was scrubbed white and the furniture was plain scrubbed deal. They scrubbed the wood with pumice stone till the floornails shone. There would be stone flags on the floor and an echo. And the old balustrades and the stairs with the easy tread. The heavy drape curtains. Those people, even when they were stricken, they never lost their dignity.

LORCAN Ó DILIÚN
from 'Growing up in the Liberties',
The Liberties of Dublin, edited by Elgy Gillespie (1973)

Taking Liberties

Whitelaw in his *Population of Dublin* describes how he worked in the summer of 1798 'undismayed by degrees of filth, stench, darkness inconceivable'.

The filth and stench were in the darkness of the tenements of the parishes of SS James, Catherine, Luke, Nicholas Without and Within, Audoen's, Michael and John, Werburgh, Bride, Peter, Ann, Andrew, Mark and Deaneries of Christchurch and Saint Patrick's. The population he gives for this area is 112,497 (he calls it south-side of the Liffey and adds 'Harold's Cross, Sandymount and Black-rock cannot with any propriety be considered as part of Dublin'). The numbers nesting in single rooms 'tend to 16 persons of all ages and sexes in a room not fifteen foot square', meant a festering slum. And as their poverty made it impossible to levy a rate for a sewage system it further meant that the Poddle and courses became open sewers. This explains the anomaly whereby the silk weavers of Dublin *c.* 1220 petitioned for water, while those of 1800 on, petitioned for the filling in of all courses. Death and disease were rampant.

As to why this area became so overcrowded we might begin from 1685 and the arrival of the Huguenots. This started the Liberties on its career as the industrial centre. The Coombe, Pimlico, Spital-fields, Weavers' Square were built at this time.

The highly skilled and educated Huguenot industry allied to the guild system (then almost 600 years old) should have been an irresis-tible combination in terms of industry, but that would be to reckon without English sanctions. Protection of rival British industry how-ever is only half the story. Between 1700 and 1840 the Guilds went into decline – capitalism set apprentices up against their masters, a long painful climb not to be resolved until after the 1920s. But the real rot which destroyed the Guild system was injustice – the old story, religious discrimination. No 'Roman' Catholic could be a member of a Guild till 1793, so the decline went on and on. (And Whitelaw noticed 'an influx after the late 1798 Rebellion' hiding among the swarming poor.)

ANN DOMINICA FITZGERALD
from 'Down the Old Poddle',
The Liberties of Dublin, edited by Elgy Gillespie (1973)

Heathens

The Belfast Protestant family were getting on the train and the little girl turned and said: *Goodbye God, we're going to live in Dublin.*

SEAN McCANN
from *The Wit of the Irish* (1968)

Margins

Living on the margins leads to feelings of alienation and powerlessness and rejection, and a sense of helplessness and dependence on others. The physical surroundings increase the sense of alienation and powerlessness. Dublin is the best example of geographical segregation of rich and poor, but every town in Ireland has its own example of the marginalised working-class estate cut off from the rest of the community.

A comprehensive report on Dublin county's deprived areas highlighted the lack of services coupled with the ghetto effect of concentrating masses of unemployed and low income groups together.

The CODAN reports, published in 1988, compared the choice and facilities available in the affluent suburbs of south County Dublin, with the local authority communities of west Dublin, devoid of adequate shopping and transport facilities. In Fettercairn in West Tallaght, over 3000 people have only one shop, along with a few visiting mobile shops. There are no neighbourhood centres, the nearest shopping centre is several miles away, and there is no proper footpath for pedestrian access.

The reports profiled the poorer areas of Dublin, where unemployment was almost triple the county average; the proportion of the population with higher education is 7%, while the proportion of the population with primary education only is twice the average. The proportion of the population aged 15 and under is 40% higher than average, and the ratio of unemployed to employed persons is 2 and a half times the average. In some areas, the rate of unemployment is 70%. Rent arrears are an accurate indicator of need. In areas of Tallaght, built betweeen 1982 and 1986, accumulated rent arrears are over 33,000.

In Brookfield in Tallaght, over one third of the 700 households depend on unemployment assistance – the lowest welfare payment. One in ten is an unmarried mother, and one in 13 is a deserted wife. Yet services and amenities in the area are scarce there. A corporation house is used as a doctor's surgery, a playgroup and a meeting place for local groups.

In the local authority estate of Jobstown, over 50% of heads of households are unemployed; in the neighbouring private estate, the figure was 5%.

AILEEN O'MEARA
from 'Women & Poverty',
Letters from the New Island, edited by Dermot Bolger (1991)

Gli Scalpellini

They came from sunny, vine-clad hills,
or fields that knew the arid drought,
And forever said farewell to homes
Destroyed by despots in the south.
To the grey-damp cities of the north
(Where bitter tears are better lost in rain)
They marched away in dark defeat
Through mists that blurred the shape of pain.

They were artisans and peasant men
From the sun-rich Roman shore
And to a timeless Celtic isle
They brought their ancient lore;
In this alien, green and fertile land
Where famine late held sway
They found a kindred suffering
And they vowed to halt and stay.

They unpacked their age-old secrets
Like peddlers at the fair
And they pointed to the graveyards grey
And the churches gaunt and bare:

And they spoke with simple gestures
Of how they shared a common creed
And the native people nodded
As they sensed the strangers' need.

Then they carved their simple effigies –
The Crucified – The Thief –
And they mingled all their heartbreak
With a hapless nation's grief.
They worked with stone and chisel sharp
With the marble and the tile;
They carved, and cut, and painted...
And with time began to smile.

Then the native notes of wistfulness
Joined their lilting, sunlit songs
And with the sharing and the singing
Each forgot their ancient wrongs.
For they hoisted rough-hewn granite
And they struck with ringing tone
And they hammered out a victory
And composed their hymns in stone.

Many of the Italian immigrants who arrived in Ireland in the middle and latter
half of the 19th century were stonemasons, church decorators and terrazzo
tile workers. A great number of them were political refugees displaced by the
Risorgimento wars and fleeing from the oppressive regimes of the Hapsburgs
and the Bourbons.

In Ireland, after the winning of Catholic Emancipation in 1829, there was
something of a boom in church building and decoration, and in the decades
immediately following the Famine years of 1845-48 there was a considerable
demand for ornamental gravestones, family memorials and statuary etc...Italian
craftsmen – with names like Pacini, Bassi, Arigho, Nannetti, Caprani, Deghini
et al – found not only employment for their skills but a welcoming new homeland.

VINCENT CAPRANI
from *Vulgar Verse & Variations, Rowdy Rhymes & Rec-im-itations* (1987)

Cabra People

Men and women of Cabra
Stand up and take a bow
Through hard work and honesty
We showed our children how.

Some have gone into Mission fields
Ambassadors of faith
Cabra footballers around the world
Built the soccer gates.

Our famous singer Dickie Rock
Is a Cabra lad at will
Our children played in safety
On that railway hill.

Cabra gets no handouts
They stand on their own two feet
Cabronians and North Stranders
Real people hard to beat.
Pope John Paul crossed the world
And embraced the Cabra people
He saw Cabra caring, Cabra sharing
With the old and feeble.

Our Church and Parish Centre
A tribute to Cabra West
Cabra people, real people
They have stood the test.

It's the togetherness in Cabra
Round the Church with no steeple
A closely-knit community
Children, priests and people.

ROSE O'DRISCOLL
from *Rose of Cabra* (1992)

The Lazy Life

For some months after my entrance into the university I did little or no work. I attended lectures, but the rest of the day I spent exploring the old streets, looking at the old houses and squares, meandering along the quays. I wandered through Phoenix Park and climbed the Dublin Hills. It became one of my chief delights to lie up there and watch the great plain, the Plain of the Birds, stretching far away to the Gap of the North, and west to Galway Town. I thought of Red Hugh, the last of the Irish Chieftains, wandering through these hills, cold and frost-bitten, after his escape from Dublin Castle. I remembered how at last he had turned his face north again making for his own mountains in Donegal. I used to follow his path through the mountains, knowing that from that day to this nothing had changed of what I saw around me.

I found the lazy life of Dublin soothing after the harshness of the North, and the indifference of the people charming. No one troubled about me, no one inquired what I was doing, or why I did no work. If I did not attend lectures, I would lose my term, that was all. The examinations were a long way off and did not trouble me. I did not worry about anything, my work, my future, the human beings around me.

MARGARET BARRINGTON
from *My Cousin Justin* (1939)

Leaving Dublin

The outside-car swung along down Dorset Street; where Sean had first seen the peep of day; past George's church, in the pocket of which had lived the Dalton family with whom he had trod, as a youngster, the stage of the old Mechanics Theatre, now known the world over as The Abbey; down Cavendish Row where the Dispensary had been from which the gentle Dr Oulton had come to cure Sean of a fever; down Sackville-O'Connell Street, catching a good glimpse of the Post Office, where Padraic Pearse had sounded the horn

that roused Ireland out of her sleeping. In this very street, on the
top of a horse-drawn tram, when a little boy safe beside his mother,
he had swept into the galaxy of illuminations, lit to honour an English
Queen; and, years after, had been almost suffocated in this very
street by the surging crowd escaping from the batons of the police.
In this very street.

The car turned down Abbey Street and swung into Beresford
Place, trotting past Liberty Hall, once the sweltering, weltering
University of the Dublin workers, now a dead tomb held by an
enemy, with Ichabod written all over it, for Larkin had gone, and
its glory had departed; down Tara Street, surely the drabbest and
dirtiest street in Dublin, looking as desolate as Tara itself; wheeling
into Brunswick Street, passing the Queen's Theatre where Sean
had seen his first play, *The Shaughraun*; past the ancient Concert
Rooms, where the National Theatre performed some of its early
plays, before it had a habitation or even a name. It was this street
that had been Sean's *via dolorosa*, through which he had passed,
three times a week, year after year, for fifteen or more of them,
with his mother first, then on his own, to the Ophthalmic Hospital
to seek ease for aching eyeballs. Ah, here was Westland Row Station
– the last spot of Dublin that would feel his footfall. It was from
this sad site that the coffin holding Parnell came slowly out, borne
by strenuous, tearful men, hesitating to part even with the dead
body of their persecuted Chieftain. Oh, God Almighty, the life he
was living now had almost all been spun from what he had felt, had
seen, had touched in these few Dublin streets!

He was on the deck of the mail-boat, feeling her sway and shyly
throb beneath his feet; watching the landing-stage drift far away,
getting his last glimpse of Eireann – separated for the first time from
her, and never likely to stand settled on her soil again. It was bitterly
cold, with a fierce, keen wind blowing, and soon it was sending
sharp sleety hail and salty spray into his face, stinging it deeply –
Ireland, spitting a last, venomous, contemptuous farewell to him.

Well, everything of any value he was carrying away with him:
the moral courage and critical faculties of his father, and his love
of good books; the gay humour and dogged resolution of his mother,
and her love for, and understanding of, the bright colours among
dead, drab things; the remembrance of the warm clasp from the
Reverend Mr Griffin's firm, white, delicately-shaped hands; the
love of his comrade workers, catholic and protestant, with whom
he had fought and starved and fought again; all the fair things he
had learned during his sojourn with the Gaelic League; the affection

and goodwill of Lady Gregory; the reluctant godspeed from Dr
Cummins; a fond recollection of brother Tom; pity for his sister
Bella, and a little less of it for Mick; and, above all, a strict and
determined confidence in himself. Jewels he could never sell; jewels
that no thief, however cute, could take out of his hands.

> Sail on, sail on, thou fearless bark,
> Wherever blows the welcome wind,
> It cannot lead to scenes more dark,
> More sad, than those we leave behind.

The ship turned giddily to right, to left, plunged with upturned
bows, dipping them again as quick, for there was more than a
half-gale blowing. Sean had been anxious about sea-sickness, but
he felt no discomfort. He was a good sailor. He faced resolutely
towards where the ship was going. Sweet Inishfallen, fare thee well!
Forever!

SEAN O'CASEY
from *Inishfallen, Fare Thee Well* (1949)

Suffer the Children

I was born in Dublin in 1856, which may be taken as 1756 by
London reckoning. I was contemporary with Swift and Johnson,
and even with Samuel Pepys; for the smoke of battle from the Boyne
had not cleared away from my landscape, nor the glorious pious
and immortal memory of Dutch William faded from my conscious-
ness, when my sense of history was formed...The fact that I am
an Irish Protestant, and that I published a volume called Three
Plays for Puritans, has created a legend about the gloomy, sour,
Sabbath-ridden, Ulster-Covenanting home in which I was brought
up, and in which my remarkable resemblance to St Paul, St Anthony,
and John Knox was stamped on me...(As a matter of fact I was
brought up in an atmosphere in which two of the main constituents
were Italian opera and complete freedom of thought; and my attitude
toward conventional British life ever since has been that of a mission-
ary striving to understand the superstitions of the natives in order
to make himself intelligible to them.)

I believe Ireland, as far as the Protestant gentry is concerned,

to be the most irreligious country in the world. I was christened
by my uncle; and as my godfather was intoxicated and did not
turn up, the sexton was ordered to promise and vow in his place,
precisely as my uncle might have ordered him to put more coals
on the vestry fire. I was never confirmed; and I believe my parents
never were either. Of the seriousness with which English families
took this rite I had no conception; for Irish Protestantism was not
then a religion: it was a side in political faction, a class prejudice,
a conviction that Roman Catholics are socially inferior persons who
will go to Hell when they die and leave Heaven in the exclusive
possession of Protestant ladies and gentlemen. In my childhood I was
sent every Sunday to a Sunday-school where genteel little children
repeated texts, and were rewarded with cards inscribed with them.
After an hour of this we were marched into the adjoining church
(the Molyneux in Upper Leeson Street), to sit round the altar rails
and fidget there until our neighbours must have wished the service
over as heartily as we did.

  ...To sit motionless and speechless in your best suit in a dark
stuffy church on a morning that is fine outside the building, with
your young limbs aching with unnatural quiet, your restless imagin-
ation tired of speculating about the same grown-up people in the
same pews every Sunday, your conscience heavy with the illusion
that you are the only reprobate present sufficiently wicked to long
for the benediciton, and to wish that they would sing something
out of an opera instead of Jackson in F, not to mention hating the
clergyman as a sanctimonious bore, and dreading the sexton as a
man likely to turn bad boys out and possibly to know them at sight
by official inspiration: all this is enough to lead any sensitive youth
to resolve that when he grows up and can do as he likes, the first
use he will make of his liberty will be to stay away from church...
I suffered this, not for my salvation, but because my father's respect-
ability demanded it. When we went to live in Dalkey we broke with
the observance and never resumed it.

BERNARD SHAW
from *Composite Autobiography*, edited by Stanley Weintraub (1969)

Doorways

I have found Barnaby and Bartleby. They are all day and every day in the doorways of Abbey Street. I call them Barnaby and Bartleby but I do not know their names. They must have some shelter to go to, for they disappear from the doorways about eight in winter, an hour later in the summer. I have never seen them leave. They seem to be there one moment and gone the next. I have never watched them go. I feel it would be an intrusion to draw too close at that time and that they mightn't leave if watched. The early morning is the one time they are busy, searching the bins with total concentration before the garbage trucks come by. They never search the same bin together or stand in the same doorway. Only in freezing weather do they come close, just inside the door of the Public Lavatory, and even there they keep the red coinslot weighing machine between them, their backs to the wall, above their heads the black arrow pointing to the urinal stalls within.

They seem to change doorways every two hours or so and always to the same doorway at the same time. I thought at first they might be following the sun but then noticed they still changed whether the sun was in or out. They wear long overcoats, tightly belted, with pleats at the back, that had been in fashion about fifteen years before. Often I want to ask them why have they picked on this way to get through life, but outside the certainty of not being answered I soon see it as an idle question and turn away. They never answer strangers who ask about the times of the buses out of Abbey Street. They have their different ways, too, of not answering. Bartleby, the younger and smaller, just moves his boots and averts his face sideways and down; but Barnaby stares steadily over his steel-rimmed spectacles into his interlocutor's eyes. Otherwise, they seem to take a calm and level interest in everything that goes on outside their doorway. They must be completely law abiding, for the police hardly glance at them as they pass on patrol.

JOHN McGAHERN
from *Getting Through* (1979)

An Insolent Brat

When we crossed the bridge to Seville Place, an expanding family making the move from the three-roomed Abercorn Road imperative, another waterway came to dominate – the 'naller' (Royal Canal). Frozen in winter and a public baths in summer is how it is etched in my memory. I can still see James Mulally disappearing beneath the ice and our impotence as we ran back and forth trying to break the grey ice cover with our fists to find him. Later on it claimed two members of another family, the Kavanaghs from St Brigid's Gardens. They lost another child beneath a lorry in Sheriff Street. Their particular streak of blond hair I have never seen since, nor will I again, anywhere.

In summer all thought of death was buried as we raced from the North Wall side in a great splash to the broken ship on the far East Wall bank. We travelled many times around the world in that ribbed shell.

When the swimming became proficient and the broken ship became nothing but a broken ship again, we left the little kids to paddle in the Canal while we took on the heady current of mother Liffey. Those first tentative sorties from the bottom steps soon gave way to dives, flips, and back somersaults from the bank opposite the cobble stones and horse trough of Guild Street. And if the 'captain' was in good form, and you possessed sufficient bravery, a dive from the Corpo ferry meant instant exaltation to a special league of heroes. But the ultimate test was the jump from Butt Bridge to the shadows of the Loopline Bridge and the long swim to the steps at the Custom House. Many times I saw that cause cars to make involuntary stops and men and women to clap, though there was no audience to hear. To this day I regret that I never made the jump. Oh, the unfulfilled exploits of youth.

And if water dominated play, then blood replaced it at school. Blood, as in definition of manhood, jackeen, Irishman, Christian. In its ideal state that blood should produce a Gaelic speaking and Gaelic loving youth; one who enjoyed to excess the exploits of our native games, by definition loathed all foreign ones (they had a ban just in case the blood was contaminated), a man who would see the reunification of his country while living and working in England (you couldn't pay for a flight to America with blood in those days) and who would shun pagans as they lay in bed on Sunday Mornings and get up to go to mass.

My blood was severely diluted. I captained Sheriff Utd FC from under 11 and took my responsibilities seriously. That meant not turning out for the school gaelic team. The tension of the situation became so bad that I confronted the CB concerned. I asked him what he had against soccer? He paled. He asked me did my father know I was such an insolent brat? I persisted, what was wrong with soccer, a game like any other? I was told I would have to take my bag and baggage and go elsewhere. I played my final ace. The man Gal, who runs our team was studying to be a priest, so what could be wrong with playing for the team. The CB stared me straight in the face and said, 'Judas was an apostle'.

Every play I've written has been an attempt to emulate that riposte.

PETER SHERIDAN
from 'Growing Up in Abercorn Road and Seville Place',
Invisible Dublin, edited by Dermot Bolger (1991)

Saturday Afternoon in Dublin

Dietrich Fischer-Dieskau is in the process
of depressing me singing
the 'Der Einsame im Herbst' section
of *Das Lied von der Erde.*
A flute is playing as I look
at my sisters photographed in New York
in a crowd of twenty-five thousand people
getting ready for a bicycle tour.
I meet them for a few days
every two years or so
but I don't know them anymore;
only how they used to be
before I went away.
Are you crying yet?
Sometimes you get to know your relatives
better when they're pinned down
like butterfly specimens
wearing baseball cap and crash helmet respectively.

Kate, I see, has a blue-faced watch
with snappy red band.
Ellen has let her hair grow.
They both smile nervously
because my father is taking the picture
in the middle of the throng.
Dietrich, meanwhile, has moved on to a beautiful, sad,
song with harps – I'm glad I don't know any German –
it's even sadder hearing words sung
that make no sense.
He says, 'Ja, ja' better than anyone.
It isn't music for New York, really.
A Hopper etching: 'Night Shadows',
an afternoon in Dublin looking
out the arid window for inspiration,
wanting so many things to happen –
that's when it gets to you.
Are you crying yet?

JULIE O'CALLAGHAN
from *What's What?* (1991)

Culchies

'Culchie,' Loretta shrieked.

Jo stopped dead, like her heart had stopped. Slowly she turned and looked at her.

'Bloody culchies, all the same. Where's your mammy and daddy?' Loretta put on a country accent as she said it. 'Go back to the bog. You don't belong round here.'

Other kids gathered round, egging Loretta on. 'Bogtrotter!'

'Culchie,' they squealed in delight. Jo didn't know what to do. She wasn't a culchie. She was from Dublin like the rest of them. Loretta was in a frenzy of screaming now, her face as red as her pixie.

'Burns in the red hat,' Jo shouted inspired. 'Burns in the red hat.'

All the kids roared with laughter. Now they began shouting at Loretta. Everyone knew her ma made her wear the pixie because she got earaches. It was something to jeer at. Loretta lunged at her.

Sensing victory, Jo grabbed at the hat, almost pulling it off. Loretta began to cry. Fixing it on again she mumbled through tears, 'I'm never speaking to you again, Jo Nowd.'

'Culchie,' she spat over her shoulder.

*   *   *

Jo lay curled on top of her bed, her hands between her legs to keep warm. Dublin, she was from Dublin. Her parents were bloody culchies. It was their fault. Why had they moved to Dublin when they bloody hated it? Hated Dublin people, hated her, that meant. But she wasn't like a Dublin kid. She didn't speak like them, she didn't dress like them and she didn't even have any relations here except her Auntie Sally and Uncle Kevin and only her uncle was from Dublin. She bashed the wall with her fist. A dent appeared in the insulation paper her daddy put up for the damp. Good! She poked and pulled at it until a whole strip came away. Now he'd kill her. She didn't care. How could she live in Dublin where all the kids had easy parents and hers were strict? And they never went to the seaside in the summer like everybody else on the road. All they did was go to their granny's in the country. They never had ice-cream and lemonade on a Sunday after Mass either. Jo went over the list of grievances in her head like a litany. She knew it by heart. And her mammy's answer.

'Dublin people are different. Your daddy wants to educate yous so he puts money away. Loretta will go into a factory the day she's fourteen. And your daddy has terrible bills to pay because of my health.'

She always took his part. That was because her mammy hated Jo being different from her. She stared at the hole she'd made in the paper. If she looked at it one way it was like the map of Ireland with a bit missing. If she looked at it another way it was like a beautiful woman laughing. Why wasn't her mammy a proper Dublin mammy who kept the house shining and was always laughing?

MOYA RODDY
from *The Long Way Home* (1992)

A Late Christening

I discovered at the age of twelve that I hadn't been christened. My parents had decided that they would be terribly liberal about religion and they would not have either Michael or myself christened until we were old enough to decide what religion, if any, we wanted to adopt. I have a very clear memory of the local curate, Mr Hanson, coming to the house one winter's evening and saying to my mother, 'I've just come to talk about Jennifer being confirmed.' My mother burst out laughing and said, 'She hasn't even been christened!' I was appalled at this because it carried a terrible social stigma, apart from the fact that I had within me the awful mythology of Limbo which I had acquired from Catholic friends. I was quite convinced that if between that moment and the moment of being baptised I were to fall off my bike and be run over by a No.8 tram, I would go straight to Limbo where I would spend a horrible eternity. I wasn't going to school on my bicycle for six weeks until the christening actually happened.

Michael and I were duly christened. I never told any of my friends; it was all too embarrassing. The grown-ups thought it was a great idea. We had a great lunch party before the christening and I remember my mother handing around bunches of parsley to everyone to eat. She didn't want the guests to arrive at the church smelling of gin and tonic!

JENNIFER JOHNSTON
from *A Portrait of the Artist as a Young Girl*,
edited by John Quinn (1986)

In the City

Gently in the night flows my river, the Liffey.
It is mine by right of love, this river always
Running, since childhood, under my feet, always
Branching along my veins – this river of birds,
Avenue of serene, Ascendancy swans,
Trail of the single gunman cormorant,

Stage of the seagulls' ballet – those faery visitors
Who cry and perch and fly, blown in the air
Like paper toys.
                              Tonight there are no birds;
The thickening mist blinds me to all but light.
By day small painted boats, wings
Of coloured parrots, tighten their holding ropes
And lie beside the wall. Pale women
Hurry across the bridges, dawdle at windows,
Treasure their handbags, intent on finding bargains.
Crowds at the rush-hour of a Spring afternoon
Move in the clean patterns of thrown confetti.
                                        But now
In fog the city covers all its candour.
From windowed vehicles the light
Imprints a moving tartan on the water;
And where a street-lamp hangs a luminous triangle,
There, mirrored, a three-sided corresponding
Euclidean figure breaks the river's blackness,
Base to base applied, with lamp-post perpendicular
And tree subtending.
                              Now
Where are the seabirds? Do they fly
At day's end to the sea, to spend the night
One-legged on rock, in thought?
When, rarely, moves a patch
Of faint illumination on the darkest water,
Then are discovered small waiting forms,
Patiently floating, homeless, through the dark
They do not understand. Silence
Holds them, until daylight.

RHODA COGHILL

6. DUBLIN DESTROYED EMERGING

Dublin has been embattled during most of its existence.
Today many citizens would perceive the enemy as the mugger,
the joyrider, the burglar, the drug pusher, the developer
and the vandal whose depredations are encouraged by the
absence of vigilant protection of property and the public
interest. This kind of lawlessness is neither new nor unique to
Dublin. It's the revival of an eighteenth – and nineteenth-
century situation which has been brought about by much
the same social conditions: too many people without jobs
and without hope of them.
In its early years Dublin had to live with the constant threat
of invasion by Danes and Scandinavians coming in from
over the sea, and by the native Irish attacking by land. In
later years there was always the uneasy wondering about
when social unrest would once more erupt into an attempt
at revolution, an uneasiness which was easily stampeded
into panic during the Fenian era. (It's touch and go whether
this situation might not recur today.)

JOHN O'DONOVAN

Gaelic Dublin

The history of Dublin as a town is normally said to date from 841, when Vikings established a fortified stockade on high ground overlooking the Liffey. Yet there is little doubt that there was some scattered settled life in the area before their arrival. Not only was Dublin Bay one of the finest on the east coast with many places where one could beach the small coracles, or curraghs, then in use for travel to Britain, but also it included several natural harbours where larger craft could land. The best of these was at a black pool (*linn dubh*) where the River Poddle entered the Liffey. This appears to have had some importance as a point of entry from and departure for Britain, as many of the most important roads or *slighte* seem to have met in its vicinity. Slige Midluachra, the main road from the North was linked to the southern roads by a ford of hurdles across the Liffey at a shallow spot near the present Whitworth Bridge.

There seem to have been at least two Gaelic settlements in the area, *Ath Cliath*, which was on the ridge above the ford, and *Dubhlinn*, a monastic enclosure of the sixth or seventh century. These settlements, however, could not be called a town in the accepted sense of the word, for, although goods may have been imported on a large scale into the country, the Irish tended to regard ports as merely points of entry, not as centres of economic activity. At that time monasteries were the main concentrations of settlement in Ireland, and as such were the destinations of most of the goods that passed inward through Dublin Bay. No doubt the wealth accruing from these trading activities, when added to the gifts bestowed by local rulers in return for blessings and invocations, made Irish monasteries all the more attractive to raiders and pirates, including those from the Scandinavian peninsula.

Hiberno-Norse Dublin

It did not take the Irish long to realise that Dublin's wealth made it an immense source of power, and that if any chief wished to be known as king of Ireland, he had to have control of the town. At the turn of the eleventh century the Norse of Dublin became embroiled in the conflict between the ambitious Brian Boru and Mael Morda, the king of Leinster, whom they supported. In 1012 there were a number of serious engagements, and 1013 was marked by continuous warfare as Brian, his son Murchad and Maelsechnaill II of Meath plundered and burned Leinster, and unsuccessfully attempted to break through the defences of Dublin, despite a four-month siege.

Early in 1014 the Dublin Norse began gathering allies from the Hebrides, the Orkneys and the Isle of Man, to support the Leinstermen in what they knew would be the decisive battle with Brian. The two sides met in battle on Good Friday, 23 April 1014, at Clontarf. The two armies were almost equally matched, the battle was hard fought and lasted all day. Eventually the Leinstermen and their Norse supporters were defeated with heavy losses on both sides. Most of the Norse leaders were killed, as was Brian Boru, who was slain by Norsemen fleeing from the battle. His son Murchad and many other Munster leaders also died. Mael Morda, king of Leinster, was killed, but Sitric, ruler of Dublin, survived as he had stayed within the town walls.

The battle of Clontarf has often been portrayed as a major defeat for the Vikings, and one which turned the tide against them in Europe. There can be no doubt that they suffered great losses, and the overthrow seems to have made a great impression on their saga writers, who spoke of strange and terrible omens before the battle, such as boiling blood raining down on warriors, weapons fighting of their own accord, and ravens attacking them with iron beaks and claws. Other marvels were reported after the battle. In the Hebrides, for example, it was claimed that Valkyries were seen weaving a web of battle with swords on a loom of death and singing.

> The men of Ireland
> Will suffer a grief
> That will never grow old
> In the minds of men,
> The web is now woven
> And the battlefield reddened
> The news of disaster
> Will spread through lands
>
> [from *Njal's Saga*]

CURRICULUM DEVELOPMENT UNIT
from *Viking & Medieval Dublin* (1978)

Surrender

Here comes Paudrig Pearse down the silent street, two elegant British officers waiting for him. He comes steadily, in no hurry; unafraid, to where two elegant British officers are waiting to meet him. His men have been beaten; the cordon of flame has burnt out their last fading hope. *The struggle is over; our boys are defeated; and Ireland's surrounded with silence and gloom:* the old ballad is singing in his ears. He wears a topcoat, for the Easter sun has gone west, and a nipping breeze blows. It is the wind of death blowing keenly on this brave man's pure face. His eyes droop, for he hasn't slept for days. He has lain down, but not to sleep. Soon he will sleep long and well. He feels this is no defeat; that to stand up in an armed fight against subjection is a victory for Ireland. So he stands silently, and listens to the elegant British officer demanding unconditional surrender. The fools, the fools! So he agrees, and hands over his sword; bows, and returns to marshal his men for a general surrender.

SEAN O'CASEY
from *Drums under the Windows* (1945)

On Sandymount Strand

These long years
Watching the seagulls bank and retreat daily
And the tide's remorseless flowing on the wrinkled
Forehead of the strand, I have been happy here,
Stealing apples from orchards and being chased,
Playing football and more mysterious games
Lost to me now, or breaking my heart
For a girl who broke her eight-year life she was so eager
To live and to experience everything well.

And there was poetry. When I found
Lines detonating in my mind and my pen
Stabbing the pages of my memory, I would have sold
My sister to the devil for a poem

Complete and lucid as spring-water, to startle
God and rock his gold throne.
It never came; yet I was happy, too,
With the snapping swords of words and the shields
   of tinsel phrases.

Gone, now, the adolescent swagger and closed
The book of my youth, ruled, and a trial
Balance extracted for my future use.
I thought today
As still the gulls banked and the evil tide
Crept nearer from the horizon while I walked
By Sandymount Tower, now decrepit and strewn
With rubble borne there by the wind and water,
How my youth wore down like an old shoe-sole
Sodden with age,
Leaving between me and the hostile, hard
Ground of society, nothing – nothing at all
Now to prevent the damp and the needling chill
Eating into my bones and burrowing to my heart.

VALENTIN IREMONGER
from *Sandymount, Dublin* (1988)

A Private Place

I, at least, was thoroughly urban. The Dublin I had known until then was a sympathetic prospect of stone and water and wet dusks over Stephen's Green. It was a convivial town of coffee and endlessly renewable talk... By the time I came to know it, other cities had prepared me to relish a place which had something of the theatre of a city, and all the intimacy of a town. These were the early sixties. There were still coffee bars set into the basements of Georgian houses, where a turf fire burned from four o'clock in the afternoon and you could get brown scones with your coffee.

None of it prepared me for a suburb. There is, after all, a necessity about cities. By the time you come to them, there is something finished and inevitable about their architecture; even about their grime. You accept both.

A suburb is altogether more fragile and transitory. In one year it can seem a whole road is full of bicycles, roller skates, jumble sales. Garages will be wide-open with children selling comics and out-of-date raisin buns. There will be shouting and calling far into the summer night. Almost as soon, it seems, the same road will be quiet. The bicycles will be gone. The shouting and laughing will be replaced by one or two dogs barking in the back gardens. Curtains will be drawn till late morning and doors will stay closed.

The main feature about such quick and even violent transition is that it demands participants, not just witnesses. A suburb is made of lives in a state of process. 'There is properly no history; only biography' wrote Emerson. To look down our road at lunchtime on a schoolday was to realise the force of his words. The public calendar defines a city; banks are shut and shops are opened. But the private one shapes a suburb. It waxes and wanes on christenings, weddings, funerals. I found this potent mix everywhere in Dundrum. Obviously, it was a place with inevitabilities and schedules. There were buildings, shops and visible progresses to prove it. But it was the hidden history that drew me. I had missed this before. I knew too little of the countryside to find it there; I recoiled too much from cities to search for it in them. But here, in my own home, on my own road, the private history which is to be found in the unique transaction between a life and a place began to unfold in front of me.

EAVAN BOLAND
from 'The Need To Be Ordinary',
Object Lessons (1995)

Decline and Fall

Dublin's municipal corruption passed belief. The Corporation having annihilated countless thousands of children in the municipally controlled Foundling Hospital, went on to facilitate regular cholera epidemics by their treatment – or rather their non-treatment – of the city sewage. The Liffey was an open sewer, the streets, even in fashionable areas, were muddy cart tracks that became almost impassable after heavy rain. The city fathers weren't going to raise the rates on themselves (many being extensive property owners) in the cause of civic improvement. Besides, anyone with 6d (2½p) to spare needn't dirty his boots because he could have himself driven by horse cab from one end of the city to the other. Sixpence was the legal fare, and though the cabby might picturesquely curse the passenger who forced him to get the last ounce out of the half-starved horse, little could be done about it.

Except in the newer suburbs squalor was to be found everywhere, even in mansions. Fastidious persons had to resign themselves to dust and grime. It came from open coal fires in inefficient hearths, from the unpaved unswept streets, from what would nowadays be an intolerable want of sanitation and personal hygiene that produced plagues of flies, bluebottles and cockroaches, and from the irredeemable sluttishness of servants. Thackeray, visiting Dublin in the summer of 1842, memorably sketched a window in the city's leading hotel, the Shelbourne, being propped open with a hearth brush because its cords and weights had long since gone out of commission.

But Thackeray was able to add that the tariff was more than reasonable. Bed and breakfast cost 6s 3d (32p), meals were lavish, wine unstinted. Such were Dublin's priorities. The insidious decline in standards in the once exclusive districts was hardly noticed. The grand houses, put up in spacious squares during the upsurge in national prosperity in the second half of the previous century, had been so handsomely and so durably furnished that after three quarters of a century they were by Dublin standards presentable. But carpets and hangings were seldom replaced when necessary, upholstery and fittings became shabby. Income went mainly on entertainment and the upkeep of wine cellar and carriage. It was not unknown for the mistresses of Merrion Square mansions, when ready money was scarce, to make ball dresses for themselves and their daughters out of curtains. (So, at any rate, alleges Percy Fitzgerald in his *Recollections of Dublin Castle and of Dublin Society.*) The beggar at the gate, telling the emerging gentleman that he didn't know where his next dinner was coming from, might well have got the reply: 'Neither do I.'

JOHN O'DONOVAN
from *Life by the Liffey: A Kaleidoscope of Dubliners* (1986)

Building Bollox

Wood Quay became the most potent symbol of the Corporation's determination to have its way with the city, regardless of the cost or the consequences. The bureaucrats wanted new civic offices, and they were prepared to stop at nothing to achieve their objective. It didn't matter to them that the office blocks were to be built on the most important Viking site ever unearthed in Ireland containing as it did, the very story of Dublin's birth and early development. With the connivance of the National Museum authorities, they brought in bulldozers to remove much of the archaeological evidence and only grudgingly consented to an incomplete excavation of what was left. Prominent conservationists pleaded with them not to enter a construction contract for the offices, but they ignored this earnest plea and went ahead anyway. They spurned appeals to cease and desist from over eighty social and cultural organisations, including the Council of Europe, and contemptuously cast aside a petition signed by more than 200,000 people. They shut their eyes to mass meetings in the Mansion House and protest marches through the city. And when the High Court declared the site to be a National Monument, they conspired with the Commissioners of Public Works to subvert this judgment by drawing up an order for the monument's destruction. Then, after Dubliners had elected a new City Council pledged to defend Wood Quay, the petty officials warned the people's representatives that they would all be personally surcharged if they welshed on the civic offices project. And with the Fianna Fáil government remaining stone-deaf to demands that it should foot the bill, the councillors caved in and the officials got their way. All in all, as Ulick O'Connor has said, this bureaucratic triumph over a clearly-expressed democratic consensus, was 'the most terrifying event in this country over the past twenty years'.

In the wake of the longest and most intense environmental controversy in Dublin's history, the Corporation has nothing to show for it but two great block-houses, which have been likened to huge filing cabinets or over-sized nuclear shelters or even to the concrete bunkers built by the Germans around the coast of continental Europe during World War II. 'It's a real *Guns of Navarone* job,' one taxi driver laconically observed. 'All that's missing are the big guns in the slits.' The architect, Sam Stephenson, whose passion for mega-structures is well known, has said his civic offices are supposed to be 'making a statement'. But what is the nature of this 'statement'?

Certainly, the design does not suggest that these buildings are to be the hub of local government in Dublin. Stark, cold and monstrous, they convey a totalitarian image, which is not too surprising given Stephenson's undisguised admiration for the work of Hitler's architect, Albert Speer. And their very totalitarianism is almost tailor-made for Dublin Corporation, whose officials will now be able to insulate themselves against the city they seem to despise so much.

The high price ordinary citizens have been forced to pay for these so-called civic offices was not merely environmental. It could be measured in pounds and pence: *their* pounds and pence. At £20 million plus, the two granite-faced blocks are the most expensive buildings ever built in Dublin – and this enormous outlay covered only the first stage of a much larger project. Still to come are two more office blocks as well as goodies like the sunken council chamber, terraced park and underground Viking museum. However, the cost of the first two blocks has spiralled out of control, jeopardising the rest of the scheme. Incredibly, it works out at triple the contract price quoted by Messrs John Paul in October 1977 and *ten times* the original estimate for the entire complex when it was first conceived in 1967.

FRANK McDONALD
from *The Destruction of Dublin* (1985)

Dirty Old Town

Well-to-do-Dublin dribbled out to nothing. The air grew thick with fumes from the brewery. The derelict sites off Clanbrassil Street were dark and empty except for the orange pool of a huge bonfire lighting up a circle of young faces, mesmerised by the one colourful thing in sight. Everything was sodden, dirty. There was nothing she could do about it, it had gone wrong long before she was born. She reached the cathedral and found she was crying, but she didn't bother wiping her face because it had started to drizzle. Her jacket drank it in and she felt cold. She walked on, down the winding streets towards the amusement arcade. It was dark inside except for the lights on the machines. Warlord, Spacebuster. The figures did not turn to look.

VICTORIA WHITE
from 'Eva', *Raving Autumn* (1990)

Ecclesiastical

The Dumays' house was not the finest in the street, nor was it the shabbiest. The door had been painted dark green some six years ago. It had a large brass knocker in the form of a wreath which the servant Jinny, a single girl of advancing years, who was paid eight shillings a week and lived in some nearby tenements affectionately called 'the little hell', occasionally polished when the matter came into her mind. On entering the house the first impression was of an ecclesiastical darkness and of the smell referred to by Mrs Chase-White. The ecclesiastical air was contributed by a window on the half-landing which was in fact inside a lavatory, the door of which, when untenanted, stood always open. This place may also have accounted for the smell. The upper landing, which was long and lit by a skylight, was divided into two, for no very clear reason, by a faintly jangling bead curtain; while along the walls stood a series of shrines or side-chapels containing stuffed birds, cairns of wax fruit, and cascades of disintegrating butterflies under glass domes.

The drawing-room in which Cathal was now prancing was a long brown room, dimmed by brownish-white lace curtains, and very full of bulbous mahogany furniture. There were a number of coloured pictures of flower gardens, a large pinkish print called *The Love Letter*, and a prominent crucifix. Both Kathleen and Pat were indifferent to their surroundings and accepted the miscellany of brass bowls, ginger jars, embroidered clothlets and photos in upholstered frames as a natural part of the daily scene, as little remarkable as the rocks upon the seashore. Only Cathal displayed any concern with interior decoration and his interests so far were limited to the collecting of model animals, which now jostled the other inhabitants of the tall and extremely complicated overmantel, causing Jinny, when the day for dusting them came round, to utter under her breath words which would have startled Father Ryan. In the midst of the overmantel, whose unsymmetrical undulations suggested a natural growth rather than the workings of the human mind, was a slim, extremely tall elliptical mirror, which showed in reflection an even more melancholy room filled with an atmosphere the colour of strong tea.

IRIS MURDOCH
from *The Red & The Green* (1965)

A Mask Like Castlereagh

The House of Lords, decorated (if I remember) with hangings representing the battle of the Boyne, was nearly empty when we entered – an accident which furnished to Lord Altamont the opportunity required for explaining to us the whole course and ceremonial of public business on ordinary occasions.

Gradually the House filled: beautiful women sat intermingled amongst the peers...Then were summoned to the bar – summoned for the last time – the gentlemen of the House of Commons; in the van of whom, and drawing all eyes upon himself, stood Lord Castlereagh...

At which point in the order of succession came the Royal Assent to the Union Bill, I cannot distinctly recollect. But one thing I *do* recollect – that no audible expression, no buzz, nor murmur, nor *susurrus* even, testified the feelings which, doubtless, lay rankling in many bosoms. Setting apart all public or patriotic considerations, even then I said to myself, as I surveyed the whole assembly of ermined peers, 'How is it, and by what unaccountable magic, that William Pitt can have prevailed on all these hereditary legislators and heads of patrician houses to renounce so easily, with nothing worth the name of a struggle, and no reward worth the name of an indemnification, the very brightest jewel in their coronets? This morning they all rose from their couches Peers of Parliament, individual pillars of the realm, indispensable parties to every law that could pass. Tomorrow they will be nobody – men of straw – *terraefilii*.

'What madness has persuaded them to part with their birthright, and to cashier themselves and their children forever into mere titular Lords?'...

'You are all,' thought I to myself, 'a pack of vagabonds henceforward, and interlopers, with actually no more right to be here than myself. I am an intruder; so are you.' Apparently they thought so themselves: for, soon after this solemn *fiat* of Jove has gone forth, their lordships, having no farther title to their robes (for which I could not help wishing that a party of Jewish old-clothes men would at this moment have appeared and made a loud bidding), made what haste they could to lay them aside forever. The House dispersed much more rapidly than it had assembled...

One person only I remarked whose features were suddenly illuminated by a smile, a sarcastic smile, as I read it; which, however, might be all a fancy. It was Lord Castlereagh; who, at the moment when the irrevocable words were pronounced, looked with a penetrating glance amongst a party of ladies. His own wife was one of that party; but I did not discover the particular object on whom his smile had settled...

THOMAS DE QUINCEY
from *Collected Writings of Thomas de Quincey* (1896)

First Impressions

I was disagreeably struck with the shabby, ruinous appearance of the streets in the Liberty; but was nearly terrified by the amazing height of St Patrick's steeple, after I had made my way to a clear view of it through the old rag and crockery fair held on the Coombe.

Then I added to my stock of knowledge by a glimpse of a soldier with an ordinary hat on his head, and cross belts over a blue coat standing sentry near the Deanery house. On enquiry I found he was only a policeman. I gazed with veneration on this old red building, owing to our great interest about its former occupant, Dean Swift...

I paid a visit to the outsides of St Patrick's, and Christ Church, and the Castle, and the College, and the old Parliament House, and the Royal Barracks to see the Highlanders on parade; and when the first impulses of curiosity were satisfied, and not a single known face to be seen, I began to feel the time dreadfully wearisome...This desolation fell on me at Carlisle Bridge; but looking up the river I bethought me of the Four Courts and the old book stalls. Oh, joy! I find there an odd volume of *Ossian* at one shilling, and, to enhance my good luck, Miss O'Reilly, who keeps a circulating library in the open air...offers to lend me *Waverly* at one penny per night...

PATRICK KENNEDY
from *Evenings in the Duffrey* (1869)

Torn Apart

They've torn this street apart now, the carriageway sliced open its soul. This clanging metal bridge links the two halves, the noise of my boots and stick telegraphed through the hollow steel to echo down at the far end. The top of the trucks almost touch my feet, the bridge trembles in their slipstream. The view from up here is like what I remember as a child before the estates cut off the sweep of the hills down to the city. Ten minutes it often takes me to crawl across its back. I feel like I'm crossing the hunched skeleton of some metallic dinosaur, a ghost from a future age who came this far and withered in the dead world of what was once my home. Those cottages down there which I often sat in with the carts creaking in from the countryside. Plunkett tuning his accordion while his wife fetched the oil lamp down. The roofs are gone from them now, a single rafter standing like a naked bone. The children have torn the corrugated iron from one of the windows to use it for parties. You can see the glint of smashed bottles there, the blackened stains in a corner where somebody's lit a fire and still a small square of wallpaper hanging on one wall like an epithet. I've watched them sink this far, pitying their dilapidation, but now with this cough they'll live to see me buried.

DERMOT BOLGER
from *The Woman's Daughter* (1987)

Heroine

It was spring; spring in Dublin. In the gardens, parks and orchards of the town, apple trees blossomed, chestnuts, limes, oaks were heavy with leaves. Flowersellers, their baskets ablaze with the colours of daffodils, lilies, peonies, forget-me-nots, paraded the streets calling their wares. Winter was gone and the Liffey sparkled with light; small boats bobbed and great white ships' sails softly billowed. Children played in the river Poddle that ran through the Liberties, screaming with laughter. Small dark weavers with high-crowned wigs left their looms idle while they gossiped with friends; nursemaids took the air with their charges in Grafton Street; the Beaux Walk on St Stephen's Green was crowded with fops in fancy waistcoats and powdered wigs; well-appointed matrons shopped in the markets of the High Street for brandied apricots, chocolate, marzipan for special supper parties. In Patrick Street their poorer sisters haggled with dealers at makeshift stalls, smelling fish for freshness, pressing stumpy fingers into fruit and vegetables, testing for soundess. Beside the cathedral a ballad singer sang in a cracked voice:

> Come buy my fine wares,
> Plums, apples and pears,
> A hundred a penny,
> In conscience too many,
> Come, will you have any;
> My children are seven,
> I wish them in heaven,
> My husband's a sot,
> With his pipe and his pot,
> Not a farthing will gain 'em,
> And I must maintain 'em.

A sardonic-looking clergyman emerged from the cathedral close. He it was who had written the verse. He was in the habit of composing such doggerel when he worked on his sermons and pamphlets, in much the same way as the early monks had scribbled in monastic scriptoriums, filling in the margins of their manuscripts with strange and wonderful animals.

Peg, making her way along Patrick Street, had a sudden urge to accost the dean, to pour out her troubles to him, to tell him of the storm which she feared would shortly break about her head. Surely he of all men would understand. For as long as she could remember he had been the subject of scandal. His book *Gulliver's Travels* had been mocked as childish, satirised as an attack on humanity, labelled obscene, fit only to be burnt in the market-place. Yet it was as widely read as popular romances, like *Moll Flanders* or *Robinson Crusoe*.

More scandalous still, at least in the eyes of the authorities, were the *Drapier's Letters*, published anonymously in 1724, denouncing Hanoverian George and his government in London for their attempts to foist a worthless currency on downtrodden people. Dublin Castle had offered a reward of £500 for information about the author. But though £500 was more than a man might earn in a lifetime and the very dogs on the street knew who the Drapier was, none could be got to betray the dean.

BRID MAHON
from *A Time to Love: The Life of Peg Woffington* (1992)

Heroin

Heroin was introduced very cunningly and deliberately into the inner city of Dublin. First the area was "flooded" with hash. In the pubs, pool-halls etc., there was open and massive selling, but no one really minded because hash wasn't seen as particularly dangerous. When the pushers had introduced a significantly large number of youngsters to hash and the idea of using drugs, a block was put on hash and heroin, palf and dike were brought in. The local teenagers didn't know about the dangers of using heroin. Those in the 17-18 age group had reached the age when joy-riding and so on had lost its glamour and become boring. Very few pubs would serve them – in the pubs they would at least have been under some minimal supervision. Hard drugs could be taken just about anywhere. They saw it simply as a good turn-on, a new trend, cool...and were easily led into using them.

I remember talking to women after heroin had got a grip, where it had got to the stage that it was almost too difficult to combat. How had they let it get so far? They said they simply had no experience. They didn't know what the hell it was. The kids that went on it went straight on it. It arrived. It was made available free. People saw kids injecting themselves and didn't know what they were doing, until they had the addictions at a rate that they just didn't know how to respond to it. It wasn't just the people in any particular block of flats. It was priests, social workers and people like myself. We just didn't believe it. I remember I used to go down to a certain bar where it was on sale. I didn't believe it. I couldn't come to terms with it. I had been in contact with all sorts of drugs. I couldn't come to terms with the fact that heroin was openly on sale and people were taking it. So how the hell do you expect a woman in, say, Hardwicke Street to see that?

The people who first became conscious of the horror were the women who lived in areas where the pushers plied their trade:

> There was plenty of drug addicts. You couldn't open your doors. I was going to keep on throwing buckets on my steps, and over the balconies – sick everywhere, syringes, matches, cider bottles everywhere. There was a lot of addicts coming from surrounding areas.

I've spoken to people in flats where heroin has now become a frightening part of everyday life. Two years ago they would not have believed it possible and two years ago they had never seen a hypodermic syringe except in a hospital ward. Now people talk of

the horror of seeing young girls knock on doors asking for water
to dilute the drug; people stumble over addicts injecting themselves
in darkened stairways, and later, are reminded by the spatters of
blood on balconies and stairs. One mother told me of her ten-year-old
boy being used by the pushers to carry 'packs of smack' from hiding
places, back to them. Local people remark on the 'lovely young
girls and boys' who come into the area for drugs. They are horrified
to see the pushers use a needle on the young addicts in full view
of children at play.

RONAN SHEEHAN & BRENDAN WALSH
from *The Heart of the City* (1988)

Serving Them Right

This is a tale of two women and two cities. The first woman is
Beate Weber, formerly a German MEP and head of the women's
group in the European Parliament, now Oberburgomeister – that
is, boss – of the city of Heidelberg. The other is a woman called
Liz, housewife and mother, of Wood Lane, off Benburb Street, which
is behind the Liffey quays near Heuston station in Dublin. Liz and
Frau Weber are both trying to influence the way their cities respond
to the needs of the half of the citizenry who are women. That's all
they have in common.

Frau Weber is a politician, but the job of mayor of Heidelberg
combines the political and administrative functions separated else-
where, so she is the finance and planning director as well as the
ceremonial head of the city. She disposes of a huge budget all round,
but the bit that interests us here is that she spends DM 1,330,000
a year on specifically woman-sensitive initiatives. That's about half
a million pounds, Liz, on the other hand, just has a few tea-chests
and a hand-written placard with which to make Dublin responsive
to her needs. As I say, they haven't all that much in common.

Liz lives in a narrow street which motorists use as a short-cut.
Her house has no yard or garden back or front. She has two small
boys and is afraid to let them out to play. She tried to get Dublin
Corporation to declare her street a cul-de-sac. Or if not, to prohibit
a right turn out of her street, because that's the way the cars want

to turn. No luck. She went to Bertie Ahern's people. Eventually, she got the sign, but at the *exit* to her street, not its entrance.

This means, of course, that cars come in, find they can't turn right, and – feeling cheated – turn right anyway. Her traffic problem is almost as bad as before. Appeals to Dublin Corporation to put up a sign at the *entrance* to her street have got nowhere. They may yet work because recently, Jim Mitchell TD, took an interest in her case. But in the meantime, she's out on the street, trying to block the right turn with her tea-chests and her placard. And getting a lot of ugly abuse which by rights, it seems to me, somebody in the Corporation should be getting.

I bumped into Liz's little protest last week, when I was just walking along. I'd heard Frau Weber talk about her work in Germany a few days earlier. The contrast vividly suggested to me that Dublin Corporation does not see itself as a body which exists to serve the citizens. That its governing self-image is of put-upon, low-paid and unvalued civil servants, trying to deal with an unruly and undeserving populace. The bunkers at Wood Quay illustrate this cosmos. They are there – I presume – because the corporation people wanted to be together. The citizen is to travel to the bureaucrat, not the bureaucrat to the citizen. Wait for the bus (if Dublin Bus and the unions ever condescend to run a bus service again), haul the buggy on the bus, pay the fares, trudge along to Wood Quay, take a queuing ticket, and so on.

In Heidelberg, there are one-stop shops in the suburbs. They link with each other of course, by computer and telephone. You can get a passport there. Pay car tax. Make enquiries. Take advantage of services. If a husband walked out, leaving a family with nothing, the wife could call to her nearest office and get all the information she might need about emergency assistance available from the city. Secretive old people can conceal the fact that they're looking for benefits when they visit these offices, because of the many reasons there are for being there. Liz could have gone to her local office, were she a citizen of Heidelberg, to discuss the traffic problem in her street in the first instance, and to make an appointment for the traffic planners to come to talk to her.

Accessible one-stop shops are particularly useful to women citizens of course. They also offer rewarding jobs to female – and male – bureaucrats. They're interesting to run. That's the kind of thing Frau Weber thinks of: she looks at the women working for the municipality, as well as the women the municipality contains. She is disgusted, for example, by the idea of a typing pool.

She's interested in streets. How can you make the streets of a city safe to walk in at night? So that women who work in offices all day could go, say, window-shopping, without fear? Could you arrange points at which groups would collect? Why should public space, after all, paid for by both sexes, become the exclusive property of men? And the city of Heidelberg subsidises a night-cab service, an anti-rape measure which means that elderly women now take part in social and cultural life. Previously, they, of all citizens, were confined to their homes after dark. Ideas like these just don't come from Dublin Corporation.

As for traffic – Liz in Dublin will be interested to know that Heidelberg is seeking to feminise its transport policy. The city carried out a study of men and women of different ages and their access to cars on a steady or frequent basis. Need I say that in the 45-65 age-group, for example, 70 per cent of men have cars available, but only 30 per cent of women.

In general, male planners think of themselves and their cars as being what traffic is. That's why there are so many roads. It is women who know what it's like to be outside that – to be the ones dependent on public transport, or – as in Liz's case – the ones paying in loss of amenity for the convenience of car-owners. Heidelberg is trying to work out a transport policy that serves *all* the people.

Had Liz despaired of getting a hearing, and lived in Heidelberg, she could have gone to the Ombudsfrau. The latter is a retired judge, entirely independent of government at any level, and she adjudicates on problems that arise between the citizen and the city administration. Imagine that! And dream on. It could never happen here, because it would make redundant the efforts of the Bertie Aherns and the Jim Mitchells. If the Corporation really, really believed that it is there to serve the people, and towards that end devised flexible and quickly-reacting systems, the citizens could deal with it as equals. There'd be no need of favours from any politician. Liz is an example of someone more than competent to run her own affairs forced, by the way things are here, into looking for favours.

Women experience the city differently from men. That's because they have life-patterns that differ from those of men. Hitherto, men have planned modern city systems. When a feminist like Beate Weber gets power she brings another perspective to the task. It is exhilarating to listen to her, and frustrating too, when one compares the situation in Ireland. She got in through being elected, and she's in for eight years. We don't even get to elect the mayor here, much less the city manager.

Liz, too, is a modern woman. She is as resourceful and determined, in her sphere, as Frau Weber is in hers. But there are no people like them at or near the top in Dublin Corporation, because there are no women. The city manager is male. The four assistant managers are male. Of the 10 principal officers, one – the head of libraries – is female, the other nine are male. There are 54 administrative officers: 45 of these are male. There are 127 staff officers: 66 of these are male. This imbalance is a disgrace in an institution which so powerfully affects the lives of the citizens, half of whom are female. The factors that have led to the imbalance should be identified. Women citizens have a right to ask that, at least.

Because if you've pushed a pram yourself you have more sympathy with the pram-pushers. If you been terrified by the sound of footsteps you arrange the night streets differently. If you've tried to keep two little boys indoors all the time – like Liz – you know what it means to be able to let them play out the front. And all of us would be the better for feeling, as citizens, that our problems are respected – that there's some middle way between doing nothing and going out with your tea-chests and your placard. In The Hague, for example, the meetings of the city council are held in an information centre and everyone has a right to express an opinion on any subject on the agenda, by arrangement. Germany and the Netherlands, it seems, have a different concept of the citizen's rights from ourselves, and that concept includes a superior sensitivity to the difference between men and women as citizens.

NUALA O'FAOLÁIN
from *The Irish Times* (1993)

Things Fall Apart

MRS GOGAN (*to the two men*). Were yous far up th' town? Did yous see any sign o' Fluther or Nora? How is things lookin'? I hear they're blazin' away out o' th' GPO. That th' Tommies is shtretched in heaps around Nelson's Pillar an' th' Parnell Statue, an' that th' pavin' sets in O'Connell Street is nearly covered be pools o' blood.

PETER. We seen no sign o' Nora or Fluther anywhere.

MRS GOGAN. We should ha' held her back be main force from goin'

to look for her husband...God knows what's happened to her –
I'm always seein' her sthretched on her back in some hospital,
moanin' with th' pain of a bullet in her vitals, an' nuns thryin'
to get her to take a last look at th' crucifix!

THE COVEY.   We can do nothin'. You can't stick your nose into
O'Connell Street, an' Tyler's is on fire.

PETER.   An' we seen th' Lancers –

THE COVEY (*interrupting*).   Throttin' along, heads in th' air; spurs
an' sabres jinglin', an' lances quiverin', an' lookin' as if they were
assin' themselves, 'Where's these blighters, till we get a prod at
them?' when there was a volley from th' Post Office that stretched
half o' them an' sent th' rest gallopin' away wondherin' how far
they'd have to go before they'd feel safe.

PETER (*rubbing his hands*).   'Damn it,' says I to meself, 'this looks
like business!'

THE COVEY.   An' then out comes General Pearse an' his staff, an',
standin' in th' middle o' th' street, he reads th' Proclamation.

MRS GOGAN.   What proclamation?

PETER.   Declarin' an Irish Republic.

MRS GOGAN.   Go to God!

PETER.   The gunboat *Helga*'s shellin' Liberty Hall, an' I hear the
people livin' on th' quays had to crawl on their bellies to Mass
with th' bullets that were flyin' around from Boland's Mills.

SEAN O'CASEY
from *The Plough and the Stars* (1926)

The Centre Cannot Hold

It is a very intimate place for a city of close on a million inhabitants.
This is because the main centre of business, social and cultural
activity is confined to a small area close to where the Vikings founded
the original Dubh Linn (Black Pool), not far from Dublin Castle
and Christ Church cathedral. This intimacy may not last into the
next century. Recent years have seen some of its institutions move
to the suburbs. The headquarters of the national broadcasting service,

Radio Telefís Éireann (RTE) and University College Dublin, for instance, are now located in Donnybrook, once noted for its disputatious fair.

* * *

Dublin was once a city of Georgian squares and the sweep of streets leading from them to the city centre. Unfortunately, political independence did little to preserve and much to destroy its architectural distinctiveness. The Georgian Fitzwilliam and Merrion squares have so far escaped unscathed, but St Stephen's Green has been badly dented, although the green itself, the park and lake at the centre of the square, retains its individuality and style. Mountjoy Square, on the north side of the city, with close associations with Sean O'Casey, has been virtually destroyed. The centre has also suffered at the hands of the "developers" and the majority of its inhabitants were banished to a series of hideous suburbs before a movement to preserve what was left gained strength.

Dublin's problems have been compounded by the ugliness of some of its most recently erected public buildings. The Central Bank headquarters in Dame Street might be acceptable in a different location, but it is clearly out of sympathy with the street that it dominates. The new municipal offices at Wood Quay, behind Christ Church, are no addition to the city skyline and would not be easily accepted anywhere. It is difficult to explain how the city that was so proud of Gandon's Custom House, near Butt Bridge, could have tolerated the overhead railway bridge that obscured the public's view of it from O'Connell Bridge, and the addition of the terrible Liberty Hall and Busaras (the central bus station) that now loom over it have compounded the original act of philistinism.

A tantalising glimpse of how imaginative commercial development can be located in an unlikely setting is provided by the Powerscourt Centre near Grafton Street where a modern shopping centre has been most tastefully installed in an old town house. Unfortunately, of the city's old hotels only the Shelbourne, overlooking Stephen's Green, and the Gresham, at the top of O'Connell Street, have survived.

A positive effect of what preservationists call the destruction of Dublin has been to make the public more aware of the capital's heritage of stone and more critical of large-scale commercial development. The pity is that this awakening of interest and concern did not come earlier.

BREANDÁN Ó hEITHIR
from *This Is Ireland* (1987)

Everything Must Go

Meeting of Dublin Destroyers

The Dublin Vandals Association had their largest ever attendance at the Annual General Meeting in Development House, Dublin. The meeting unanimously congratulated Bord na Móna for their splendid work in the destruction of Georgian Dublin. The chairman, 'The Knocker' Muldoon, said that Bord na Móna were following in the footsteps of their colleagues in the ESB who had done a good job on these same Georgian slums.

The honorary secretary reported an extremely destructive year. Their forces in the field had destroyed 10,000 newly-planted trees in Dublin. This year, according to reports, the Corporation had planned to plant twice as many trees next year. 'All members must be vigilant to stop this city being turned into a jungle,' he said.

The secretary said that it had been an extremely good year in the telephone field. Reports from Foxrock, Ballyfermot, Dun Laoire, Howth, Drimnagh. Rathmines branches say 7000 telephones had been broken and kiosk doors knocked off.

The Bus and Train Branch Secretary in a special report said that 11,000 seats had been ripped, 11,000 windows rendered useless and straps had been cut on all CIE trains. In general, the general secretary said, they had maintained a reasonable rate of steady chaos.

At the close of the meeting members broke fifty chairs and the windows of seventy cars. Before leaving, there was a chorus of 'Ireland Boys Hurrah'.

The Paras Strike in Dublin

A group of bogmen paramilitaries describing themselves as the Semi-State Destructive Group (S.S.D.G.) emerged yesterday from a house in Pembroke Street, Dublin, with pickaxes in their hands. They had just destroyed the interior of a number of Georgian houses in the street. Their sergeant, who wore dark glasses and black beret, said: 'We are spearheading a scheme which we hope will modernise old Dublin.'

The sergeant said that their first action was totally successful and they looked forward to further destruction work. He then left by a fast car accompanied by a Garda escort for Newbridge, the HQ of the SSDG. (It is also used by Bord na Móna).

It is no secret that the militant SSDG has government support, although that has been clouded in semi-State secrecy. It has been

known unofficially, however, for some years that the central areas
of Dublin, particularly the draughty old Georgian houses and the
great waste of space of the Georgian Squares has been an irritant
to official Dublin people.

The people of An Lár, Dublin's mythical centre, have been under
constant pressure from secret agents of overseas developers and on
many occasions they have suffered from the Gardai's well known
blind eye. Remember the British Embassy?

Nowadays they only emerge at night to grab a pint of plain and
get back to their back room hideouts.

The SSG (2 Coy.) were drilling with pick axes last night in the
Furry Glen, Phoenix Park, and were hourly expected to converge
on Merrion Square. Present plans, it is believed in bog circles, are
to convert the square itself into a car park and make the houses into
a battery egg factory. 'This will mean cheap eggs on their doorsteps
for Dubliners,' said a delighted Bord na Móna top executive.

DONAL FOLEY
from *Man Bites Dog*

Nothing Vulgar

Alison's house was one of a row of artisan's dwellings dated from
the turn of the century but recently discovered by the young middle
classes. It was sturdily built of brick and stone, and it faced the
river Dodder only a few steps away from Ballsbridge. Where once
plumbers and carpenters and coopers and bricklayers had reared
huge families without benefit of a bathroom, rich young couples
had moved happily in and set about building sun-rooms and
patios and bathrooms and au pair rooms and conservatories and
playrooms. Because so many of them were architects or engineers
or advertising people it was all done in excellent taste, nothing
vulgar, nothing that wasn't sure to be in perfect harmony with the
character of the little houses. But it all meant that they were now
removed for ever out of reach of the ordinary Dubliners for whom
they had been built. Such Dubliners now lived miles away from
their work in huge suburbs clawing out into the countryside, each
with the population of a large town and a multiplicity of social

problems. Alison, on the other hand, could easily walk to work for her advertising firm in Harcourt Street or wheel her children along the river bank when she was free or down to Baggot Street and back with her groceries slung from a net on the underside of the pram. Her husband was a junior partner in a firm of architects and was sometimes away, but Alison never felt isolated. The river splashed and broke over its weir within sight of her front gate and she knew most of her neighbours. Besides there was Monique, specially acquired a few weeks before the baby was born and said to be a treasure by the family who were unloading her.

*   *   *

Ben sat for a while longer nursing his pint and watching the bar fill up with lush types as the afternoon became evening. It used to be mainly students here, scruffy, noisy, buying their grass for the weekend, making a couple of pints last until hunger drove them elsewhere, so unused to any more that some of them became truculent if four pints came their way. Now shorts rather than Guinness were the order of the day, though the pub's former clientele (who had moved along when the prices rocketed) were the reason why a good pint was still pulled here for those who wanted it. But looking along the tables he could see few pints. The beautiful people, together after work before they tragically parted for the weekend, favoured tequila or Pernod or gin and tonic or cocktails. They dressed brightly as tropical birds and they sought one another out from table to table, frequently shrieking with delight on discovering some-body, embracing theatrically and loudly exchanging gossip. Very few of these people were in fact theatre people – their watering place was across the road and that was where new productions were frequently cast. But here the common link was business, advertising, travel, sound recording, and the happy sloshers all around him were probably at the top of the heap.

VAL MULKERNS
from *Very Like a Whale* (1986)

Ascendancy

'Dirty Protestant', he shouted
When I was surrounded.
He was gap-toothed, carrot-haired,
Snotty-nosed, six inches taller,
In command of seven or eight
Equally menacing.

Only a hundred and fifty yards
From Donegan's shop to home;
But that lay round the corner,
Up the hill. And I was
Surrounded.

I had been sent on a message,
Was clutching some parsley,
Had never known hatred before,
And found it inexplicable,
As well as terrifying.

Someone had seen them
And shouted something.
I thought I was lucky
To get away with a split lip,
To get away at all,
Up the hill.

DERRY JEFFARES
from *Brought Up in Dublin* (1987)

Dead Bones and Chickens

A new path has been laid at one end of the green in Kilbarrack.
There are other paths missing and there's a scabby old field beside
the tracks doing nothing, but when I saw this new path a month
ago the thought hit me – it's finished. They've finished building
Kilbarrack.

I can now get to the Giant shopping centre without getting muck on my trousers. It's a pity it's closed down.

The green is a great place. It has a weather system all of its own. The rain doesn't fall on the green. It gallops across it. It waits for you. It surrounds you like the Apaches, jabs at you and wriggles in under your coat. It breaks the nose off you. Even on a dry day you can get drenched crossing the green.

On summer evenings the green is full of people. Thin kids in tracksuits run round and around it and stockier kids run quicker across it. There are Golfing Prohibited signs and the golfers lean against them while they wait for the lads in front to finish. Sometimes there are horses. Polo isn't prohibited. And there is soccer, what looks like three matches being played on the one pitch at the same time. The fathers stand on the sideline and shout, Good lad Darren and Mind your house. The kids all run after the ball.

Last September there was a dead body on the green for a couple of hours. RTE came out. The next Saturday there was another dead body there.

Ah Jaysis, not another one!

But he was only drunk. The guards took him home.

At Halloween there are bonfires on the green; cardboard boxes, wooden pallets from the supermarkets, bags of rubbish, sometimes a tyre and, once, the clinic. The day after that one the road was covered in nappies and files.

Yesterday my first year Group Cert class recited the Great Deserts of the World for me.

Sahara, Kalahari, Gobi, Dollymount. Sahara, Kalahari, Gobi, Dollymount.

They burst out laughing everytime they got to Dollymount.

The church in Kilbarrack is one of those pyramid jobs, with a tape of a bell instead of a real one. The old church is now the snooker hall. The old church isn't very old. I was delighted when it was built. It meant that I could now go to mass on my own and, later, pretend to go to mass on my own. Before that we had to go to Baldoyle for mass, the whole family. By the time my parents got their act together there was usually only the half-twelve mass left, and we weren't allowed out because we were in our good clothes. We drove to Baldoyle. My father pointed up to a window in the convent there and told us that that was where they kept the black babies. Sometimes the half-twelve mass was a Requiem mass and it went on forever. I sat there, squashed and sweating, hoping that someone would faint, especially an altar boy, especially the one

holding the bell. Kilbarrack's own church was a great escape. I'll
never play snooker in it.

Last week I met a past pupil at Kilbarrack station. He's twenty
two. He left the army last year.

They made us get up before the fuckin' seagulls, Mister Doyle.

He's back home now. They call the house Vietnam because they
never cut the grass.

From our house on Kilbarrack Road, Howth Junction seemed
like miles away. But then they widened and straightened the road
and chopped down the hedges and there it was, the station, just
down there. They dug up the road and put down pipes. Then they
dug it up again and put down more pipes. Houses were replacing
the cows, first private ones and then the corporation ones. Young
ones and young fellas took over the paths. I'd heard the word Fuck
for the first time in Ballybunion in August 1966. I heard it a lot
now. I heard off a lot as well. They put down more pipes. Then
the grocer's was sold and became the chipper, and that was it. Kil-
barrack had become a new place.

The third years had their town plans on the desks. We were
doing street names.

Cooper's Lane?, I asked.

A man that makes barrels lived down there.

Good man. Pearse Street?

Padraic Pearse, said Debbie.

Good. Who was he?

He won the Eurovision Song Contest.

I looked at her. She was grinning.

Mick King was one of the new people. One of us would say –
Here's Mick King, and we'd be legging it down Kilbarrack Road
or up Kilbarrack Road, anywhere to get away from him. Before
Mick King the wildest man in Kilbarrack was the one who'd pissed
in the letterbox of one of the shops. And there were the older boys
who'd put aspirin in a bottle of coke and got sick over each other
and passed out in the fields where Bayside was being built. But
Mick King was – Mick King. There were dozens of stories. Mick
King broke all the windows in the school, Mick King threw roof
slates down at the guards, Mick King skulled a man with a hammer,
Mick King set his ma on fire, Mick King hijacked Mister Whippy.
I believed all of them. I knew all about Mick King but I don't
think I ever saw him.

The day after Hector Grey's warehouse burned down I watched
a child emptying his schoolbag. He took out a biro, half a pencil

and twenty seven fancy pencil parers. He lined them up at the top of his desk; Papa Smurf, Paddington Bear, Metal Micky, Darth Vader, Zebedee. He let the girl beside him sharpen her pencil with Dougal's arse.

There's still a farmyard in Kilbarrack, on the corner of Kilbarrack Road and Thornville. There are chickens in there, and a smell. I've been told that if you hang around long enough on a Saturday night you'll see all the mammies climbing up over the wall for the Sunday dinner.

Last October I saw Christy on the corridor just outside my room. He was holding a magnifying glass to the crotch of his trousers and everytime a girl walked past him he made it go bigger, smaller, bigger, smaller.

I roared at him.

Christy! Stop that. He grinned.

Ah now, Sir, he said. They'll have to learn about it sooner or later.

I'm glad I come from the same place as Christy.

RODDY DOYLE
from *Invisible Dublin*, edited by Dermot Bolger (1991)

Temple Bar

Where and what is Temple Bar and why is it so called? Strictly speaking Temple Bar is a short, modest city-centre street near the south banks of the river Liffey. In itself the street has no great significance or historical connections but in the last few years the Temple Bar area has taken on a national prominence and has become a byword for urban regeneration, restoration and cultural development.

Temple Bar was ostensibly named after Sir William Temple whose residence and gardens previously stood on the site in the early 17th century. However, as there was already a Temple Bar leading onto Fleet Street in London, it might be correctly supposed that these names were imported both as a memory of England's Capital (the native city of many of Dublin's administrators and developers) and at the same time to coincidentally honour the well-regarded Temple family. The earliest record of Temple Bar on a map of Dublin is 1673 .

A "bar", originally barr, is an estuary sandbank or, as in the case of the London version, a barrier or gate blocking the entrance to the city.

Today Temple Bar is taken to mean the area bordered by Fishamble, Dame and Westmoreland Streets and Wellington Quay. It has been given a special status for building and residential renewal and development as a Cultural Quarter by legislation and tax incentives.

From the 1950s this whole area began to decline as businesses and shoppers moved elsewhere. From 1981, CIE (the state transport company) started to buy up property to build a transportation centre. However, the plan ran into difficulties and while awaiting a resolution CIE leased out premises at low rents which attracted creative and fringe activities. These, in turn, breathed new life into the area.

The upsurge in a whole range of activities brought a fresh focus to the charming characteristics of Temple Bar and after intensive lobbying by various groups including the Temple Bar Development Council and the preparation of an Action Plan by Dublin Corporation, the government took decisive action by introducing the Temple Bar Area Renewal and Development Act.

Opportunities now exist for Temple Bar to relate to the essence of each stage of its colourful past, a past that was inextricably bound up with the genesis and development of Dublin.

The rest will be history.

PAT LIDDY
from *Temple Bar* (1992)

Note from the Dead

One evening in 1974, I took a stroll through the old house in Mountjoy Square where I was living in a flat, poking into dead rooms, toeing odds and ends of boxes and drawers. You could walk a big dog through a place like that and count it exercised. No one else was in; or maybe the scholar who lived upstairs was picking over some page of Joyce above, silent and mesmerised. And I felt that sense of other lives, I saw clearly, separately, the old brownness of the paint that was no longer paint in the halls, but a ghost, a coffin-coloured remnant of true paint. I heard the steps, the countless steps, the privacy of those roomkeepers going out for whatever private purchases into the greater city.

Dark winter as always, the late day full of gloom outside the windows, every object I saw beginning to speak its story, to clamour to be heard, to explain, to detail disaster and the victory of sudden joys. Each old table had been picked and purchased new once, pennies pinched to have it, each door had been opened and shut a million times, by twenty generations in as many ragged fashions. Now no one was there to disturb the hinges and they creaked with that complaint.

The lower landing was readying up for revelation, for a tiny information to me, a preparation, a hint at the very stuff of life and the use of a life. I wandered into the most battered room of the house where there wasn't even a frame in the window, only a jagged sheet of thick plastic over the hole, and the night wind icing in, and the streetlamps forward and blunt in the debris.

Here was a little tin box. I prised it open with a nail and took out a piece of old blue writing paper, the sort I used to write to my father on when he was away in London, old blue paper folded a few times into a small irregular shape. It had the dirt outside of something often handled but less often unfolded, as if it had been taken from spot to spot, extracted from book to niche to tin, over the span of a life. So settled in its folds it was almost difficult to open it.

The surface inside looked quite crisp and new, as if it had just been written on, and the writing was in a fresh pencil. The paper spoke, you could hear its voice, in the list of names and the few bleak sentences:

> In this room on the night of January the 2nd the coldest night of the year we went to bed all hale, and awoke to find three of our number dead,
> Jamie (Brown) aged 7 Mary and Christie Finlay, 3 months, 11 years from a suffocation. And the rest not much better

Under this, there was an entry in a different hand, or the same hand at a different time, a tireder hand perhaps, listing two others, two of the old ones, who had died

> we suppose from the late effects of the same cause.
> I, Jane Finlay, mother, write this down, the names of our loved ones. We must never forget this.

What was to be done with such a discovery? What did it mean? When I was long gone out of that house I used to think of that room, think of that family sleeping there in the great privacy, the secrecy of poverty, and that coldest night of the year, and that woman of the elegant words writing down the record of the event. This was her *Book of Kells,* her illuminated text. Still sticking to it in that dreadful room were the ribbons of their lives, the faintest sounds spiralled around the note, vague faces appeared under the force of such a signal, the small corpses of her children, the big corpses of her elders. One morning in winter – and when was this, the twenties, the thirties, the sixties? – she had awoken to find half her family suffocated, all the air in the stifled room used up. The cold absences of that day! Even now seventeen years later that note, a few words in pencil, affect me more than many a fine book has, many an excellent and resplendent play.

I suppose I was the first person to read that piece of notepaper since the last hand belonging to it had passed away from the world so thoroughly that even it, a precious document, an heirloom, a history, had not been safekept. It had lain in its tin box for decades in a room of rubble – the scholar above poring over his Joyce – its tiny message silent, waiting for a foolish student to wander about the deserted house.

I'm sure I took it with me, stuffed it in my jacket. I'm sure I took it with me out of that room and I'm equally sure I lost it. Not in safe hands! Or at best it sits among old papers of mine in some old box in my mother's house, waiting for a fresh reader, a second hearer, a better seer. I hope Jane Finlay died a nicer death than her people did that night, when it got so cold, and they stopped up the window with rags, that fine old Georgian window, and minute by minute their lungs used up the precious air, and warm enough they died, and cold she awoke, to rise, and shake her dead, and write her note.

SEBASTIAN BARRY
from *Invisible Dublin,* edited by Dermot Bolger (1991)

Heritage Trail

I went to see Dublinia to learn about my home town, first of all,
but also to try again to come to terms with this theme-park thing.
In the contemporary world, they're inescapable. In New England,
I noticed recently, whole villages are inhabited by girls and boys
wearing historic costumes and doing historic things, like grinding
corn, or quaffing ale, for the benefit of tourists.

In contemporary Derry, the quayside is all motorway and Chinese
restaurants. But in the museum-park near Omagh, they've recon-
stituted the real, so to speak, Derry quayside. What's more, you
can step from it on to an emigrant ship, and step off the other side
into replica Pennsylvania.

Dublinia is not so ambitious. It doesn't really aim to induce the
suspension of disbelief, even though there are tapes of street-noises
and the crackle of burning flames, and real onions and garlic hang
in the merchant's kitchen, and so on. These are more teaching-aids
than sensory wraparounds.

And the teaching is quite conventional. If I'd been listening at
school I'd know it. Strongbow, and trade, and Art MacMurrough
Kavanagh and Silken Thomas and all that. To tell you the truth,
after the exhibition the history of Dublin is as much of a blur as
ever. But it's a fondly familiar blur. It'll do me.

It is history of the one-important-bloke-after-another-important-
bloke kind. You don't learn anything interesting, like what time
people got up, or who got educated, or at what age people had sex,
or how much a clerk earned, or what kind of burial rituals there
were, or what happened at Christmas.

The nearest Dublinia gets to domestic detail is in the exhibition
of little things for playing gambling games that are shown with
other finds from Wood Quay. As usual, the past seems very clean.
And very underfurnished – bits of jugs, combs, clasps don't suggest
a world to the non-archaeologist. There is a magnificent model of
medieval Dublin which fixes its geography in your head for all
time. But it is almost empty of people, like the rest of the show.

It ends with a split-screen, audiovisual thing. It has Laurence
O'Toole in it, and an Irish king-type person, and a foreigner who
is very likely Strongbow – I missed the beginning and never caught
up. At one point Laurence O'Toole says to the other chaps: 'It
seems each of us has his own agenda.' Verisimilitude, plainly, is not
the point. The very last line has the city's first historian, Stanyhurst,

in the 16th century, exclaiming: 'Dublin could be heaven!' Then the lights come up and all the split screens show pictures of bottles of Bailey's Irish Cream.

But then the first of the good transitions happens. You're decanted (through a souvenir shop, naturally) across the mock-Gothic bridge and into Christ Church Cathedral itself. And there is St Laurence O'Toole's real heart, and the inscription from the real Strongbow's tomb. It will be a first time in Christ Church for many Irish people, and even if that were all that Dublinia achieved it would be worth it. Not that Christ Church has anything like the personality and beauty of St Patrick's, in my opinion. But it is as ancient a site as this city has, and that it should at last be incorporated into the general sense of the city is a very good thing.

If it were ever really hot in this country then the crypt of Christ Church would be the place to go. There's even a memorial down there to a man called Henry Mathias who went to the Arctic, showing the little 19th century ships, sailing past a huge iceberg. And the cathedral itself is shiny and cool, with a floor of wonderful tiles. By the time you get there, from first going in the door of the Dublinia exhibition, you've been maybe an hour trying to learn about the city, trying to imagine it, to feel it. You're sensitised to things like tiles, by the end.

It is the best transition of all, to come out of the cathedral into the real city. The office workers, and the buses squealing, and sea-gulls wheeling around in the blue, spring sky. That crest of the ridge, there above the river, even damaged by road widening, is full of presence.

The elements of the city are there. The airiness. The churches. The absorptions of pavement life, along Thomas Street and Wer-burgh Street and Dame Street. The poor and disadvantaged, piled along the balconies of Oliver Bond House. And the outsiders and tourists, carrying handbags carelessly, where they should not. There's a new hotel now, opposite Christ Church. Visitors seem, at the moment, to leave their cars outside. Has the city as a whole, then, or that part of it, become so peaceful?

What the mid 20th century did to Dublin was to all but destroy the poorer enclaves through unemployment, and the coming of drugs, and all that drugs entail. Individual people were ruined, and people as neighbours. Below the Dublinia building, on Merchants Quay, there is a place were HIV-positive people can go for help. Anyone there can tell you of the abject misery of parts of inner Dublin.

The physical city, equally, was treated as if nobody loved it. The old buildings were torn down: sterile roads were driven through irreplaceable streetscapes; medieval Dublin – Victorian Dublin, if it comes to that, which means more to me – was sacrificed to the Wood Quay bunkers. Until the inner-city tax-relief policies began to pay off, the area around Christ Church looked like a ruin. The Corporation planners could sit in their Wood Quay offices and look down on ruin, human and urban.

Now, there is, at least a physical improvement. There's the hotel, and terraces of bijou residences, and a patisserie as well as a great chip-shop, and Kinlay House and the College of Art and all the young people going to and fro. The old Dublin didn't have so many young people: it had brown, narrow streets, and there was a square with plane trees off Clanbrassil Street, and little dairy shops that reminded you of the roads from the country leading into the town.

That Dublin was unique. Now, it is quite like anywhere else. Except for the people, spilling along the streets, crossing through the traffic as if cars are unimportant. And for the friendly distances between things. And for the fact that this is a place where as long as your heart is high you can have a fine time, money or no money. It's a city where you can still belong if you're poor or old.

The loss and the profit in a city's mutations can't be captured in exhibits. Dublinia is carefully and brightly done, within its genre, and I wish it great success, for the sake of the people who work in it or who've invested in it. But this city to me is all the bedsitters I ever woke up in, and the afternoons in pubs, especially in the winter, and the things I've seen happen in streets – people knocked off bikes, women pushing buggies and crying, film stars coming out of hotels.

Meandering along, in love. The dawn coming, in love. Being hungry, having no money, and hanging up your coat in warm restaurants. All the emotions felt on these streets. The books read in it. About it. Music heard. Shoes bought. Funerals gone to. What can an exhibition be, compared with this huge, redolent mass, these memories inside each person which – if they could be added together – would be the city?

The contemporary world seems often to pose the question: is a bit of something better than nothing at all? Are the melodies from the slow movements of concertos transcribed for electric guitar better than no knowledge of them at all? Is a *Reader's Digest* condensed book better than no book? Is a visit to a theme-centre better than nothing? I'd swap a thousand Dublinias to have the Wood

Quay offices unbuilt or even to have someone just *apologise* for building them. But that deal wasn't on offer.

In the end, how you value Dublinia depends on how you classify it. If you take it as a responsible introduction to the history in which Christ Church Cathedral is important, it is satisfying. If you bring to it all the feelings a person might have towards the arena in which their lives are played out, then it, or any exhibition, must disappoint. When it comes to renewing your affection, or teaching affection to your children, better by far to saunter across Dublin in the sun, looking at all the details by yourself.

NUALA O'FAOLÁIN
from *The Irish Times* (1993)

A Second-Rate Knackers Yard

No city, and certainly not a small, coherently-planned one like Dublin, can endure the thoughtless, day-by-day destruction of its older architecture without endangering its particular identity.

The Official Guide to Dublin is positively lyrical about the city's charms. Dublin, says the guide, is 'a city of spacious streets, fine buildings and friendly people; a city which combines the beauty of more leisured centuries with modern progressiveness'. That's not all: incredibly, tourists are told that Dublin is 'one of the most charming cities in the world...an important capital and, at the same time, the most perfect intact example of an eighteenth-century European city'.

Nobody could blame Dublin Tourism for trying to present their product in the best possible light, but even transient tourists are not that easily conned, which is why their average stay in Dublin is less than two days. They come here expecting to find something of the city of James Joyce, of Behan and of O'Casey. Instead, they discover the terrible truth – that Dublin is probably the shabbiest, most derelict city in Europe, chaotic and disorderly like the capital of some Third World country. The tourists, no more than the inhabitants, cannot walk more than a few hundred yards without being confronted by shocking evidence of urban blight. The eyesores are everywhere – weed-strewn derelict sites surrounded by decaying hoardings, dilapidated buildings boarded up and left to face the elements, gap-toothed streets and grotesque modern office blocks. Indeed, the cratered roads and scarred footpaths would do credit to war-torn Beirut.

For those of us who were born here, the sad reality is that we can no longer take pride in calling ourselves Dubliners. The state of the city is a cause for shame, a cause for outrage. Even our City Fathers are prepared to concede that Dublin is rotting at the core. One former Lord Mayor, Jim Mitchell, confessed some years ago that the city centre had 'about as much character as a second-rate knacker's yard'. And one of his colleagues, battling Alice Glenn, was so embarrassed by the appalling dereliction that she pretended to visiting councillors from abroad that it was all the result of terror-ist bombings.

Most of us, having lived with the degradation on a daily basis, are now so de-sensitised that we don't even bother to make excuses anymore. Only visitors and prodigal sons, seeing it afresh, are truly horrified. Stephen Gardiner, architecture critic of *The Observer*, is more shocked every time he comes here. 'Suddenly Dublin has become a shabby city – shabby because its centre is peppered with crude concrete structures, flashy mirror-glass façades and other inappropriate schemes which have no connection at all with the spirit of the place,' he wrote in 1979. 'Some say what's happening in Paris is just as bad – look at La Défense. It is appalling; but at least the French have made sure that, on the whole, developers go mad outside the city's centre. In Dublin, the destruction is from within.'

Almost fifteen years ago, Lewis Mumford, the distinguished American urban philosopher, gave his stark verdict. 'Dublin,' he said, 'exhibits the worst aspects of the collapse of twentieth-century urban structure and is on its way to becoming a non-city.' The chilling route charted by Mumford had its landmarks – the ESB's gutting of Fitzwilliam Street, the battle for Hume Street, the row over the Central Bank, the rape of Wood Quay – but these were merely the more notorious milestones on the relentless march of destruction. Nothing, it seemed, was sacred. For John Simpson, the BBC's diplomatic correspondent, the demolition of the Royal Hibernian Hotel in 1984 was the final straw. 'Eleven years ago, when I was the BBC's correspondent in Dublin, the Hibernian was my office and sometimes my home, and I am naturally sad that it too should have fallen victim to the developer,' he said in a letter to the *Irish Times*. 'But the loss of this fine building is not simply a personal one; it is Dublin's and Ireland's loss as well. No city, and certainly not a small, coherently-planned one like Dublin, can endure the thoughtless, day-by-day destruction of its older architecture without endangering its particular identity.'

Bob Geldof, characteristically, was rather less diplomatic. At a civic reception at the Mansion House to mark his outstanding success in raising millions for Africa's famine victims, the outspoken rock singer laid it squarely on the line. In front of the Lord Mayor, the City Manager and other big-wigs, he railed against the destruction of his native Dublin. 'This city has become increasingly brutalised,' he said. 'The people have lost some of their openess, and I think a lot of it is largely due to the destruction of the city itself, which was once one of the prettiest cities in these islands and is now a shambolic mess, at best. Tomorrow, I have to bring some of the BBC around the city to show them some of the things I remember and love about the place. Unfortunately, when I went through the list of my memories, 50 per cent of the things I liked had disappeared, to be replaced by the most mediocre, unaesthetic, architecturally inarticulate buildings I've ever seen in my life. They are a scandal. They can only be the product of back-handers, political corruption and moral degradation.

'When a city is being destroyed by its custodians, then what are the people who live in it supposed to think? The brutalisation seeps through, in the increased use of drugs, which is epidemic in this city, the street violence and the rudeness that is almost everywhere. And I'm sorry if my image clashes with the tourist image of it, but that's what I've seen over thirty-two years. As I say, it's very nice to come home and it's particularly nice to be honoured in this way. But please stop destroying Dublin, and please get rid of those buildings that offend us all, that make us so depressed. And, please, bring back to this city some of the life and beauty that was there when I grew up with it, and make it somewhere that's nice to come home to – especially if you've been somewhere like Ethiopia.'

The City Fathers, assembled in the Oak Room of the Mansion House, were taken aback by Geldof's outburst; it cut them to the quick. More than twenty years earlier, they had been give a legislative mandate to make Dublin a better place to live in. And much as some of them might not like to admit it, deep-down they knew that they had failed – and failed miserably. The 1963 Planning Act was supposed to herald the dawn of a new era. It was as the long-title proclaimed, 'An Act to make provision, in the common good, for the proper planning and development of cities, towns and other areas, whether urban or rural (including the preservation and improvement of the amenities thereof)...' The legislation contained ninety-two sections, running to more than two hundred pages, and it gave local authorities – including Dublin Corporation – wide powers to further the cause of 'positive planning'. Bureaucratic cobwebs were to be swept away and the Corporation was to prepare a Development Plan for the city, to be reviewed and updated every five years.

Back in 1963, when the Planning Act was passed by the Oireachtas, Dublin was certainly a poorer place, but at least it had some coherence. After twenty-two years of "planning", the city is a mess. Sure, there has been "urban renewal", lots of it, but mostly in areas that didn't need to be renewed. We have had an uprecedented boom in office development. Almost three hundred new blocks have been built, producing a total of ten million square feet of modern office space with a combined capital value exceeding one billion pounds. Yet scarcely a dozen of these buildings could be regarded as good modern architecture. But then, aesthetic considerations played almost no part in their design, construction or location. For office blocks are not like other buildings; they are crude investment vehicles for pension funds and insurance companies. By allowing them to be built here, there and everywhere, regardless of the social and environmental cost, we have effectively sacrificed our city for the sake of our pensions.

Office blocks didn't just deface the city; they helped to kill it as well. Once-thriving streets, where people used to live above the shops were ruthlessly denuded of their population. The inhabitants were uprooted and forced to move to the suburbs or, worse still, to the "new towns" far out of the city's perimeter. As the office blocks took over, streets were left for dead after six o'clock every evening, to become mugging alleys where people walked in fear and dread. Belatedly the Corporation tried to staunch the population haemorrhage with its much-praised inner city housing programme. At the same time, however, the Corporation's own engineers were reinforcing the trend towards a lifeless city through their destructive road plans. And it's not as if nobody shouted stop. Fierce battles were fought along the way by intermittently well-organised conservation groups. But at the end of the day, the city is in such bad shape that one is left wondering would it have been any worse if they hadn't intervened. Indeed, the Georgian lobby's only real success was entirely unintentional; by campaigning so hard to save the threatened eighteenth-century terraces in the city centre, they helped in no small way to spawn the mutant of fake-Georgian semis in the suburbs.

FRANK McDONALD
from *The Destruction of Dublin* (1985)

The Old Lady Says *Yes!*

Dublin is an enigmatic old lady. She celebrated her millenium in 1988 with a facelift highlighting many of her features. She emphasised some of her outstanding assets by restoring the Royal Hospital, Dublin Castle and Government Offices in Merrion Street.

It's strange how obsession with the past sometimes obscures the achievements of the present. The first phase of the Civic Offices was born amidst much frustration after a gestation period racked with controversy. Opponents vied with each other to find the most colourful vituperative language. And yet the second recently completed linking phase which stands boldly on the banks of Anna Livia gets comparatively little mention. Its beautiful new outdoor Amphitheatre and Pedestrian Way which beckons people in from Temple Bar are ignored. Strange, because it is an award-winning building which many select as the outstanding building in Dublin in recent years, an inner city architectural gem fronting the river in the tradition of those great buildings of the eighteenth century, the Custom House and the Four Courts.

People have come back in their thousands to live in the heart of the city. Decrepit sites have undergone a metamorphosis and the Quays have taken on a fresh look with new developments looking out over the river. The last decade has seen the advent of many new pedestrian-friendly areas – Grafton Street is a good example – where people can saunter in a pleasant atmosphere and become intoxicated with the gaiety and the buzz of the living city. In the grandeur of College Green at night, now beautifully floodlit, the memory resounds with the oratorical skills of the many famous people who spoke there.

There is a bounce to the lady's step and a new song in her heart.

FRANK FEELY (DUBLIN CITY MANAGER)
from *Whither Dublin* (1995)

The Fall

The Garden of Eden (described in the Bible)
Was Guinness's Brewery (mentioned by Joyce),
Where innocent Adam and Eve were created
And dwelt from necessity rather than choice;

For nothing existed but Guinness's Brewery,
Guinness's Brewery occupied all,
Guinness's Brewery everywhere, anywhere –
Woe that expulsion succeeded the Fall!

The ignorant pair were encouraged in drinking
Whatever they fancied whenever they could,
Except for the porter or stout which embodied
Delectable knowledge of Evil and Good.

In Guinness's Brewery, innocent, happy,
They tended the silos and coppers and vats,
They polished the engines and coopered the barrels
And even made pets of the Brewery rats.

One morning while Adam was brooding and brewing
It happened that Eve had gone off on her own,
When a serpent like ivy slid up to her softly
And murmured seductively, Are we alone?

O Eve, said the serpent, I beg you to sample
A bottle of Guinness's excellent stout,
Whose nutritive qualities no one can question
And stimulant properties no one can doubt;

It's tonic, enlivening, strengthening, heartening,
Loaded with vitamins, straight from the wood,
And further enriched with the not undesirable
Lucrative knowledge of Evil and Good.

So Eve was persuaded and Adam was tempted,
They fell and they drank and continued to drink
(Their singing and dancing and shouting and prancing
Prevented the serpent from sleeping a wink).

Alas, when the couple had finished a barrel
And swallowed the final informative drops,
They looked at each other and knew they were naked
And covered their intimate bodies with hops.

The anger and rage of the Lord was appalling,
He wrathfully cursed them for taking to drink
And hounded them out of the Brewery, followed
By beetles (magenta) and elephants (pink).

The crapulous couple emerged to discover
A universe full of diseases and crimes,
Where porter could only be purchased for money
In specified places at specified times.

And now in this world of confusion and error
Our only salvation and hope is to try
To threaten and bargain our way into Heaven
By drinking the heavenly Brewery dry.

FERGUS ALLEN
from *The Brown Parrots of Providencia* (1993)

The End

I will take this earth in both my hands and batter it into the sem-
blance of my heart's desire! See, there by the trees is reared the
gable of the house where sleeps my dear one. Under my feet the
grass is growing, soft and subtle, in the evening dew. The cool, clean
wind is blowing down from Killakee, kissing my hair and dancing
with the flowers that fill the garden all around me. And Sarah...
Sarah Curran...you are there...waiting for Robert Emmet.

I know this garden well for I have called it into being with the
Credo of the Invincibles; I believe in the might of Creation, the
majesty of the Will, the resurrection of the Word, and Birth Ever-
lasting.

(He flings aside his sword and looks around him in triumph. It is very dark, so dark that for all we know perhaps it may be the garden of the first scene. Perhaps those may be the trees and the mountains beyond the Priory. For a moment we hear the tramp of feet and the distant sound of the Shan Van Vocht. His voice falters and he staggers wearily.)

My ministry is now ended. Shall we sit down together for a while? Here on the hillside...where we can look down over the city, and watch the lights twinkle and wink to each other...Our city...our wilful, wicked old city...

(The gauze curtains close slowly behind him.)

I think...I would like to sleep...What?...On your shoulder?...Ah, I was so right to go on!

(His head sinks drowsily and his eyes stare out into the auditorium. He is lying just where the Doctor left him some time ago.)

Strumpet city in the sunset
Suckling the bastard brats of Scot, of Englishry, of Huguenot
Brave sons breaking from the womb, wild sons fleeing from their
      Mother.
Wilful city of savage dreamers,
So old, so sick with memories!
Old Mother
Some they say are damned,
But you, I know, will walk the streets of Paradise
Head high, and unashamed.

(His eyes close. He speaks very softly.)

There now. Let my epitaph be written.

(There is silence for a moment and then the doctor reappears bearing a large and gaudy rug. He looks towards the audience, places one finger to his lips, and makes a sign for the front curtains to be drawn. When last we see him he is covering the unconscious speaker with his rug. That is the end of this play.)

DENIS JOHNSTON
from *The Old Lady Says 'No!'* (1929)

ACKNOWLEDGEMENTS

The titles given to prose extracts have in most cases been coined for this book, although many are quotations. All titles given to complete works such as poems (and articles or stories which are not extracts) are the authors' own.

Acknowledgements are due to the following authors for their kind permission to reprint work in this book: **Sebastian Barry**, from *The Water-Colourist* (Dolmen, 1983) and *Invisible Dublin*, ed. Dermot Bolger (Raven Arts Press, 1991); **Brian Boydell**, from *Irish Childhoods*, ed. A. Norman Jeffares & Antony Kamm (Collins, 1987; Gill & Macmillan, 1992); **Maurice Craig**, from *Dublin 1600-1860* (Allen Figgis, 1980); **Anthony Cronin**, from *Dead As Doornails* (Dolmen, 1976); **J.P. Donleavy**, from *The Ginger Man* (The Olympia Press, Paris, 1955); **Eamon Dunphy**, from *Invisible Dublin*, ed. Dermot Bolger (Raven Arts Press, 1991); **Anne Haverty**, from *Constance Markievicz: An Irish Revolutionary*, 2nd edition (Pandora, 1993); **John Healy**, from *Healy, Reporter* (House of Healy, 1991); **Peter Murphy**, for 'Town of Little Stars'; **David Norris**, from the *Irish Times* (25 June 1993); **Sinéad O'Connor**, for 'The Pigeon House'; **Martin Roper**, from *The Close* (1992); **Mary Russell**, from the *Irish Times* (9 July 1992); **Peter Sheridan**, from *Shades of the Jelly Woman*, in collaboration with Jean Costello (1986); **Paul Smith**, from *The Country Woman* (Scribners, 1961; Heinemann, 1962).

Acknowledgements are due to the following literary agents, estates and executors for their kind permission to reprint work by these authors: **John Banville**, from *The Book of Evidence* (Secker & Warburg, 1989), copyright © John Banville 1986, to Sheil Land Associates Ltd; **Margaret Barrington**, from *The Lazy Life* (Jonathan Cape, 1939; Blackstaff Press, 1990), to Peters Fraser & Dunlop Group Ltd; **Kathleen Behan**, from *Mother of All the Behans* (Hutchinson, 1984), to Brian Behan; **Samuel Beckett**, from *Murphy*, copyright © Samuel Beckett 1938, 1963, 1977 and © Samuel Beckett Estate 1993, to The Samuel Beckett Estate and The Calder Educational Trust, London; **Dermot Bolger**, from *The Woman's Daughter* (Raven Arts Press, 1987; Penguin Books), to A.P. Watt Ltd; **Elizabeth Bowen**, from *Look at All Those Roses* (Gollancz, 1941), to Curtis Brown Group Ltd on behalf of the Estate of Elizabeth Bowen; **Austin Clarke**, from *Twice Round the Black Church* (1962) and 'Abbey Theatre Fire' from *Too Great a Vine* (1957), to R. Dardis Clarke, 21 Pleasants Street, Dublin 8; **Oliver St John Gogarty**, 'Ringsend' from *Others to Adorn* (1938), to Oliver D. Gogarty; **James Joyce**, extracts from *Dubliners* (1914; The Corrected Text, Jonathan Cape, 1967), *A Portrait of the Artist as a Young Man* (1916; The Definitive Text, corrected from the Dublin holograph by Chester G. Anderson and edited by Richard Ellmann, 1964, Jonathan Cape, 1968), *Ulysses* (1922; Bodley Head, 1960), and *Finnegans Wake* (Faber, 1939), to the Estate of James Joyce, and Stephen James Joyce exceptionally authorised the extract on page 156 from a letter by his grandfather to Grant Richards (15 October 1905); **Patrick Kavanagh**, 'Tale of Two Cities', 'On Raglan Road' and 'Elegy for Jim Larkin' and an extract from *Collected Pruse*, to Peter Fallon, literary agent to the Estate of Patrick Kavanagh; **Patrick McDonogh**, 'No Mean City' from *One Landscape Still* (1958), to Caroline McDonogh; **Louis MacNeice**, 'Dublin' from 'The Closing Album' (August-September 1939), to David Higham Associates Ltd; **Val Mulkerns**, from *Very Like a Whale* (John Murray, 1986), to Peters Fraser & Dunlop Group Ltd; **Sean O'Casey**, from

The Plough and the Stars (1926), *Drums Under the Windows* (1945) and *Inishfallen, Fare Thee Well* (1949), to Macnaughton Lord Representation Ltd on behalf of the Sean O'Casey Estate; **Ulick O'Connor**, from *Biographers and the Art of Biography* (Quartet, 1991), to Eugene Downes; **James Plunkett**, from *Strumpet City* (Hutchinson, 1989), to Peters Fraser & Dunlop Group Ltd; **V.S. Pritchett**, from *Dublin* (Hogarth Press, 1991), to Peters Fraser & Dunlop Group Ltd; **Bernard Shaw**, from *Composite Autobiography*, ed. Stanley Weintraub (Max Reinhardt, 1969) and *Music in London* (1931), to the Society of Authors on behalf of the Bernard Shaw Estate; **James Stephens**, from *The Charwoman's Daughter* (1912) and 'The James Joyce I Knew' (1946) from *James, Seumas and Jacques*, ed. Lloyd Frankenburg (Macmillan), to the Society of Authors as the literary representative of the Estate of James Stephens; **William Trevor**, from *The News from Ireland* (Bodley Head, 1986), to Peters Fraser & Dunlop Group Ltd. Permission for reprinting work by **W.B. Yeats** was pending from A.P. Watt Ltd when this book went to press, subject to clarification of matters affected by recent copyright legislation. The extracts from articles by **Bernadette Doorley, Deirdre Lindsay** and **Imelda Brophy** are reprinted from *The Gorgeous Mask: Dublin 1700-1850*, ed. David Dickson, published by Dublin TCD History Workshop in 1987, with permission sought from that source.

Acknowledgements are due to the following publishers for their kind permission to reprint work from their books or newspapers: **Anvil Books**, Dublin, for Tom Corkery from *Tom Corkery's Dublin* (1980); **Appletree Press**, Belfast, for Peter Somerville-Large from *Dublin: The First 1000 Years* (1988); **Attic Press**, Dublin, for Mary Black, Clare Boylan, June Levine, Nuala O'Faoláin and Maureen Potter, from *Alive, Alive O!* ed. Mairín Johnston (1988), Carol Coulter from *Web of Punishment* (1991), Moya Roddy from *The Long Way Home* (1992); **B.T. Batsford Ltd**, London, for Desmond Clarke from *Dublin* (1977); **Bloodaxe Books Ltd**, for Julie O'Callaghan from *What's What* (1991), Micheal O'Siadhail from *Hail! Madam Jazz: New & Selected Poems* (1992); **Brandon Book Publishers Ltd**, Cooleen, Dingle, for Anthony Cronin from *An Irish Eye* (1985), Ronan Sheehan & Brendan Walsh from *The Heart of the City* (1988); **Carcanet Press Ltd**, Manchester, for Eavan Boland from *Object Lessons* (1995); **Constable & Co. Ltd**, London, for Mary Lavin from *The Stories of Mary Lavin* (1974 & 1976); **Dedalus Press**, Dublin, for Valentin Iremonger from *Sandymount, Dublin* (1988), Gerard Smyth from *Painting the Pink Roses Black* (1986); **Faber & Faber Ltd**, London, for Fergus Allen from *The Brown Parrots of Providencia* (1983), Seamus Heaney from *North* (1975), John McGahern from *Getting Through* (1979), Donagh MacDonagh from *The Hungry Grass* (1947), Constantia Maxwell from *Dublin Under the Georges* (1979); **W. Foulsham & Co. Ltd** for Harry Ludlum from *A Biography of Dracula: The Life Story of Bram Stoker* (1962); **The Gallery Press**, Oldcastle, for Thomas Kilroy from *Talbot's Box* (1979), Paula Meehan from *The Man who was Marked by Winter* (1991); **Gill and Macmillan Ltd**, Dublin, for John O'Donovan from *Life on the Liffey: A Kaleidoscope of Dubliners* (1986), Frank McDonald from *The Destruction of Dublin* (1985); **HarperCollins** *Publishers* **Ltd**, London, for Mary Rose Callaghan from *Kitty O'Shea* (1989), Flann O'Brien from *At Swim-Two-Birds* (1939), Margaret Ward from *Maud Gonne* (1988); **The Harvill Press**, London, for Paul Durcan from *The Berlin Wall Café* (Blackstaff Press, 1985; Harvill Press, 1995), © Paul Durcan 1985, 1988, 1993, 1995; **The Irish Times Ltd**, Dublin, for Donal Foley (from *Man Bites Dog*), Frank Kilfeather

(28 February 1982), Sean Kilfeather, Frank McDonald (1988), Nuala O'Faoláin (28 September 1992, 10 May 1993 & 5 July 1993); **Lenhar Publications**, Dublin, for Bernard Neary from *Lugs: The Life & Times of Jim Branigan* (1985), Rose O'Driscoll from *Cabra People* (1990); **Macmillan General Books** for Bob Geldof from *Is That It?* (Sidgwick & Jackson, 1985); **Mercier Press Ltd**, Cork & Dublin, for John D. Sheridan from *The Best of John D. Sheridan: I Have Been Busy with Words*, ed. Gay Byrne (1979); **MO Books**, Dublin, for Vincent Caprani from *Vulgar Verse & Variations: Rowdy Rhymes & Rec-imitations* (1987); **O'Brien Press**, Dublin, for Curriculum Development Unit from *Viking & Medieval Dublin* (1978), Ann Dominica Fitzgerald, Robert Wyse Jackson and Lorcan Ó Diliún from *The Liberties of Dublin*, ed. Elgy Gillespie (1973), Eamonn MacThomáis from *Janey Mack Me Shirt Is Black* (1982), Paul Ryan from *Street Talk* (1986); **Penguin Books Ltd**, London, for Richard Ellmann from *Oscar Wilde* (1988), Hugh Leonard from *Home Before Night* (André Deutsch, 1979); **Poolbeg Group Services Ltd**, Dublin, for Art Byrne & Sean McMahon from *113 Great Irishwomen & Irishmen* (1990), Mannix Flynn from *Nothing to Say* (Ward River Press, 1983), Bill Kelly from *Me Darlin' Dublin's Dead and Gone* (1983), Joe Joyce & Peter Murtagh from *The Boss* (1983), Nell McCafferty from *In the Eyes of the Law* (Ward River Press, 1981), Brid Mahon from *A Time to Love: The Life of Peg Woffington* (1992), Breandán Ó hEithir from *The Begrudger's Guide to Irish Politics* (1986) and *This Is Ireland* (1987), Sheila O'Hagan from *The Peacock's Eye* (Salmon, 1992), Victoria White from *Raving Autumn* (1990), Michael O'Toole from *More Kicks Than Pence* (1992); **Random House UK Ltd**, London, for Brendan Behan from *Borstal Boy* (Hutchinson, 1958) and *Brendan Behan's Island: An Irish Sketch-book* (Hutchinson, 1962), Iris Murdoch from *The Red and the Green* (Chatto & Windus, 1965), Somerville & Ross from *The Real Charlotte* (Chatto & Windus, 1894); **Raven Arts Press**, Dublin, for Philip Casey from *The Year of the Knife* (1991), Aileen O'Meara and John Waters from *Letters from the New Island*, ed. Dermot Bolger (1991), Fintan O'Toole from *A Mass for Jesse James* (1990), Roddy Doyle and Peter Sheridan from *Invisible Dublin*, ed. Dermot Bolger (Raven Arts Press, 1991); **Reed Books**, London, for Christy Brown from *Down All the Days* (Secker & Warburg, 1970), Roddy Doyle from *The Commitments* (Heinemann, 1988), Anne Enright from *The Portable Virgin* (Minerva, 1991), Jennifer Johnston from *A Portrait of the Artist as a Young Girl*, ed. John Quinn (Methuen, 1986); **Seven Towers Publishing**, Dublin, for Pat Tierney from *The Moon on My Back* (1993); **Sinclair-Stevenson Ltd**, London, for Joseph O'Connor from *Cowboys and Indians* (1991); **Colin Smythe Ltd**, Gerrards Cross, for Derry Jeffares from *Brought Up in Dublin* (1987), Denis Johnston from *The Old Lady Says 'No!'* (1929); **Sunday Independent**, Dublin, for extracts from articles by Terry Keane (1993); **Temple Bar Properties**, Dublin, for Pat Liddy from *Temple Bar* (1992); **Weidenfeld & Nicolson**, London, for Christopher Nolan from *Under the Eye of the Clock* (1987); **Wolfhound Press Ltd**, Dublin, for Dorothy Nelson from *In Night's City* (1982). Thanks are also due to Stuart Cole of James Adam Salerooms, Dublin, for help with the cover picture, and to the photographer Gerry Farrell.

Every effort has been made to trace copyright holders of material reprinted in this book. The editors and publisher apologise if any material has been included without permission and would be glad to be told of anyone who has not been consulted.

INDEX

Index compiled by Salma Blackburn